THE RIALTO
IN RICHMOND

The Money War Between the States & Other Mysteries of the Civil War

JOSEPH P. FARRELL

Adventures Unlimited Press

Other Books by Joseph P. Farrell:

THE RIALTO IN RICHMOND

The Money War Between the States & Other Mysteries of the Civil War

The Rialto in Richmond

by Joseph P. Farrell

ISBN: 978-1-948803-73-1

Published by:
Adventures Unlimited Press
One Adventure Place
Kempton, Illinois 60946 USA

auphq@frontiernet.net

www.adventuresunlimitedpress.com

Cover by Joe Boyer

10 9 8 7 6 5 4 3 2 1

THE RIALTO IN RICHMOND

For all the Gizars, in thanks for the wonderful
conversation of the past several years,
and especially to Chuck McCorkle
and Catherine Austin Fitts and all the good people
who brought music back into my life with "Bruno,
And to Walter Bosley who boldly went where no
man had gone before,
To T.S.F. and G.A.H. and M.T.C.
Who made it all possible,
And to Shiloh
Who encouraged in the writing of this book with the
well-placed wag-of-tail, barks, whines, and canine
kisses; each and all a
DUR-AN-KI...

TABLE OF CONTENTS

PART ONE:
THE TWO PRESIDENTS

"The Government had ceased to answer the ends for which it was ordained and established. To save ourselves from a revolution which, in its silent but rapid progress, was about to place us under the despotism of numbers, and to preserve in spirit, as well as in form, a system of government we believed to be peculiarly fitted to our condition, and full of promise for mankind, we determined to make a new association, composed of States homogenous in interest, policy, and in feeling."
Confederate President Jefferson Davis, in his second inaugural address, February 22, 1862

"Fellow citizens, we cannot escape history. We of this Congress and this administration will be remembered in spite of ourselves. No personal significance or insignificance can spare one or another of us. The fiery trial through which we pass will light us down in honor or dishonor to the latest generation. We say we are for the Union. The world will not forget that we say this. We know how to save the Union. The world knows we do know how to save it. We, even we here, hold the power and bear the responsibility. In giving freedom to the slave we assure freedom to the free— honorable alike in what we give and what we preserve. We shall nobly save or meanly lose the last best hope of earth."
Union President Abraham Lincoln, Annual Message to Congress, December 1, 1862

1

The Two Presidents:
Left: Jefferson Davis,
1ˢᵗ and Last President of the Confederate States of
America,
Right, Abraham Lincoln,
16ᵗʰ President of the United States of America

A PREFACE OF PROBLEMATICS

"The Confederate States of America was naturally engaged from its inception in a struggle for existence. The creation of a Treasury and the establishment of a revenue were a concern of vital consequence, which was to be vastly emphasized by the mounting demands of a land widely assaulted. The test from the start was the more severe in that the Treasury was engaged in deficit financiering. Every device which opportunity or necessity could urge was the subject of experiment by the Department in its efforts to supply the sinews of war."
Ernest Ashton Smith[1]

A HORRIBLE SENSE OF *DÉJÀ VU* HOVERS OVER THE WAR BETWEEN THE STATES, a sense that we've been here before, and given the semi-permanence of the human condition across the vast swaths of history and culture, there is no doubt we will be here again. History, someone once said, never repeats, but it *does* rhyme and echo, and in the current times, the echoes and rhymes with all their horrible sense of *déjà vu* are being clearly heard once again, if not equally clearly heeded and understood.

---

[1] Ernest Ashton Smith, Ph.D., *The History of the Confederate Treasury: A Dissertation Presented to the Board of University Studies of the Johns Hopkins University for the Degree of Doctor of Philosophy* (Southern History Association: January, March, May, 1901. University of Michigan Library Reprint, no ISBN) pp. 1-2. Smith's diction is itself an indicator of how sweeping the *cultural* consequences of the war were, for prior to it, the United States, when referred to, were referred to in the *plural*, rather than the singular, and this diction was continued by the men of letters in the Confederacy, as in "The Confederate States of America *were* naturally engaged from *their* inception in a struggle for existence..." &c.

3

Consider, for example, the following words:

> They organize in their midst societies to destroy our peace… they preach a crusade against our institutions: they train up their children to hate and distrust; they abuse to our destruction the power which the government has confided to them. We have surrendered to that government our arms and our fortresses—our army and our navy—our sword and purse—and soon we may find, to our cost, that they are in the hands of an open enemy.
>
> Time does not permit the further elucidation of this portion of our enquiry. Enough, however, has been said to prove that we have a union without a constitution. The Union indeed stands, but it has ceased to effect … the great objects for which it was formed. It is but the carcass of its former self – the body without the soul. The blessings which it once conferred have departed—the glories which once surrounded it have been dimmed; and its burdens remain. Pressing down… without compensation. History is not without its illustrations on this subject to teach us wisdom. Republics have, before ours, been enslaved under all the forms of free institutions. It was in the Roman Senate that Sylla sat while his soldiers were butchering the citizens of the republic. It was in the Roman forum that Antony thrice offered unto Caesar the kingly crown, which in deference to the forms of the constitution he thrice refused; and it was in a vain effort to restore that constitution, that Brutus and his confederates put Caesar to death. Long after the extinction of all liberty, the edicts of the senate professed to be in the name of the Roman people, and

the emperor himself exercised his absolute authority under the republican names of consul and imperator.

...

1. Our rulers have been educated from childhood to denounce us and our institutions; so that instead of the kindly sympathy with which a government should respond to the feelings of those whom it governs, our government is our enemy.

2. That government being composed of a sectional party, it is the interest of its leaders to keep alive all the elements of sectional strife; and the future, therefore, offers to us no prospect of relief.[2]

Reading these words, one might think that they were uttered by a modern, twenty-first (or as a friend of mine once put it, twenty-worst) century conservative talk show host or pundit, or a traditional history scholar, complaining of the rampant "wokery" and moral meltdown of the modern United States and its war against every sort of manifestation of traditional culture. In reality, they were the utterances of the man who would become the first Confederate Secretary of the Treasury, Christopher Gustav Memminger, when he was appointed to be the commissioner of the State of South Carolina to Virginia, where he uttered these words before the latter commonwealth's General Assembly, trying to persuade Virginia to secede and join the rest of the already seceded southern states. But his complaint is ironically (or perhaps, not so ironically) a familiar one: the union had become a

---

[2] C.G. Memminger, (Gale Archival Editions on Demand: No Date, ISBN 978-1432-801397) "Address of the Hon. C.G. Memminger, Special Commissioner of the State of South Carolina before the Assembled Authorities of the State of Virginia, January 19, 1860", pp. 36-37.

suicide pact where traditional culture must commit suicide to make way for the programs and agendas of a radicalized political burger and academic class that had seized control of all the levers of governmental, institutional, and cultural power in order to impose and compel their equally radical cultural program.

Because of these ominous parallels and the horrible *déjà vu,* the talk of secession once again is openly heard inside the porous borders of "the Union," as counties in California and Oregon, fed up with their radicalized state governments and the one-party machines that rule them, seek to join other states; some people in states like Texas and Florida—overrun with refugees and illegal aliens because "the Union" takes no interest in enforcing its own laws or borders—are openly considering leaving "the Union" altogether. Whatever one thinks of these people or of their movements and motivations, they all have one thing in common: the genuinely and honestly held perception and conviction that all recourse to the courts, which openly display every sign of an unequal application of law, is futile; the perception abounds that any appeal to the institutions of government are no longer viable because they are so badly corrupted and compromised they are no longer capable of enforcing the laws with impartiality.

Under such circumstances, a study of the American experiences with secession would seem advisable if for no other reason than to understand what should be done, and what should be avoided, in its eventuality. After all, if one counts both the American Revolution and the later secession of the Confederate States, the American performance is one win to one loss, not exactly a stunning nor promising record. When one considers this record in the light of the parallels between the original colonies and the Confederate States, the record becomes downright puzzling if not problematical. For

6

example, both the original colonies and the Confederacy faced an opponent that was militarily and economically vastly more powerful, and which, additionally, could (as is often rehearsed in history books) literally strangle their international trade by their possession of much larger and more powerful navies. Both the original colonies and the Confederacy faced their similarly powerful opponents from a considerable industrial, population, and financial disadvantage.

There were of course *dissimilarities* that have also often been rehearsed as explanations for the success of the one and the failure of the other. In the first case, we are told that the colonies were fighting an opponent who was fighting thousands of miles from his home base, with a long supply line, while the Confederacy, on the other hand, was literally fighting an opponent that was not only "right next door," but whose capital was less than two hundred miles from its own. We are also told that the colonies owed their eventual success to the military assistance and alliance with France, which made possible the Admiral Comte de Grasse's naval squadron's victory over the British Admiral Hood, thereby driving off Lord Cornwallis' only hope of re-supplying his army and thus making Washington's victory at Yorktown, and consequently colonial independence, possible.

The Confederacy, so this version of the story goes, and in spite of its own much greater power than the original colonies, could never translate that power into meaningful relationships with foreign powers. Thus, according to the typical "narratives" of the War Between the States, the seceding states of the South that formed the short-lived Confederate States of America from 1861 to 1865—Florida, Alabama, Mississippi, Louisiana, Arkansas, Texas, Tennessee, South Carolina, Georgia, North Carolina, the

7

Indian Territories (Oklahoma) and Virginia±never stood a chance.

Indeed, given the Union's vast preponderancy in virtually every meaningful category of strategic dominance—finance, population, industrial plant, railroad mileage and so on—it is something of a wonder that the Confederacy did not collapse within a year of its formation, much less be able to pack a punch out of proportion to its resources even as late as 1864. In some of the more nuanced versions of the narrative, we are "informed" about the collapse of the Confederate finances and currency, events which spelled the inevitability of the surrender of the Confederate armies of Generals Joseph Johnston and Robert E. Lee in the spring of 1865.

Within even these "nuanced" narratives there occasionally appear references to a "mystery." In some of the more adventurous presentations, this "mystery" assumes the grand name of "the lost Confederate treasure," and from there the "narrative" degenerates into the twin fantasies of credulous belief or equally dubious "academic skepticism."

Yet, here too there is a problematic posed by a fact that is seldom discussed nor mentioned: neither the Union nor the Confederacy operated with a central bank, and both operated with very similar (though not identical) understandings of wartime finance and of currency. This should not surprise us, for both the Union and the Confederacy shared the common history of rebellion and secession from Great Britain, and therefore share a common understanding of how such an effort was to be financed.

This problematic of credulous belief in, or dubious academic skepticism of, such a missing treasure is sharpened and enhanced when it is viewed in connection with (and as a backdrop to) the fates of their respective leaders at the end of the war: Abraham Lincoln of the Union, and Jefferson Davis of the Confederacy. The assassination of the one, and the flight and eventual capture of the other, are little understood chapters of this financial and political problematic, and accordingly, we shall spend some time with both. The Two Presidents represent not just differing attitudes to chattel versus wage slavery, they also symbolize two financial systems by and with which the War Between the States was waged.

Indeed, consider briefly the problematical strangeness of the case of Confederate President Jefferson Davis, the commander-in-chief of the Confederacy, at whose direction the armies of Robert E. Lee, Joseph Johnston, Pierre Gustav Toutant-Beauregard, Albert Sydney Johnston, and Braxton Bragg marched, shot at, and killed, Union soldiers in their tens and hundreds of thousands. Finally captured, Davis was held without appearing at a public trial for two years, being found guilty *in absentia* by a military tribunal of questionable jurisdiction, and then, he was finally released, never to mount his own defense for any crime, in spite of his own insistent demands for one. Davis is the central mystery in this story; accordingly, we shall *begin* this book with a review of all the weirdness surrounding the Confederate President.

One final note: in this book I have no intention nor purpose of rehearsing all the endless polemics surrounding Southern chattel slavery. For the record, I regard the institution as abominable, and I have no regrets as to its abolition. This does not mean, however, that I have any sympathies for the radical secularized Calvinist-Unitarian abolitionists either, nor for their *post bellum* program of "reconstruction" of the South. It is perhaps significant that no comprehensive pre-war program of manumission and compensation was vigorously advanced by the abolitionists until *after* the war had already begun, and even then only by

President Lincoln himself some months after his Emancipation Proclamation, as we shall see.

Lincoln's proposals underscore the fact that the emancipation and reconstruction could have been done much more effectively, smoothly, and in a way that may have benefitted all—both slave-holder and manumitted slave— much better than was done, and had they been urged prior to 1860, perhaps even without a war.

After all, at roughly the same time period as the War Between the States, the Tsar of All the Russias emancipated all Russian serfs. *Unlike* Lincoln's Emancipation Proclamation, the Tsar's ukase of manumission was neither hypocritically sectional (for Lincoln's proclamation freed only the slaves over which he had *no* jurisdiction nor control, i.e., in the South, and *not* those slaves in the border states that remained in the Union), nor was the Russian manumission done in a financial vacuum: the Russian landholders were compensated financially both for the loss of their serfs, and for the loss of the lands that the serfs worked. Rather, under the Russian program the emancipated serfs were able to *purchase* their lands from their former masters via a series of low interest government loans. Everyone, in other words, had a stake in the plan, and that stake was economic.

From that period to the outbreak of World War One, Russia became the "breadbasket of Europe", until the Bolshevik "revolution" took its massive step backwards into collectivization of agriculture, that is to say, back into new form of serfdom. The soil remained the same, the people remained the same. Only the policies were different; the one promoted, and the other destroyed, the productivity of the land and the freedom of the people.

Given this strange and ironic co-temporality of the Russian and American experience with serfdom, one can only speculate how very different American history might have been had a similar policy of manumission been pursued, rather than the morally confrontational policies both of the radical Yankee abolitionists and of the Southern slave holders.

Indeed, in his annual address to Congress in December of 1862, Mr. Lincoln himself followed up his Emancipation Proclamation by proposing just such a program of compensation both to slave holders and manumitted slaves, a program in some respects similar to the Russian, as we shall see.[3]

There are those who have argued that Lincoln's Emancipation Proclamation was in part designed—in yet another incongruity—to court the good will of autocratic Imperial Russia to the Union cause, just at the time that Confederate diplomacy had managed to secure "belligerent status recognition" from Spain, France, and England, the latter nation much more clearly democratic than autocratic Russia. The Russian manumission also occurred against the wider geopolitical backdrop of the Crimean War, the European and Ottoman designs on Russia, and Union and Confederate diplomacy.

Hence, the emancipation of the serfs was from one point of view a necessity if Russia was going to be able to proceed with industrialization at a similar pace as was already well underway in the rest of Europe, and thus to remain a great power.

It is against this wider geopolitical backdrop that the American War Between the States occurs, and given the decision of the Tsar in 1863 to send his fleet to San Francisco

---

[3] Q.v. Chapter two, "The Anomalies of Abe's Assassination."

and New York as a demonstration of support for Mr. Lincoln, it is a reminder that the second American secession (and the opposition to it) could easily have blossomed into a full scale world war; the Russian naval demonstration might thus have induced some hesitancy about intervention in the unwritten and secret councils of the European powers, and prevented such a war from breaking out.

Either way, all of these considerations are designed to highlight the fact that this is less a book of answers than it is of lessons, questions, and above all, speculations. I believe that the lessons to be learned from the American experience(s) with secession can only be learned by asking and highlighting the right questions. Sometimes these questions are so obvious that asking them again will seem rather pointless or a waste of time and effort, until one is forced to ponder the details, and even when the details cannot be had (or, as is also likely, when I have failed to look in the right place and uncover them), the implications for the lessons can nevertheless often be extrapolated.

For example, we can already extrapolate two lessons that we shall encounter in fuller fashion in the body of this work: before seceding, take two necessary and basic steps to succeed, by having (1) a thorough financial plan inclusive of a sound basis for currency, and (2) at least *some* foreign contacts and supports, all the better if they are at least quasi-official and governmental, but at the minimum, at least corporate and private. In this last regard, as we shall discover, what the Confederacy may have lacked in diplomatic recognition, it made up for by a well-developed network of private and corporate contacts. And what both the Union and the Confederacy may have lacked in terms of a financial plan, they made up for with enormously important experiments whose failures as well as successes are highly instructive. If

12

there were failures with the financial plans, those failures, as we shall discover, came very early on, and in the lack of adequate attention to one of the most basic steps of strategy or of any "business plan"...

One final reminder and caveat. As noted above, this is a book of lessons, questions, and speculations, and primarily focused on the Confederacy, though where necessary involving the Union as well. I do not assert any claim to exhaustive or intensive scholarly research. That would have required several extensive trips to documents held only in old state archives, and long hours pouring over them, which neither my health nor finances could sustain.

I have, however, attempted to acquire the few scholarly sources that touch upon these topics, and I can say in all honesty that I am left with as many questions and (gaping) holes in the narrative at the end of my effort as I had at the beginning of it.

My task therefore in this book is less to provide the answers, nor even so much the lessons and questions, but to enable others even to see and acknowledge that there is, indeed, a big, gaping hole in the center of the narrative. I think I've managed to assemble much of the frame of the jigsaw puzzle, and perhaps even portions of the picture. But like the three blind men trying to describe an elephant, what I have managed to assemble is a tail here, a trunk there, and a floppy ear over there. But the creature itself, the creature of the big mystery squatting in the middle of the War Between the States, remains, mysterious and chimerical, but at least now we have some ears, tails, and trunks. And we have encountered those ears, trunks, and tails before, in the forms of "missing money", "hidden systems of finance," and "occulted financiers."

Consequently, I *do* think that I have managed to clarify aspects of the Mystery of the Missing Confederate Treasure and to outline possible speculative answers to where it might have gone, or at least, the directions it was headed when it vanished.

Joseph P. Farrell
2024, from Somewhere

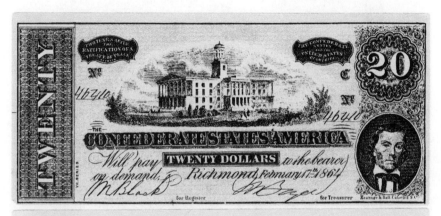

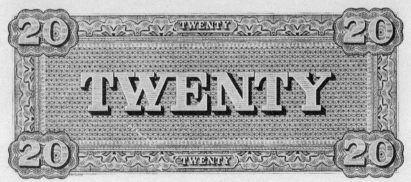

1864 Obverse and Reverse
Confederate Twenty Dollar Certificate.
The Figure in the Lower Right Oval is that of
Confederate Vice President Stevens

*Confederate President Jefferson Finis Davis,
as he appeared after the war and at the approximate time of
the composition of his memoir,
"The Rise and Fall of the Confederate Government"*

1

THE DILEMMA OF JEFFERSON FINIS DAVIS

"History cannot give us a program for the future, but it can give use a fuller understanding of ourselves, and of our common humanity, so that we can better face the future."
Robert Penn Warren[1]

"Davis died without rancor, and wishing us all well. But if he were not now defenseless in death, he would no doubt reject the citizenship we so charitably thrust upon him. In life, in his old-fashioned way, he would accept no pardon, for pardon could be construed to imply wrongdoing, and wrongdoing was what, in honor and principle, he denied."
Robert Penn Warren[2]

O N OCTOBER 17, 1978, PRESIDENT JAMES EARL "JIMMY" CARTER signed into law a resolution— Senate Joint Resolution 16—that had unanimously passed the United States Senate by voice vote, an unusual event in the normally fractious world of American "bi-partisan" politics, and an event that would be all but impossible to accomplish in contemporary twenty-first century American political culture. The resolution had been introduced by the U.S. Senator from Oregon, Mark Hatfield,

---

[1] Robert Penn Warren, *The Legacy of the Civil War* (Lincoln: The University of Nebraska Press, 1998 ISBN 0-8032-9801-3), p. 100.
[2] Robert Penn Warren, *Jefferson Davis Gets His Citizenship Back* (Lexington, Kentucky: The University Press of Kentucky, 1980, ISBN 0-8131-1445-4), p. 112

on January 25, 1976 and had finally been brought to the floor and unanimously carried two years later. The resolution was simple: it posthumously restored American citizenship to the former and only President of the Confederate States of America, Jefferson Finis Davis, who had died some ninety years earlier. Davis' citizenship was restored three years after a similar Congressional action had restored the citizenship of Confederate Lieutenant General Robert E. Lee.[3]

But if the resolution was simple, the historiographical problematic it posed and still poses was not simple at all, for it highlights all the unresolved contradictions and mysteries not only of Davis himself, but of the whole War Between the States. Here the best place to begin is at the *end* of the drama, for though most people know the general story of President Abraham Lincoln's assassination, few know of its connections to the flight and eventual capture of President Jefferson Davis, and to the gymnastic financial and policy contortions it forced on the real Lincoln conspirators, for tragic as the assassination of Lincoln was, it was not Lincoln who was the central character and the core mystery of the drama. Nor was it even Davis, but rather the financial systems—the *currency* systems—that each represented. We may highlight that mystery by asking two very obvious, though seldom-asked, questions:

Why was Jefferson Davis never tried for treason? And if he was, why was he never punished, but his citizenship restored?

As we have already noted, his citizenship was actually *restored*, though posthumously, and as the second epigraph at the beginning of this chapter indicates, Davis himself

---

[3] Ibid., pp. 93-94.

probably would have strenuously objected to the restoration in any case. Indeed, the mystery deepens when we consider that during the approximately two years he was held in federal prison, Davis himself constantly insisted he be brought to trial, a trial which was persistently dodged and evaded, and a trial that, seemingly, was all the more necessary since the conspiracy that swirled around the murder of President Lincoln went all the way up to the Confederate President himself, at least, it did according to the carefully controlled northern press and the Union Secretary of War, Edwin Stanton, who controlled it. The *other* conspirators in the Lincoln assassination *were* tried, and some of them were hung for it. No effort nor expense was spared to bring them to an appearance of justice. True, Davis was "tried" by a military tribunal just as the Lincoln conspirators were; but this "trial" was in absentia, and Davis himself was never questioned, nor able to appear to mount his own defense. There were other anomalies, but we shall return to these at the end of this chapter.

As for the rest of the Lincoln conspirators, there was no attempt to manufacture a "lone nut" shooting a misaligned telescopic rifle from a high-rise building; no effort was made to concoct a ridiculous narrative in order to disguise the conspiracy and pin the whole blame on the lone nut. The narrative that *did* result in 1865, however, was no less problematic, and indeed perhaps it even served as a template of assassination planning and action should circumstances ever require its re-use, which apparently they did in 1963, because the whole narrative of conspiracy had been dropped by then. Even so, however, there are disturbing parallels. For example, just as occurred in the assassination of President John F. Kennedy less than a century later with the appearance of more than one Lee Harvey Oswald, so too in the Lincoln assassination plotline, more than one individual looking uncomfortably like the alleged assassin, John Wilkes Booth, would emerge. And just as it did in the case of Oswald, doubts would emerge over whether or not it was actually Booth that died where and when the "narrative" insists he did.

In the case of Mr. Lincoln in 1865, the conspiracy and conspirators were thus very real, and as we shall see, there were conspirators who never faced the end of the rope. There were, of course, conspirators who evaded the hangmen but nevertheless were convicted and sentenced to imprisonment under what can only be considered to be cruel circumstances, even by nineteenth century standards.

Those who did face the gallows were the Lee Harvey Oswalds and Jack Rubys of the day. Those who didn't were, like the Dulles Brothers, ensconced in the lofty parapets and shadowy bunkers of governmental and corporate power. So once again the question: with all the rumors in the Northern press at the time that the whole thing was a vengeance plot concocted by the Confederate Secret Service and authorized by Confederate President Jefferson Davis, why was he never *properly* tried along with the other Lincoln assassination conspirators?

And more importantly, *why was he released from prison* to live out the rest of his days plying the insurance trade and able to write his thousand-and-a-half page memoir *The Rise and Fall of the Confederate Government* in comparative peace, when the tribunal had found him guilty? *Why did the trial he insisted upon never happen, and why was he released at all after a "trial" had found him guilty? Why was the former Confederate President even allowed to write memoirs at all since the potential existed that they could expose secrets that others might not wish exposed? And why is he curiously silent on so many important issues? Had he been warned not to mention them? Or did he "censor himself", daring perhaps only to draw attention to certain questions by avoiding them altogether?*

A. A Timeline of the End:
1. The End of March, 1865:
Lincoln's Wishes and his
"Captured Coon" Story told to his Cabinet

The end of March, 1865 was a busy period for both American Presidents and their staffs. The War Between the States was clearly approaching its end. The only question was what sort of end it would be. A Union victory was a probable, though even at that late period not a completely foregone, conclusion, and even though Lincoln had already begun to discuss and prepare for that possibility with his cabinet.

For example, on March 28, 1865 President Lincoln met with Generals Grant and Sherman at Hampton, Virginia, in anticipation of the capture of Richmond. There, Lincoln made it clear to his two senior generals that he would prefer that the Confederate armies simply surrender, and their personnel return to their homes to reassume their lives and production. When queried about the Confederate leadership and Jefferson Davis in particular, Lincoln made it clear that his preference was that they all flee the country, rather than remain as a problem to be dealt with. Additionally, the President informed his generals that he was not able to speak

21

his mind fully on the matter,[4] doubtless due to the internal politics and fissures within his own administration and political party.

It takes but little imagination to ascertain from this that Lincoln was conveying his wishes to his commanding generals without being on the record with a formal order, that perhaps with a little "nudge" in the right direction, or a bit of purposeful "misdirection," Davis might slip through the Union dragnet to freedom. Nod nod, wink wink.

That this seems to be the proper frame of reference by which to interpret Mr. Lincoln's remarks is strongly corroborated by a meeting with his cabinet recounted by Patricia G. Neely in her excellent study of the flight of Jefferson Davis from Richmond. At this cabinet meeting, Mr. Lincoln made it clear that his preference was simply to allow the Confederate leadership to escape, even though most of the Cabinet members—the majority of whom were staunch abolitionist Republicans—wanted to hang the Confederate leaders for treason.

> Lincoln launched into a story. "Well, Josh," replied Mr. Lincoln, "when I was a boy in Indiana, I went to a neighbor's house one morning and found a boy of my own

---

[4] Patricia G. McNeely, *President Abraham Lincoln, Generan William T. Sherman, President Jefferson Davis, and the Lost Confederate Gold*, p. 36. Ms. McNeely's book is the only single volume study of the flight of President Jefferson Davis and of the rumors of a large treasure of bullion and specie that accompanied him that is easily and currently publicly available. It is a superb one volume resource of details, information, and speculation rarely examined in other accounts of the end of the war.

size holding a coon by a string. I asked him what he had and what he was doing. He says, "It's a coon. Dad cotched (sic.) six last night and killed all but this poor little cuss. Dad told me to hold him until he came back and I'm afraid he's going to kill this one too, and, oh, Abe, I do wish he would get away."

"Well, why don't you let him loose?" Lincoln asked.

"That wouldn't be right," the boy said, "and if I let him go, Dad would give me hell. But if he would get away himself, it would be all right."

Bridging from the "coon" story, Lincoln said, "Now, if Jeff Davis and those other fellows will only get away, it will be all right. But if we should catch them and I should let them go, Dad would give me hell."[5]

The interesting thing about this anecdote is not so much the insight it provides into Lincoln's dispositions toward *post bellum* policy with respect to the South, but rather for the unanswered question that hovers over it: *Who is "Dad" in Mr. Lincoln's parable?* If Mr. Lincoln had meant to mean the people themselves, analogical aptness would seem to require some appropriate symbolism for them in the parable, such as "family." But no, Mr. Lincoln perhaps inadvertently betrays the truth of his situation by referring to some superior authority; hence, *Who is "Dad"?*

In any case, Mr. Lincoln appears to have communicated his orders to his generals in an informal fashion without expressly challenging his own cabinet, for the "coon" could always be released by "the boy" while "Dad"

---

[5] Patricia G. McNeely, op. cit., p. 38, citing Ward Hill Lamon, and Dorothy Lamon Teillard, *Recollections of Abraham Lincoln* (Cambridge, The University Press: 1911), p.p. 248-249.

was not home, or for whatever other reason he was not looking. One could always then claim that the "coon" had gnawed through the string holding him captive, and had escaped.

Problem solved, provided the "raccoon" cooperated and escaped.

Unfortunately, this "raccoon" was Jefferson Finis Davis, and while he had *every* intention of escaping, he had *no* intention of stealing away into a quiet and leisurely life of exile and not being a headache to Mr. Lincoln and his "dad."

2. A Timeline of the End and of President Davis' Flight

Most histories of the War Between the States treat of President Davis' flight and the other events that occurred during that frenetic three weeks in a few paragraphs devoid of details, and usually in a particular way. That way emphasizes the hopelessness—by that point of the war—of the Confederate cause and the implied fanaticism of the Confederate President, wandering from house to house and field camp to field camp from Virginia to the Carolinas, accompanied by a ragtag group of soldiers and followers until his eventual capture by Federal forces on May 10, 1865. In some cases, for good measure, the hopelessness of the situation (and the fanaticism of Davis n wanting to continue the war) is underscored by passing references to the surrenders of Confederate Generals Joseph Johnston and Pierre G.T. Beauregard.

But here, as in so many cases, the actual details tell a very different and much more complicated story. We shall follow the timeline of events as presented in the excellent study of Patricia G. McNeely very closely, summarizing the story, though with the understood proviso that this cannot replace actually reading her book and comparing it carefully to the studies of the Lincoln assassination that will be reviewed in the next chapter. In so doing, the purpose of most popular presentations—bereft of analysis and speculation that they are—is disclosed, because any such analysis and speculation would lead to "messy questions" and even messier implications.

§§§

a. *February 28, 1864: The Dahlgren Raid:* The first relevant contextual factor that must head any such timeline of events is the failed Union raid on Richmond known as the Dahlgren Raid. This little-known but extremely important event had its beginnings in an offhand statement made by President Lincoln in a letter to Union General "Fighting Joe" Hooker in May of 1863, just after Hooker's stunning defeat at the hands of Generals Lee and Jackson at Chancellorsville. In his letter, Mr. Lincoln relayed information that had come to him from Union cavalry forces operating around Richmond, stating that the Confederate capitol was all but bereft of soldiers, and that "our men, had they known it, could have safely gone in and burnt everything (and) brought us Jeff. Davis."[6]

---

[6] McNeely, op. cit., p. 8, citing Roy P. Basler, ed., *The Collected Works of Abraham Lincoln* (New Brunswick, New Jersey: Rutgers University Press, 1953-55, vol. 6, pp. 202-204.

This remark was converted to a plan for operational action when Union General Judson Kilpatrick with approximately 3,500 Union cavalry was ordered to raid the Confederate capital, ostensibly to free the Union prisoners of war in Libby prison. The reality was otherwise, for Kilpatrick's main force was a diversion so that Union Colonel Ulric Dahlgren could lead a raiding party of approximately 500 men to the heart of Richmond. Specially equipped for the mission with incendiary material, his men were to attempt to set fire to the government district. The raid, however, failed, as Confederate forces drove off both Dahlgren and Kilpatrick's forces, and killed Colonel Dahlgren.

When Colonel Dahlgren's body was searched, the Confederate troops made the discovery of Dahlgren's written orders titled "Special Orders and Instructions" which stated "The men must be kept together and well in hand, and once in the city, *it must be destroyed and Jeff Davis and his cabinet killed.*"[7]

b. *February 1864: President Davis' Response: Expanded Confederate Espionage and Covert Operations in Canada and Elsewhere:* The effect of this failed raid and the capture of the orders detailing its actual secret purpose electrified both Davis, his cabinet, and the entire South, for its contents were published in the Southern press. As the news and purpose of the failed raid spread, it created a backlash of opinion even in the North, where Mr. Lincoln was facing re-election and a population increasingly tired of the war. While Lincoln's

---

[7] McNeely, op cit., p. 9-10, emphasis added.

government denied the assassination plans and claimed the orders were forgeries, Davis responded by authorizing Confederate espionage operations and rings to be expanded to Canada, where an effort was organized to elect anti-war governments in Illinois, Indiana, Ohio, and the state of Kentucky, a slave state which had remained in the Union but also declared its "neutrality" in the war.[8]

The Dahlgren raid presents a conundrum, for as has already been seen from Mr. Lincoln's "coon" anecdote, *his* preference was for the Confederate leadership simply to escape altogether. Hanging for treason was *not* on his mind. And as we shall see later in this chapter, Davis himself, upon learning of Lincoln's assassination, was visibly shocked and dismayed. So which is it? Were both Presidents innocent of any involvement in the assassination plots on the other? Or did Lincoln order Davis' assassination in the Dahlgren raid, and did Davis retaliate by ordering Lincoln's, and did his secret service successfully accomplish it as was actually claimed in the Northern press after the event?

To the latter set of questions the answer is "Possibly, but probably not."

While we have yet to examination the Lincoln assassination itself, which we shall do in the next chapter, it is more likely that events and their own intelligence services, "deep states", and "continuity of government" operations, outgrew and ignored their personal control and overtook the two Presidents. In the

---

[8] Ibid., pp. 10-11 for her discussion of this raid and its effect.

case of Colonel Dahlgren's orders to kill Davis and his cabinet, therefore, it is more likely that these orders were issued by someone high enough within the Lincoln Administration as to suggest or imply presidential approval (if not origin) of those orders.

c. *March, 1865: President Lincoln's 2ⁿᵈ Inauguration, and Booth's First Plot:* By March of 1865, President Lincoln had faced down the challenge of Northern Democrat General George McClellan and the "peace party", had successfully gained re-election to a second term, and was preparing for his second inauguration. Behind the triumphant scenes and moods, however, Mr. Lincoln had been warned as early as December of 1864 of threats on his life. The threats took the form of organized kidnapping plots, one of which was orchestrated and organized by John Wilkes Booth, who had even managed to attend Lincoln's second inauguration. After Lee's surrender to Grant at Appomatox on April 9, these plans were changed to an assassination plot, utilizing the same networks and many of the same arrangements, repurposed to provide escape routes for the assassination plotters. We shall have more to say in detail on these matters in the next chapter, but take note of them here for their place in the timeline of President Davis' flight from Richmond.[9]

d. *March 12, 1865:* Union General William Tecumseh Sherman reaches Fayetteville, North Carolina. During his infamous "march to the sea", Sherman's army plundered

---

[9] Q.v. McNeely, op. cit., pp. 19-23.

the property of Southerners in his army's line of march, utilizing the confiscation law passed by the Union Congress on July 17, 1862. This law granted the Union armies the ability to confiscate and dispose of Confederate property as it saw fit, including destruction of that property. In practice this meant that Sherman's troops confiscated and plundered anything that was not fastened down and could be transported, and subjected the rest to destruction.

One gains a more accurate measure of Sherman's character and his army's conduct of war by noting how he himself reacted to a proclamation of President Lincoln and the March 12, 1863 decision of the Union Supreme court that owners of Confederate property who had their property confiscated by Union forces acting under the 1862 Confiscation Act could and did, upon pardon, have all property rights restored, and this included the proceeds from any properties seized by Union forces under the Act.[10] After the fall of Atlanta to Sherman's forces, he issued General Order 120. This order required that the officers and soldiers of his army to issue "no receipts for confiscated, stolen and destroyed property" and that any identification or other indicators of ownership be removed from cotton and commodities being shipped from Savannah. The intention was clear; the aim of all these measures was the outright theft and plunder of Southern property and to make it impossible for any claims to be presented "against the Federal government after the war."[11]

---

[10] McNeeky, op. cit., pp. 26-27.
[11] Ibid., p. 27.

These facts provoke some questions: are these actions indicative simply of General Sherman's character, of his vindictiveness, and cruelty, of personal flaws and moral defects that he through sheer willpower and force of his position stamped on his army? Or are they rather the *product* of deeply hidden policy decisions and players masking their activities behind the public face of General Sherman? Or are they a mixture of both? As we shall see subsequently in this and the following chapter, there are good grounds to believe that the actions of Sherman's army were those of a deliberate policy decision that had been taken vis-à-vis the South, hiding behind Sherman's character and personality.

The implications are clear, sweeping, and disturbing: ***Sherman's General Order 120 is thus entirely consistent with a piracy and plunder operation—a kind of nineteenth century "disaster capitalism" being practiced on the "opportunity zones" of the Confederacy—and as will be seen in the next chapter, is also entirely consistent with the motivations behind the deepest conspirators in the Lincoln murder. Sherman's General Order 120 is thus consistent with someone displaying clear understanding of the policy and intentions of his commander-in-chief, Mr. Lincoln, but also consistent with someone intending to subvert those intentions, and thus perhaps to serve the interests of other parties.***

Viewed under the light of this interpretive template, what Sherman's March to the Sea failed to accomplish, post-war Reconstruction could. There was just one obstacle, and his name was Abraham Lincoln.

e. *April 2, 1865:* While attending St. Paul's Episcopal Church in Richmond, President Davis receives a message from General Lee urging him to abandon the city. Davis finally accedes to Lee's advice and orders the Confederate government to evacuate Richmond; Mrs. Davis and the Davis children, and Mrs. Trenholm, wife of the Confederate Secretary of the Treasury, George Trenholm, depart Richmond. Mr. Davis follows later with a guard of soldiers, Confederate archives, and the Confederate Treasury that had remained in Richmond up to that point, intending to link up with Mrs. Davis and their children elsewhere. According to the statements of Captain William H. Parker who witnessed the train being loaded, the train carrying Mr. Davis, some members of his cabinet, and the Confederate archives and Treasury, was packed, inside and on the tops of the carriages, to standing room only.[12] The goal of President Davis, the archives, and the treasure, was the Trans-Mississippi department, where Davis hoped to continue the war from a "rump" Confederacy.[13] While estimations of the amount of money accompanying Davis' party vary wildly, from a few hundred thousand dollars in gold and silver coin, the Richmond bankers informed Union General Halleck that Davis' party was carrying between six and thirteen million dollars of specie.[14]

It is important to understand the significance both of the large amount of specie—whether hundreds of

---

[12] McNeely, op. cit., p. 69.

[13] Ibid., p. 66.

[14] Ibid., p. 67.

thousands or millions of dollars—that Davis took with him, and of the *archives* which accompanied him, for it is the *archives* which are forgotten in most contemporary accounts of the Confederate President's flight from Richmond. The archives get buried in a blizzard of speculation about what happened to all that "lost Confederate treasure," but if there was a treasure that accompanied Davis and his party, it was not the specie buried in some secret cache in Kentucky or Virginia or North Carolina or even Texas or Oklahoma, for while such literal treasure may indeed be there, it was the archives that were the real treasure, *for the archives contained the information about the Confederate accounts, and their agents and security procedures, abroad.* We are looking, in other words, at a continuity of government operation, nineteenth century style.

f. *April 3, 1865:* That Davis' flight should be seen as a Continuity of Government operation is further corroborated by the first stage of that flight, for on April 3, 1865, Mr. Davis and his party detrain in Danville, Virginia, where he had hoped to rendezvous with General Lee and his retreating army. Lee, who had outlined his plans for the withdrawal of his army from the Richmond environs in a letter, is unable to do so as the letter falls into Union hands unbeknownst to Lee. General Grant, knowing of Lee's planned lines of retreat, is able to order troop movements accordingly, and to finally trap Lee's Army of Northern Virginia and force its surrender on April 9, 1865. In any case, this indicates that the large and heavy train and small guard of soldiers accompanying Davis was intended to have been augmented by Lee's entire army, which could more adequately have protected the large wagon train needed to transport specie, archives, and the Confederate leadership. On April 3, 1865, however, Lee's surrender is still in the future, and thinking everything is going according to plan, President Davis held another cabinet meeting. One may reasonably assume that the purpose of this meeting was to review the plan to get the "treasure", archives, and rump government to the Trans-Mississippi department.

Davis' stop in Danville is the first clue that the treasure accompanying him may have been much more than modern scholars are willing to entertain. Confederate Captain Parker, who had helped oversee the loading of Davis' train in Richmond, stated that the "treasury contained $500,000 when it left Richmond,"[15] subsequent statements by the acting Secretary of the Treasury[16] maintained that "the treasury only contained $327,022.90 when it left Danville. Out of that, $39,000 was paid to soldiers in Greensboro, so that the treasury contained $288,022.90 ...outside of Washington, Georgia. By his accounting, $127,977.10 did not leave Danville."[17] Additionally, the acting Confederate Treasury Secretary "made no mention of 39 kegs of

---

[15] McNeely, op. cit., p. 73.

[16] The Secretary of the Treasury himself, George Trenholm, had left Richmond on board Davis' train, but had later departed Davis' continuity of government party to return to South Carolina. Trenholm, as will be seen, is a crucial part of the story.

[17] McNeely, op. ct., p. 73.

Mexican silver dollars left in Danville that the Confederacy is believed to have received through the sale of cotton to Mexico. The Mexican coins had been transported to Danville, and when the David party was forced to continue on to Greensboro, the more than 9,000 pounds of silver would have slowed down the procession."[18] This was certainly true for Davis' smaller flight party. However, it must be remembered that the *original* plan included a rendezvous with General Lee's army, whose soldiers also would have required payment.

This permits us to infer a rather astonishing implication, for the mere $500,000 reported by Captain Parker as being the contents of the treasury that left Richmond would not long have sustained the payments to the tens of thousands of soldiers in Lee's army.[19]

---

[18] Ibid.

[19] At the time of Lee's surrender, the Army of Northern Virginia was but a shadow of the army that, always outnumbered but rarely outfought, had been the bane of Union armies at the now famous battles of Malvern Hill, Gaines' Mill, Second Manasses, Antietam, Fredericksburg, Chancellorsville, Gettysburg, Spotsylvania, Cold Harbor, the Wilderness and many a minor skirmish. It is perhaps a testament to the military prowess of that army that our "public memories" of the war, of the battles that live on in our memory of that horrible conflict, are associated with Lee's command of this one Confederate field army, when in fact, there were other field armies in the Confederate military under other commanders and in other theaters throughout the war. But of those battles and campaigns, there are few that are publicly remembered beyond Shiloh, Vicksburg, or perhaps Chickamauga. Few recall the battle of Pea Ridge nor the abortive Confederate "invasions" of Missouri or Kentucky. It is rather the Army of

After all, the mere thousand or so soldiers accompanying Davis' flight party soaked up $39,000! This means that the report of the Richmond bankers to Union general Halleck, that anywhere from six to thirteen million dollars worth of gold and silver coin was accompanying Davis' party at least for *some* part of his journey is much more likely, and it likely too that it accompanied him at least as far as Danville, the intended rendezvous point with Lee's army. Nor is it surprising that this vast sum never is mentioned in the accounting of Davis' flight, for this fortune represented the specie reserves of the banks of the "Richmond Rialto", and not the Confederate treasury itself, the legal agent responsible for the salaries of Confederate soldiers.

Northern Virginia and its association with Lee that lives on and is most remembered, even though its previous commanders, Beauregard and Joseph Johnston, also distinguished it with victories. (Oddly enough, Beauregard and Johnston, the generals who gave the Confederacy the first victory of the war at First Manasses, commanded the same army when its official name was The Army of the Potomac, when its opposite Union army under Irwin McDowell was equally ironically named the Army of Virginia!). At the time of the surrender of the army, McNeely states that "only 7,892 men of the army of Northern Virginia had arms in their hands. The total number, including those who reported afterward, was between 26,000 and 27,000. Grant's army was more than twice as large at 62,239." (McNeely, op. vit., p. 52, citing Varina Howell Davis, *Jefferson davs: Ex-President of the Confederate States of America: A Memoir by his Wife*, Volume 2 [New York: Belford Company Publishers, 1890], p.. 594.)

g. *April 9, 1865:*Confederate Lieutenant General Robert E. Lee Surrenders his army to Union General Ulysses S. Grant at the McClean House at Appomatox Courthouse, Virginia. The images are imprinted on the American soul to this day; two generals, who had waged such and long and bitter campaign of cat and mouse against each other, meet in the old farmhouse where they and their staffs exchange pleasantries, and Grant dictates a surrender proposal based on the lenient terms President Lincoln had outlined to him. The document prepared and reviewed by their respective staffs is signed; Lee rises and exists the house, and mounts his horse, Traveler. Grant raises his hat in salute, and Lee does the same, riding back to his lines, where his army greets him with a tearful cheer. The war, at least for the Army of Northern Virginia and its illustrious commander, which now pass into history, is over.[20]

h. *April 12-13, 1865* Learning of the surrender of General Lee before leaving Danville, Davis informs Generals Johnston and Beauregard by telegram of the news, and orders Johnston to meet him and his party at Beauregard's headquarters in Greensborough, North Carolina. It is worth citing Davis' own account of this meeting, and of his motivations for continuing the continuity of government operation and the attempt to move the Confederate government to the Trans-Mississippi department:

---

[20] For McNeely's treatment of this poignant episode, q.v. pp. 48-52.

...General J.E. Johnson came up from Raleigh to Greensboro, and with General Beauregard met me and most of my Cabinet at my quarters in a house occupied by Colonel J. Taylor Wood's family. Though I was fully sensible of the gravity of our position, seriously affected as it was by the evacuation of the capial, the surrender of the Army of Northern Virginia, and the consequent discouragement which these events would produce, I did not think we should despair. We still had effective armies in the field, and a vast extent of rich and productive territory both east and west of the Mississippi, whose citizens had evinced no disposition to surrender. Ample supplies had been collected in the railroad depots, and much still remained to be placed at our disposal when needed by the army in North Carolina.

The failure of several attempts to open negotiations with the Federal Government, and notably the last by commissioners who met President Lincoln at Hampton Roads, convinced me of the hopelessness under existing circumstances to obtain better terms than were offered, i.e., a surrender at discretion. My motive, therefor, in holding an interview with the senior generals of the army in North Carolina was not to learn their opinion as to what might be done by negotiations with the United States Government, but to derive from them information in regard to the army under their command, and what it was feasible and advisable to do as a military problem.

The members of my Cabinet were already advised as to the object of the meeting, and, when the subject was introduced to the generals in that form, General Johnston was very reserved, and seemed far less than sanguine. His first significant expression was that of a desire to open correspondence with General Sherman, to see if he would agree to a suspension of hostilities, the object being to permit the civil authorities to entire into the needful arrangements to terminate the existing war. Confident that the United States

Government would not accept a proposition for such negotiations, I distinctly expressed my conviction on that point, and presented as an objection to such an effort that, so far as it should excite delusive hopes and expectations, its failure would have a demoralizing effect both on the troops and the people.... During the last years of the war the main part of the infantry in the Army of Northern Virginia was composed of men from the farther South. Many of these, before the evacuation of Petersburg and especially about the time of Lee's surrender, had absented themselves to go homeward, and, it was reported, made avowal of their purpose to continue the struggle. I had reason to believe that the spirit of the army in North Carolina was unbroken, for, though surrounded by circumstances well calculated to depress and discourage them, I had learned that they earnestly protested to their officers against the surrender which rumor informed them was then in contemplation....

But if, taking the gloomiest view, the circumstances were such as to leave no hope of maintaining the independence of the Confederate States—if negotiations for peace must be on the basis of reunion and the acceptance of the war legislation—it seemed to me that certainly better terms for our country could be secured by keeping organized armies in the field than by laying down our arms and trusting to the magnanimity of the victor.

For all these considerations I was not at all hopeful of any success in the attempt to provide for negotiations between the civil authorities of the United States and those of the Confederacy, believing that, even if Sherman should agree to such a proposition, his Government would not ratify it; but, after having distinctly announced my opinion, I yielded to the judgment of my constitutional advisers, of whom only one held my views, and consented to permit General Johnston, as he desired to hold a conference with General Sherman for the purpose above recited.[21]

From this point, Davis continues by stating that having given General Johnston permission to contact Union General W.T. Sherman, he then inquired of Johnston what his favored line of march would be if his proposals for a cease fire should be rejected, in order that he might arrange for supplies to be laid for his army along that line of march.[22] As we shall see in the next chapter, Davis had good reason to be concerned that the Union government would reject any negotiation proposals, for that government was about to be radically changed, and in the most radical manner possible:

i. *April 14, 1865, Good Friday:* President Abraham Lincoln is assassinated by John Wilkes Booth while he and Mrs. Mary Todd Lincoln attend a play at Ford's theater in Washington, and another assassin attempts to murder Secretary of State John Seward. A male nurse, and Seward's son Frederick, are wounded in the attempt. Both assassins get away. The double assassination and getaway indicates an organized conspiracy. Again, a more detailed discussion of the Lincoln Assassination will be undertaken in the next chapter, but for the moment its effect on Davis' flight and its motivations must be noted, for Lincoln, with his insistence on

---

[21] Jefferson Davis, *The Rise and Fall of the Confederate Government*, Volume II, pp. 679-681, emphasis added. For McNeely's account of this episode, q.v. McNeely, op. cit., pp. 80-81.

[22] Davis, op. cit., p. 681.

absolute surrender, was not nearly the radical that the Southern leaders knew that those who *surrounded* Mr. Lincoln would be, and as was evident from the terms of Lee's surrender to Grant, which they knew to have been the wishes of Lincoln.

j. *April 15, 1865*: President Abraham Lincoln dies ca. 7:20 A.M., President Jefferson Davis departs Greensborough, North Carolina for Salisbury and Charlotte on horses and wagons, due to Federal troops having destroyed the rail lines.[23] Meanwhile, Mrs. Davis and the CSA treasure reach Chester, South Carolina.

k. *April 16, 1865:* Union General William T. Sherman and Confederate General Joseph Johnston meet. Sherman, at the beginning of this meeting, shows Johnston the message that he had received announcing the assassination and death of President Lincoln. According to Sherman's account of the meeting, Johnston displayed sincere sorrow and distress over the news, expressing his hope that no one would lay responsibility for the dead at the feet of the Confederacy or its leadership. Sherman responded by telling Johnston that he did not believe that any of the Confederacy's officers or generals "could possibly be privy to acts of assassination," adding that he could "not say as much for Jeff. Davis, George Sanders and men of that stripe."[24] However, it is Sherman's attitude in the negotiations with Johnston that

---

[23] McNeely, op. cit., p. 82.

[24] Ibid., p. 119, citing William T. Sherman, *The Memoirs of W.T. Sherman* (Archeron Press, St. Louis, Missouri: 1875), Volume 13, p. 244.

are important, for like General Grant, he offers his old opponent Johnston rather lenient terms for the surrender of his army.[25] These terms were accepted, and he and Johnston sign a cease-fire based on those terms. For Sherman, it was essential to procure Johnston's surrender because, like Grant, he feared that the Confederacy would simply "disperse and begin guerrilla warfare,"[26] a fear that reflects their accurate assessment that the Confederate leadership, in its flight from Richmond, was pursuing a Continuity of Government operation. Indeed, Sherman was even prepared to offer Davis and his entourage ships to allow them to flee the country, which indicates that Sherman at least (and very likely the entire higher command of the Union military) knew of Lincoln's expressed wish that the Confederate leaders simply leave the country, rather than pose a massive post-war problem. We shall have more to say on this subject in the next chapter in direct relationship to the Lincoln assassination. For now, we take note of it only to record that the change of policy that had been effected by the assassination had not yet filtered down to the Union's field commanders.

1. Meanwhile, President Davis arrives in Charlotte, South Carolina with 1,000 cavalry, and receives a telegram announcing Lincoln's assassination. Initially Davis is not willing to believe it, but later that day the arrival of General Breckinridge confirms the details that Mr. Lincoln had been shot while attending a play at Ford's

---

[25] McNeely, op. cit., p. 121.
[26] McNeely, op. cit., p. 119.

Theater. Hearing the news, Davis responds "I am sorry to learn it. *Mr. Lincoln was a much better man than his successor will be, and it will go harder with our people. It is bad news for us.*"[27] These remarks are consistent with the motivations Davis previously displayed as to the reasons he sought to continue the war, and they are also a clear recognition that he possessed an understanding that there were divisions within the Lincoln administration regarding *post bellum* policy toward the South. Thus, the assassination of Lincoln and the looming change of government in the Union only reinforced Davis' conviction that the war must be continued until better negotiating circumstances could be brought about. This meant that the original plan for the Continuity of Government via its escape to the Trans-Mississippi Department was still in effect.

m. *April 23, 1865:* The change in post bellum Federal policy is made clear when Union Secretary of War Edwin Stanton telegraphs General Sherman and informs him that his surrender terms with General Johnston are rejected and the armistice is suspended. At this juncture, things heat up again, substantially. To begin with, on the following day, April 24, 1865, *The New York Times*, never a paper that would attempt to drive events in a particular way in response to pressure from the government,[28] ran an

---

[27] McNeely, op. cit., p. 130.

[28] This is, of course, said tongue in cheek, because as will be seen in the *next* chapter, the Northern press, particularly in New York City, had been reduced during the war to being a kind of

article implying that General Sherman, via his negotiations with General Johnston, was trying to clear an escape route for Davis, his entourage, and "treasure." The article stated explicitly that "the amount of specie taken south by Jeff. Davis and his partisans is very large, *including not only the plunder of the Richmond banks,* but previous accumulations."[29] Thus, we have not just Union General Halleck's statement that Davis' party included specie accumulated as reserves in the banks of the "Richmond Rialto," but this claim is now repeated in the *New York Times*, without mentioning that the source of the story, in Halleck's case, were those very Richmond bankers!

Needless to say, when General Sherman received orders from Union Secretary of War Edwin Stanton that his armistice with Johnston had been "cancelled", and learning of the accusations concerning him in the Union press, he was outraged. But that's not all. Patricia McNeely sums the episode up this way:

"Sherman said he had not known about the March 3 dispatch from Lincoln to Stanton that limited Grant and thus his subordinates to negotiations on purely military matters, even though at Savannah, Stanton had authorized Sherman to control all matters, civil and military. Stanton implied that Sherman had received a copy of the dispatch and had disobeyed orders. The newspaper article said that "General Sherman was ordered to resume hostilities immediately."

---

proto-typical "project Mockinbird" covert adjunct of the government.

[29] McNeely, op. cit., p. 146.

"Sherman was preparing to head back to Savannah by sea to meet officers stationed at Macon and Augusta when Stanton issued a second dispatch on April 27. The orders were for Generals Edward R. Canby and George Henry Thomas to disregard Sherman's arrangements with Johnston and to "push the enemy in every direction."

"The dispatch said that "Jeff. Davis's money was moving south from Goldsboro in wagons as fast as possible." *Thomas and Wilson were warned not to obey any orders from Sherman* and, along with Canby and all commanders on the Mississippi, were to take measures "to intercept the rebel chiefs and their plunder." Sherman was outraged. "By this time, I was in possession of the second bulletin of Mr. Stanton, *published in all the Northern newspapers*, with comments that assumed that I was a common traitor and a public enemy; and high officials had even instructed my own subordinates to disobey my lawful orders," even though Sherman's command over North Carolina had never been revoked or modified.

"Stanton was insinuating that Sherman was allowing Davis to escape with wagon loads of "specie…estimated here at from six to thirteen million dollars." Sherman was "shocked and insulted" by the tone of the dispatches coming out of Washington and the allegations that Davis had enough money to buy his escape from Sherman's army."[30]

The problem with the assertion that Jefferson Davis was trying to buy his way through Sherman's forces is absurd on the face of it, absurd because the character of the Confederate President would not have permitted such a thing, and absurd because, in the second case, we

---

[30] McNeely, op cit., pp. 146-147, emphases added.

have actually observed that Davis was trying to do no such thing.

This said, however, there are several issues worth noting. Firstly, did Mr. Lincoln *actually* issue a directive on March 3 to his Secretary of War Stanton to order his field commanders not to negotiate any surrender terms beyond those dealing directly with surrendering Confederate armies? As we shall see in the next chapter, this question is crucial, given Stanton's total control over the War Department's communications. The second thing to note from McNeely's summary of the episode is that it is clear that the Union leaders have correctly interpreted Davis' flight as a Continuity of Government operation, *not* as an attempt to plunder the treasury of the Confederacy and "escape to a rich exile in the tropics." Indeed, as will shortly become apparent, the Lincoln assassination conspirators may have had good reason to assume that Jefferson Davis was in a unique position to provide information that could have exposed them. Again, more will be said about these possibilities in the next chapter, but for the present it is now necessary to flesh out in more speculative detail the nature of the "treasure" accompanying President Davis, and why so many Union leaders were so exercised over it, and determined to prevent Davis' flight to the Trans-Mississippi Department from succeeding.

We have already noted that the specie from the banks of "Rialto in Richmond" was, for that day, a large sum, from six to thirteen million dollars. This specie has never been found, leading some people to doubt it ever really existed, and that accounts of it were merely postwar exaggerations and "the big fish that got away" stories. But again, as we have also seen, the original plan of Davis and his party was to link up with General Lee and the retreating Army of North Virginia, and thence, with the army of Joseph Johnston in concert, to make their way, and if necessary to fight their way, to the Trans-Mississippi. These armies, and their supplies, would have to be paid for, and the corresponding specie carefully guarded. This would have required an enormous sum of money, *but not one that would have likely exhausted the millions of dollars of specie reported.* So where is the "treasure"?

I submit that, again, one misunderstands the entire flight of Jefferson Davis if one understands it in any *other* way than as a Continuity of Government operation, for that government would require that its international financial contacts and resources remain intact. What the Rialto in Richmond's specie represented was therefore *the hard currency reserves of those banks necessary to the conduct of international trade and necessary to the ability to issue a stable domestic currency and to service the Confederacy's foreign debt.* Thus, contrary to all those who argue that such an amount of specie would have slowed and encumbered Davis' flight, thereby making it unlikely that such an amount was ever a component of his flight, it is an absolute requirement that such amounts of specie accompany Davis out of Richmond because the government would have required it to continue. Viewing this specie as the *reserve* of those banks also means something else, and something equally crucial: *the accounts and records of those banks* tied to the specie and its use as reserves for any loans and foreign exchange were equally crucial. These banks are, effectively, the banks of account for the Confederate Government, and thus the accounts which the specie represented are bound to be much larger in terms of dollar valuation or totals than the specie reserve.

Consequently, *three* things are present in the flight of Davis and his party that clearly indicate the whole affair as a Continuity of Government plan organized around the continuation of the "Richmond Rialto: (1) the specie alleged to accompany the party, (2) the archives and therefore the records of agents and accounts, and (3) the state seals of the departments of the Confederate government. By the time of the Union occupation of Richmond and the flight of its "rialto", intelligence about these three components of the Davis party would doubtless have filtered up through the Union chain of command to senior General officers (Grant, Sherman, and Sheridan), and to the War Department itself. Those three components would have been enough to convince the Union leaders of the real nature of the flight of the Confederate President.

It was not a plunder operation.

It was Continuity of Government.

n. *April 26, 1865,* After the original policies of the Lincoln administration, and therefore of the surrender between Sherman and Johnston, had been rejected by the new incoming Johnson administration,[31] Sherman and Johnston signed a new surrender. Notably, Johnston disobeyed orders of President Davis when he did so, for

---

[31] Oh the irony!

Davis was still planning to get to the Trans-Mississippi Department, and had good reason to believe that Johnston's army was capable enough to get him there, the number of troops under his command at that point still numbering close to 90,000.[32]

o. *April 24, 1865* "John Wilkes Booth" is allegedly shot dead at Garrett's Farm.[33]

p. *May 2, 1865:* The new Union President Andrew Johnson issues a Presidential Proclamation offering $100,000 reward for the capture of Jefferson Davis. Meanwhile, Davis' entourage burns the Confederate paper money

---

[32] McNeely, op. cit., p. 173. McNeely gives the figure of 89,360, based on Confederate prisoners from Johnston's army who had surrendered and then been released by Sherman in Florida and Georgia. Mere numbers do not tell the whole story, however, as most of these forces would have had to have been concentrated nearer to the Confederate leadership entourage to participate in enabling the flight. Nonetheless, Davis does have a point in that no effort was made to do so. In any case, it is really the surrender of Johnston, rather than of Lee, that signals the real death knell for the military fortunes of the Confederacy. There were significant forces near Davis, and these, as Davis noted after the war, might have been sufficient to enable the escape to the Trans-Mississippi. Q.v., McNeely, p. 197.

[33] Due to the fact that so much controversy surrounds Booth, and the subsequent "identification" of his corpse, we have put his name in quotation marks merely to indicate that someone is shot whom the Federal authorities maintained was John Wilkes Booth. Suffice it to say that so many anomalies crowd around the death of the assassin of President Lincoln that these will have to await the next chapter to explore.

and bonds they have with them., thus perhaps indicating that the Continuity of Government operation was now taking on the characteristics of a flight. President Davis, in response to General Johnston's second surrender to Sherman, decides to break up his command and allow subordinate units of Johnston's army to determine for themselves whether or not they wish to accept the terms of surrender or to continue fighting.[34]

q. *May 10, 1865:* President Jefferson Davis is captured by federal forces and is interred at Fort Monroe, Virginia until his release two years later. In spite of Northern calls for him to be hanged, and despite his own insistence upon a trial, he is released without trial, resumes civilian life, and writes his memoir *The Rise and Fall of the Confederate Government.*[35] In spite of being found guilty for alleged involvement in the Lincoln assassination conspiracy, there is no record of the $100,000 reward for his capture ever having been paid. Davis never appeared before a civilian court, never was able to mount his own defense in spite of insistence on both, and, as we have seen, was released, wrote his memoirs, and had his citizenship posthumously restored by a unanimous act of Congress and signed into law by President Carter.

r. *July 7, 1865:* Four Lincoln Assassination Conspirators found guilty—Mary Surratt, George Atzerodt, David Herrold,

---

[34] McNeely, op. cit. pp. 189, 193.

[35] McNeely's treatment of Davis' capture, and the origins of the notorious fiction that he was dressed in women's clothes, is found on pp. 202-202 of her study.

and Lewis Payne—are hanged. Other conspirators found guilty are sentenced to years of hard labor.

With this timeline of events now in hand, let us look more closely at the principle elements, and speculate more carefully.

B. The Evacuation of Richmond:
The Confederate Treasury and the First Signs of a Problem
1. The Confederate Treasury:
Missing Papers, Specie, and Seals of State

We have seen, firstly, the evacuation of Richmond included the following inventory:

(1) The Confederate leader, President Jefferson Davis, and certain members of his federal Cabinet, including, most importantly, Secretary of the Treasury George Trenholm, about whom we shall have more to say in part two of the present work;

(2) A large sum of money, both in specie and in Confederate paper certificates. The estimations of the amounts of this sum of money vary as much as two orders of magnitude, from hundreds of thousands of dollars to thirteen million, in specie alone. As was argued in the previous pages, while most researchers believe the lower amounts to be more accurate representations, this book argues the opposing view that the larger estimations are more congruent with the flight as a Continuity of Government operation;

(3) The characterization of the flight as a Continuity of Government operation is further buttressed by two important facts:

(a) The entourage included the evacuation of the Confederate state seals, by which is meant presumably the seals of its various executive departments of government: War, Treasury, Interior and so on; and,

(b) the goal of the operation was an evacuation of the government to the Trans-Mississippi Department of Confederate territory west of the Mississippi River, i.e., the states of Louisiana, Arkansas, Texas, and the Indian Territories.

In other words, it is a gross misunderstanding and misnomer to characterize Davis' evacuation of Richmond merely as a flight. It was that, but it was much more than that.

2. A Closer Look at the Amounts of Money and a Peculiar Point

The Continuity of Government operation becomes even more apparent when one considers just exactly what the inventory of what was traveling with Davis and his entourage included. By one estimate, the amount of gold and silver specie traveling with the Confederate President was considerable, some $500,000.[36] But this is a mere pittance considering the testimony of James Jones, President Davis' personal paid bodyguard. Jones, who would remain with Davis even during the latter's two years imprisonment at Fort

---

[36] Ibid.

Monroe after the war, gave a very different account in 1913, when he was 80; Jones was reported to have said:

> "When defeat became certain, just before the close of the war, during which I had constantly served as Col. Davis' body guard and servant, he intrusted (sic.) to me the sum of *thirteen million dollars in gold, silver coin **and English notes**,* to convey from Richmond to South Carolina… This sum was under my exclusive charge for four weeks.[37]

It should be noted that Jones' destination in South Carolina, to which he was to convey this treasure, was Newberry. In addition to this treasure, however, there was something far more important in Davis' party.

This quotation is crucial for a very important reason, for its explicit mention that, included in the inventory of money being evacuated from Richmond along with the government, an *unspecified sum of "English notes" were included.* These "notes" were actually the reserve currency of the day, the British pound sterling. There is no indication of the amount of this money, but we may assume that it was possibly considerable, and most likely constituted portions of the reserves not only of the Confederate Treasury but more importantly of the banks of the "Richmond Rialto." For any such posited Continuity of Government operation, it would have been vitally important to preserve any foreign currency reserves, especially of the international reserve currency, and to evacuate it with the government. It is to be carefully noted that *the burning of the paper currency recorded by McNeely makes no mention that the "English notes" were burned. In fact, after this one brief mention, they disappear entirely from*

---

[37] McNeely, op. cit., p. 56, emphases added.

all versions of the story of the flight. Thus, one may add to the inventory of unaccounted for missing specie, an unspecified but probably significant amount of British pound sterling notes.

However, the centerpiece of attention in Jones' story was not the "English notes" but the amount of thirteen million in specie, which Jones maintains travels *ahead* of Davis. This raises the following questions:

(1) Did the thirteen million in specie leave *with* Davis and his entourage? Or,

(2) *Ahead* of Davis and his entourage as Jones indicated; or,

(3) Were there two entirely different evacuations of millions of dollars of specie from Richmond? Did the six million dollars in specie of some reports constitute one of the evacuations, followed by another of seven million, for a total of thirteen? Or were there two evacuations of unspecified amounts? Or were both evacuations of thirteen million? In any case one is looking at the possibility of missing money.

Lest the argument thus far has been missed, let us summarize it:

(1) The flight from Richmond is clearly a Continuity of Government evacuation;

(2) The immediate intended goal was a link up with the armies of Lee and Johnson, with the ultimate goal of the Trans-Mississippi Department;

(3) As such, the continued operations of the Confederate government and military would have required much more vast sums of money, than the mere hundreds of thousands of dollars contained or mentioned in many reports. This would have required the transfers of the reserves, both specie and foreign currency and especially British pounds sterling, to enable those operations, and to provide a continuing basis for international trade.

With these thoughts firmly in hand, we turn to the other critical component of this Continuity of Government operation, the state seals of the Confederacy.

3. A Closer Look at the State Seals: Davis' Servant Jim Jones' 1913 Account of a Missing Seal

In her critically important study of the flight of Jefferson Davis, Patricia G. McNeely states that the silver seals of the Confederacy *and the engraving plates for them* were also smuggled out of Richmond. The Confederate Secretary of State, Judah Benjamin, who would end up in Great Britain after the war practicing law(!), had most of his department's papers, and its seal, entrusted to his secretary, William J. Bromwell, whose wife then hid the seal in her skirts to smuggle it from the Confederate capitol. The seal "passed through several hands before being sold in 1912 to the Confederate Museum at Richmond for $3,000, which is where it is today, in its leather case."[38]   Secretary of State

---

[38] McNeely, op. cit., p. 57.

Benjamin additionally disposed of the other official seal engraving plates by throwing them into the Savannah River.[39]

Such steps—preserving the seals themselves while destroying their engraving plates—are commensurate with a government in flight, and undergoing a nineteenth century version of what we would now call Continuity of Government operations.

There is one final story surrounding the Confederate seals, and this one only sharpens the mystery. When in 1913 he related the story of the Confederate treasure that he conveyed to South Carolina, Davis' servant Jim Jones also told another story. According to Jones, upon his return from conveying the treasure to Newberry, South Carolina, President Davis entrusted him with yet another version of the Great Seal of the Confederacy, a massive silver seal weighing ten pounds.[40] According to Jones in his 1913 story, this seal had actually been engraved in London, and smuggled into the Confederacy by its blockade runners.[41]

As one might expect, there is a problem with this story. According to Jones, whose story is recorded in the *Newberry Herald and News* in its Tuesday, Oct. 28, 1913 edition, President Davis gave Jones this seal with the following charge:

> In describing the manner and the emotions of Mr. Davis while entrusting him with this charges, ("the tears coming into his eyes") when he spoke, Jones said, 'James, I hereby

---

[39] Ibid.

[40] At a price of $25 per ounce, the silver alone in this seal would be worth $4,000. The intrinsic historical value of this seal, if ever found and if indeed it ever existed, would be much greater.

[41] McNeely, op. cit., p. 59.

hand you solemnly and sacredly, the seal of the Confederate States of America. The Southern government is about to fall. This seal, which we must and do hold sacred and undefilable, must be secreted, where no man in future (sic.) shall profane it, by public gaze and examination, I intrust (sic.) this mission to you. I hereby charge you with this seal's disappearance. Hide it and let no man know where it is. Tell not even me. And let the secret die with you."[42]

If one views President Davis' flight from Richmond as a nineteenth century "Continuity of Government" operation—which it clearly was—then this story presents a significant problem to that approach.

If Mr. Davis was intending to move the Confederate executive to another region of the Confederacy in order to continue the fight, why then would he entrust the official Great Seal of the country itself to his servant, with words acknowledging that the fight was lost, and that the seal should be hidden? Was Jones simply making the whole thing up?

The problem does not disappear if one assumes the truthfulness of Jones' story. In fact, the problem becomes much more acute *unless* one assumes that Jones' story was somehow a component of that "Continuity of Government" operation. Consider the following questions, all of which are based on the assumption that the core element of Jones' story—that there was such a seal, and that Davis entrusted it to him to hide—is true:

---

[42] McNeely, op. cit., p. 59, citing the *Newberry Herald and News,* Tuesday, October 28, 1913.

1) Did the Confederacy itself place an order for such a seal to be engraved in London, via its agents in Great Britain? Or,

2) Was the seal a gift from unknown parties in Great Britain—the Crown? The governors of the Bank of England? The Privy Council? – *to* the Confederacy? If so,

3) Did President Davis' alleged orders to Jones to *hide* the seal have some *other* purpose, namely, to conceal the fact that possession of the seal might have disclosed some hidden and unknown relationship between the Confederate government and parties in Great Britain or Europe at large? This emerges as a possibility because it is customary on such items – and especially if they are gifts – to engrave the name of the giver of the gift somewhere on the item. Similarly, if it was *not* a gift but rather a purchase from some London jeweler, again, it is customary for such items to be engraved inconspicuously with the name of the firm or individual doing the engraving, and this might again disclose relationships best kept hidden. Any such group, for diplomatic reasons, had strong reasons to keep its existence secret. However, Britain had already openly granted the Confederacy belligerent status, and thus there was less reason to disguise any support for the Confederacy from circles of power in the United Kingdom. But such support, while not entirely *secret* would therefore have wished to remain *quiet* and out of the limelight, and the Confederate executive branch and War Department would have

known this. Thus, taking the seal in Davis' treasure train on his flight from Richmond might have risked disclosure of a relationship that was best kept carefully hidden. Taking such a seal with him during his flight may have subjected that relationship to potential exposure that, in the Continuity of Government circumstances under which Davis had begun to operate, would have been better to leave unexposed, and hence, rather than run that risk, David ordered his servant to hide the seal. And finally,

4) It is possible, even at that late date, that a misdirection was being continued, that the story of the seal having been hidden by Jones somewhere in the southern states was a fabrication, while in reality, Davis may have taken it with him, and subsequently had some member of his party hide it. It is even possible that this seal, had it ever existed, was evacuated from Richmond by some other route, and was never part of Davis' treasure train, nor ever entrusted to Jones. Again, this would be classic Continuity of Government types of operation.

Viewed in *this* way, then, Jones' story of the missing Confederate Great Seal still contains the ring of truth, for nothing about it is ultimately contrary to Continuity of Government operations, especially to the types of carefully orchestrated obfuscations and deceptions that accompany them.

While there is not a shred of hard evidence to back it up other than Jones' own 1913 story, in my opinion, the seal probably existed, and probably *was* engraved in London and smuggled into the Confederacy by one of its blockade runners. And in my opinion, it was most likely a gift of some sort, by a prominent person or persons within the British power structure.

This raises the possibility that Jones' whole story of *hiding* the seal was one big misdirection. This possibility emerges when one asks the following question:

Assuming the basic story of a ten pound silver Great Seal that had been engraved in London and smuggled into the Confederacy by blockade runners to be true, into what part of the Confederacy was it smuggled?

To answer this question we have to do a bit of preliminary detective work. For such a seal to be professionally engraved and struck, one has to have time to find the jeweler via Confederate agents in Britain, which agents have to be first put into place; the design for the seal must be created (and the artist found to engrave it) and this design must, moreover, be exact replications of any designs created within the Confederacy itself and to any other Great Seals cast by the Confederacy, that is to say, must have the official approval of Confederate officials. Then the piece must be engraved and cast, and then smuggled into the Confederacy from Great Britain. As will be discovered in subsequent pages, the Confederate corporate network and agents within Europe would not really begin to coalesce until 1863 even though they were present from 1861. Thus, placing an order for such a seal, or conveying the *gift* of such a seal, would to my mind be an operation requiring perhaps a year to two years, and this would place the entry of such an object into any Confederate port within a time span from late 1862 to 1864, and probably sometime in 1863.

Given this time frame, one then has to look at the typical pattern of Confederate blockade running, and here is where our speculation regarding the alleged missing Great Seal becomes much more interesting. Most standard histories of the War Between the States stress the effectiveness of the Union blockade in shutting down the key ports of the Confederacy: Norfolk, Virginia, Wilmington, North Carolina, Charleston, South Carolina, Mobile, Alabama, New Orleans, Louisiana.   But the plain fact of the matter was that the Confederacy, much more than the Union, had an enormous coastline, and that the Union blockade was, at best, porous. Until those ports could be invaded and occupied, they remained open. But they were also, by dint of their sheer volume-handling capacity, easily subject to interdiction by Union naval forces.

Thus, the overwhelming *pattern* of most Confederate blockade running ran through the Bahamas, Hispanola, and Cuba, into the Gulf of Mexico, and thence into *Louisiana and Texas* directly, or alternatively, through Mexico, the only country with which the Confederacy shared an international border, a neutral.

To put it country simple: the Trans-Mississippi Department of the Confederacy—the states of Arkansas, Louisiana, Texas, and the Indian Territories (modern day Oklahoma)—was a lifeline of supply that it was difficult if not impossible for the Union to cut, since supplies could always be smuggled via neutral Mexico, and across its border with Texas (and obviously, trade could and did flow from the Confederacy to Europe in the reverse direction). Either a complete military occupation of the Rio Grande river would have to be made, or the Mississippi River itself would have to be occupied, which, as is now known, was the strategic course of action that the Union pursued.

And so we return to our speculations about the version of the Confederate Great Seal recounted by Davis' servant Jim Jones: where would such a seal, if it ever had existed, have been likely to have entered Confederate territory? And the answer, based on the pattern of most Confederate blockade running, must be that it most likely entered the Trans-Mississippi department of the Confederacy where it possibly remained (and possibly remains hidden to this day, on the view that Jones' story was deliberate misdirection). Our reasons for advancing this speculation must, however, await our brief exploration of the Trans-Mississippi department, the role they played in President Davis' Continuity of Government plans.

4. State Bullion Depositories

We have observed that the specie and "English notes" referred to as part of the inventory of what was evacuated from Richmond most likely formed the *reserves* of the Confederacy, and that the archives were also part of this "treasure," and indeed, the most *important* part of it. Patricia McNeely rightly draws attention to this by noting that, whatever the *actual amounts* of the treasure smuggled out of Richmond were, these were

> only a small part of the government and civilian financial holdings held in the Confederacy *and foreign countries*. Most of it would fall into the hands of looting Federal armies *and the U.S. government, which would soon send agents and soldiers accompanied by a wide-range of*

61

imposters into the former Confederacy to tax and seize gold, cotton and other commodities while an avalanche of lawsuits was launched against banks, civilians, and England.[43]

One sees in these words the *post bellum* "policy" of the new Johnson administration, a policy of plunder of the defeated Confederacy under the euphemistic name of "reconstruction." While we shall have to say more about *why* such a policy had to be adopted in Part Two, suffice it for the moment to note that the closest analogy to this *post bellum* plunder of Southern resources, already severely depleted by the war, is the "Rape of Russia" after the collapse of the Soviet Union, and includes, conspicuously enough, "carpetbaggers" buying up assets on the cheap.

The reason for this widespread plunder operation may, perhaps, be more readily appreciated by recalling a salient feature of the pre-bellum banking system both in the Union and in what would become the Confederacy: there was *no* national banking system, nor any such thing as nationally chartered banks. In so far as banks had charters, these were from individual states. Thus, states could (and did) appoint banks to be their agents of account, and as such, these banks functioned as state depositories of bullion, in the form of gold and silver coins. In effect, *the system was one of "bi-metallism"*, an important point with massive repercussions after the war, as we shall see.[44] This is an important point, for

---

[43] McNeely, op. cit., pp. 61-62, emphasis added.

[44] McNeely discusses the largest banks with the largest such reserves in the Confederacy on pp. 61-62, but without explicit reference to the concept of "bi-metallism" in connection to its huge importance to the *post bellum* monetary debates.

it means two significant things: (1) while the Confederacy did not enter the war with a central bullion depository nor even a *plan* about its finances, it did nevertheless have (2) several state banks that acted as bullion and specie depositories and in some cases as the agents of account for the state governments. This fact, plus its commodities based economy, provides the basis from which to understand its financial and more specifically currency experiments during the war.

5. General Sherman's Curious and Very Telling Omissions

In the timeline previously recounted, we noted General Sherman's outrage at the suggestion that he was committing treason by allegedly aiding and abetting the flight of Jefferson Davis to the trans-Mississippi, and via the initial surrender terms imposed upon and accepted by General Joseph Johnston. But there are a number of curiosities that surround the Union General and his army. The story of Sherman's "march to the sea" is well known to both to scholars and amateur historians of the War Between the States. Sherman's army, using the confiscation acts, literally loots, plunders, and burns its way in a wide swath from eastern Tennessee to the Georgia Atlantic coast, before turning its tender attentions northward to the Carolinas.

While this plunder, notes McNeely, "was apparently never documented in any official reports,"[45] there *does* exist a letter from a Lieutenant Thomas G. Myers to his wife, dated February 26, 1865, which describes how Sherman's army regulated its plunder operations and booty distribution to the soldiers. After noting that Sherman's army was nothing but a

---

[45] McNeely, op. cit., p. 64.

"universal license to burn" and that "plunder was the order of the day,"[46] Myers goes on to state how the spoils were divided:

> The valuables procured we estimate by companies. Each company is required to exhibit the result of its operations at any given place. One-fifth and first choice falls to the share of the Commander-in-chief and staff, one-fifth to field officers of regiments, and three-fifths to the company. *Officers are not allowed to join these expeditions without disguising themselves as privates....* Officers over the rank of Captain are not made to put their plunder in the estimate for general distribution.[47]

Several important points are to be observed about this statement:

(1) Sherman's army's plunder operation was a well-organized *and regulated* affair, and extended up to and inclusive of Sherman and his command staff, as they were personal recipients of some of the plunder; but,

(2) Officers were *not* permitted to appear in the uniforms of their rank while conducting or overseeing such operations, indicating that while the plunder operations were organized, the army was maintaining a public posture of what would now be called "plausible deniabity", giving the

---

[46] Ibid.

[47] Ibid.pp. 64-65, emphasis added, citing James G. Gibbes, *Who Burnt Columbia* (Newberry, South Carolina: Elbert H. Aull Company, 1902), pp. 60-61.

appearance that the plunder operations were not those of *policy*, but of a *rabble*.

There is one final point that emerges from Myers' letter, and that is his claim about what happened when Sherman's army reached Columbia, South Carolina. So vast was the plunder seized at Columbia that Myers wrote his wife that "We took gold and silver enough from the d----d rebels to have redeemed their infernal currency twice over," a currency which, Myers went on to notice—without apparently being aware of his glaring contradiction—the Union soldiers burned whenever they encountered it because, as Myers noted, "we consider it utterly worthless."[48] So the third point to be observed and carefully noted is this:

(3) The amount of gold and silver plundered at Columbia, South Carolina was so large that a Union officer resorted to a bit of hyperbole to convey how much had been plundered: enough to redeem the Confederate certificates "twice over" is described in the next breath as "entirely worthless." Which is it? Entirely worthless? Or redeemable to some degree, if even not the extravagant degree indicated by Myers? In any case, the Myers letter is testimony to the fact that, for however much the Confederacy was struggling economically (and it was), it was *not* bereft of financial resources for a Continuity of Government effort.

---

[48] McNeely, op. cit., p. 65.

This is not all, however, for Lieutenant Myers also explicitly states that General Sherman himself had acquired enough gold and silver "to start a bank," noting that his personal share of booty from Columbia alone came to two hundred and seventy-five dollars. He then ends his letter to his wife with a warning not to make its contents known to anyone outside their family.[49]

For those seeking contemporary analogies to Sherman's Union plunder operation, the closest analogy to its efficiency would be Operation Golden Lily, the plunder operation of the Japanese imperial family conducted by its military throughout occupied China, Asia, and the Pacific Islands. In this regard it is also intriguing and necessary to note while General Sherman was outraged over the implication that the missing thirteen million dollars of C.S.A. specie was used by Confederate General Johnston (whom, let it be noted, at no point ever had access to it) to bribe Sherman to allow Davis to escape, amid all his huffing and puffing, Sherman never mentioned, much less denied, the allegations explicitly![50] Rather, in his post-war memoirs, General Sherman maintained that Davis, during his flight, had somehow managed to *spend* and squander this enormous amount of money, in coins no less (!), during his flight, and in open contradiction to the fact that one witness who accompanied Davis' party and who had charge over the

---

[49] McNeely, op. cit., p. 65.

[50] McNeely, op. cit., p. 56. This is McNeely's observation. Personally, reprehensible as I think Sherman's army's behavior and some of his own to be, I have difficulty believing that he could be bribed in such a blatant manner.

66

party's treasury funds, maintained that Davis had no gold![51] Sherman's plunder activities were all done under color of law, under the Union confiscation act of July 17, 1862,[52] an act and policy that were at some variance with Lincoln's own thoughts and policies.

Before ending our review of President Davis' Continuity of Government operation, a final word is necessary. The inevitable post bellum Union-Federal effort to recoup monies from foreign Confederate accounts and operations and to pursue damages through legal actions is a hint at the sheer scale of the short-lived Confederacy's international financial operations. While we shall have occasion to refer to these in more detail later in this book, we note for the present only another analogy to more recent and similar events. The United States government at the end of World War Two made every effort to shut down *all* surviving financial operations and corporate fronts of the defeated Axis powers and to recover those assets as war booty. Those operations were to a great degree successful. However, considerable sums and fronts were never exposed, nor recovered. And that is the case here: to assume that the *post bellum* Union was completely and one hundred percent successful in recovering lost Confederate accounts or pressing damages against the Confederacy's foreign corporate and private connections is to assume an absurdity.

---

[51] Ibid., p. 207.
[52] Ibid., p. 231.

C. Some Remaining Glaring Anomalies

We began this book and this chapter by pointing out that President Carter signed into law a Congressional resolution posthumously restoring the American citizenship of Confederate President Jefferson Davis. Despite Davis' own disgusted shock at the news that someone had murdered his Union counterpart, and despite all the strange twists and turns of his own flight from Richmond to his eventual capture by Union forces, there is one final and glaring spotlight on the bizarre nature of the posthumous restoration of his citizenship:

> Two American Presidents were accused of having had a hand in Lincoln's murder.
>
> Jefferson Davis, President of the Confederacy, was named as a leading assassination conspirator in an official indictment set forth by the U.S. Government. While held as a Federal prisoner in Fortress Monroe, *Davis was found guilty as charged by a United States Military Commission trying Booth's accomplices in Washington, D.C.*
>
> **But Davis himself was never put on trial. All efforts to bring him to court were eventually quashed. Although he had been found guilty in absentia, the Confederacy's President was finally granted official amnesty.**
>
> *(Union Secretary of War Edwin) Stanton's Bureau of Military Justice had claimed there was a great deal of evidence linking Jefferson Davis to the assassination conspiracy. But this evidence, like the indictment, somehow dissolved. In the end a cloak of censorship was thrown over*

the whole Davis case. The modern historian endeavoring to investigate the records finds himself groping in a vacuum.[53]

The question is, what was it about Jefferson Davis that merited such a wild spectrum of responses and complete reversals? Tried *in absentia* by a military tribunal of questionable jurisdiction to begin with, found guilty while the Union's War Department and its Secretary Edwin Stanton carefully avoided allowing him to ever appear personally and state his case and defense for the record, and *then* to be granted amnesty, and *then* a century later, regaining citizenship? Extraordinary indeed!

It is almost as if someone, even in the middle of the twentieth century, wanted either to keep something very secret, something that perhaps Jefferson Davis knew, but which he was not talking about, or the converse, that by restoring his citizenship, they wanted to draw attention to. At the end of this book I shall offer a few speculations—wild and bizarre though they may be—as to what Davis may have known, and what he may also have known not to talk about.

As for the other American President, Abraham Lincoln, he too invites analogical comparisons, for yet a *third* American president is suspected of having *some* sort of role and hand Lincoln's murder: his very own Vice President, Lyndon Baines Johns... er... Andrew Johnson:[54]

---

[53] Theodore Roscoe, *The Web of Conspiracy: The Complete Story of the Men Who Murdered Abraham Lincoln* (Englewood Cliffs, New Jersey: 1959), pp. 25-26, emphases added.

[54] It's very difficult at times to keep the parallels separate in one's mind.

Could Johnson conceivably—just conceivably—have had a hand…?

The question stems from three others.

Was Andrew Johnson personally acquainted with John Wilkes Booth?

Where was Andrew Johnson during the dark hours Lincoln lay dying?

Why did Johnson himself never answer these questions? Or, if he did answer them, why were the answers withheld from the public?[55]

And as if those ominous parallels between the Lincoln and John F. Kennedy assassinations were not enough, consider this evaluation of Vice President Johnson:

> Censorship condemned him to a sort of historical mediocrity. Today's American histories and standard biographies do not answer the questions which compose the "incubus" that haunted … Johnson. If honest, the historians confess they do not know the facts because the facts were never fully disclosed.[56]

At the ellipsis in the quotation, I have deliberately deleted the name "Andrew" in order to make the parallelism between the two infamous presidential assassinations, and their respective Vice Presidents, clearer. It is even more disturbing to note

---

[55] Theodore Roscoe, *The Web of Conspiracy*, pp. 26-27.

[56] Ibid. p. 27. At the ellipsis in the quotation, I have deliberately deleted the name "Andrew" in order to make the parallelism clearer. It is even more disturbing to note that Roscoe's book was published *before* the assassination of President Kennedy, and the subsequent suspicions cast on Vice President (Lyndon, not Andrew!) Johnson.

that Roscoe's book, from which this quotation was taken, was published *before* the assassination of President Kennedy, and thus before the subsequent suspicions cast on Vice President (Lyndon, not Andrew!) Johnson.

The anomalies continue to pile up. Lincoln's Vice President, Andrew Johnson, upon assuming the office of the presidency, issued Presidential Proclamation No. 131, offering a $100,000 reward for the live capture and arrest of Davis. In the Proclamation, Johnson stated that "evidence from the Bureau of Military Justice in the murder of Lincoln and the attempted assassination of (Secretary of State) Seward were *'incited, concerted, and procured'*"[57] by Confederate President Jefferson Davis.

Again, this proclamation only serves to highlight the glaring anomalies surrounding President Davis, for President Johnson's Proclamation clearly and squarely fixes the ultimate foreknowledge and responsibility for the murder of Lincoln and the attacks on Secretary of State Seward on Davis himself. Yet, in spite of being tried *in absentia* by a military tribunal—a legally dubious procedure—Davis himself was never brought before that tribunal nor before any other court, *when he was clearly in Federal custody and it would have been easy to do.* In yet another anomaly, and in spite of the fact that President Johnson had publicly offered a reward for Davis' capture, "there is no record that any of the reward money…was ever paid."[58]

---

[57] Patricia G. McNeely, *President Abraham Lincoln, General William T. Sherman, President Jefferson Davis, and the Lost Confederate Gold* (Personal Publication: 2015, ISBN 13-978-1517212384), p. 189, emphasis added.

[58] Ibid. p. 220.

Rather, as has been stated, Davis is granted amnesty, and over a century later, his citizenship is posthumously restored!

We are *still* not yet quite done with all this truly high strangeness!

As has already been stated, after his amnesty and release from federal custody, in the final years of his life, Davis wrote *The Rise and Fall of the Confederate Government*, a massive two-volume study of over fifteen hundred pages' length.[59] Davis' knowledge, wide reading and education are in clear evidence in the work, as is his mastery of the Philadelphia Constitution of 1787, the writings not only of the Federalists, but of the Anti-Federalists, and his skill as a lawyer. Even his thorough exposure to classical Latin and Greek authors comes through with elegant diction or turns of phrase.

But in all that massive work, there is *no* mention of Lincoln's murder, the trial of the conspirators, his own trial in absentia, nor of his never appearing in person before *any* court or tribunal. As is to be expected in a book about the rise and fall of the Confederate *Government*, there is a great deal of discussion of its military operations, its foreign affairs, and so on. For all that, however, there is but one *very* brief mention of the Confederate Government's financial system. And more importantly, there is no mention, in all that

---

[59] Jefferson Davis, *The Rise and Fall of the Confederate Government* (London and New York: Thomas Yoseloff, 1958, no ISBN). I was fortunate enough to discover this edition in a hardcover, slipcase reprint by the publisher in the early 1980s while I was in graduate school in Oklahoma being sold for a mere $25.00.

verbiage, of the Trans-Mississippi Department of General Edward Kirby Smith—or "Kirby Smithdom" as it was known in the day—that was the ultimate *goal and objective* of Davis' Continuity of Government flight!

All of this compels more questions: Was someone trying to cover-up something by the posthumous restoration of Davis' citizenship, or the converse, was someone trying to draw attention to something? In either case, what was *"something"*? Or was the whole thing simply what it was presented to be, an innocent attempt at the binding of the nation's wounds and the recognition that, for whatever else he was, Davis was not an unprincipled nor evil man, and had no hand in nor foreknowledge of the assassination of his Union counterpart.

Taking the telltale omissions from Davis' memoir as clues, one may draw the following conclusions and implications that will guide the inquiries in subsequent chapters:

Something is massively, massively wrong, it may have something to do with money, finance, and Davis' attempted flight to and Continuity of Government in the Trans-Mississippi department; that "something" has also to do with Lincoln's assassination. In order to gain more clues as to what that "something" might be, we must look more closely at America's first and most infamous presidential assassination, that of Abraham Lincoln.

Joseph P. Farrell

Judah Benjamin, Confederate Secretary of State
March 18, 1862—May 10, 1865

Salmon Chase, Union Secretary of the Treasury
March 7, 1861—June 20, 1864

74

2
THE ANOMALIES OF ABE'S ASSASSINATION

*"Seventy years after the crime, writers were garbing it with a
dignity it did not deserve: Lincoln, the stereotyped martyr; Booth,
the stereotyped villain; the assassination avenged by classic
justice; conspiracy strangled; Virtue (in the robes of Government)
emerging triumphant, and Lincoln 'belonging to the Ages.'... thus
a towering edifice of so-called history was erected on sand."*
Theodore Roscoe[1]
*"...(The) case is an omnibus of mysteries,... a labyrinthian
anthology."*
Theodore Roscoe[2]

AS WAS EVIDENT FROM THE PREVIOUS CHAPTER, strange financial details and military circumstances surrounded Confederate President Jefferson Davis' flight from Richmond and attempted escape to the Trans-Mississippi Department or "Kirby-Smithdom." As a result, the War Between the States did not so much "end" as it simply petered out, sputtering and wheezing to a stop from sheer exhaustion, coughing out one last steamy spin of the crankshaft as the over-heated engine gave its last effort before it simply seized up and stopped.

This seems completely contradicted by the images carefully implanted in the public consciousness; it is thus important to note that this public consciousness is not uniquely American, and this fact—that the images of the end

---

[1] Theodore Roscoe, *The Web of Conspiracy: The Complete Story of the Men Who Murdered Abraham Lincoln* (Englewood Cliffs, New Jersey: Prentice-Hall, Inc., 1960, no ISBN), pp. vii-viii.

[2] Ibid., p. 27.

of the war are not confined to Americans – should be the first clue that something is very wrong with those images, for virtually every educated person in the globe "knows" that there are two archetypal events that brought the war to a sudden and very clear stop. There was, firstly, the "movie" that plays out in our minds: the iconic surrender of Confederate Lieutenant General Robert E. Lee, his bag of tactical tricks finally exhausted, outfought, out-supplied, outnumbered, and outgunned by his arch-rival, Union General Ulysses S. Grant, at Appomattox Courthouse on April 9, 1865. The two generals and a small number of their staffs meet, salute each other, exchange pleasantries, and discuss the terms of surrender. The terms are agreed upon, the documents drawn up, copied, and signed by the respective generals and witnessed by a few of their staff officers. Then General Lee rises, shakes hands with Grant, and exits the courthouse. General Grant and his officers raise their hats in respect, and Lee rides off on his favorite white horse, Traveler, and the first Confederate field army to surrender is accomplished. It is only a matter of time now. Somewhat later the rest of the Confederate field armies under Joseph Johnston surrender, Jefferson Davis is captured; case closed, war over, movie ends.

The second iconic event signaling the finale was, of course, the sudden and bloody end of Abraham Lincoln himself at the hand of an assassin while the President and his wife and a small entourage of guests attended an evening play at Ford's Theater in Washington, D.C. on Good Friday Evening, April 14, 1865. The assassin murdered him with a small pistol with a shot to the head behind the President's left side, execution-style, in an act curiously all-too-similar to more modern Mafia-style "hits". At this point, the crazed assassin takes no pains to disguise his identity, for he leaps from the President's box to the stage and injures or twists his left (or was it the right?) foot in the effort. He is widely recognized by the theater goers and the thespians on the stage as the noted and famous actor John Wilkes Booth, who shouts "*Sic semper tyranis!*" (Thus always to tyrants) before running from the theater. Lincoln himself, mortally wounded, is carried to the Petersen house across the street, where he lingers until approximately 7:22 of the next morning, when he finally expires. The accomplices of Booth are rounded up, the "more guilty" are tried and hung, the others given long prison sentences. Booth himself is shot in the barn of a farm while trying to escape, and buried. Case closed, justice served, movie ends.

And thus, we are "informed", did the terrible four years' War Between the States "end."

As was seen in the previous chapter, many questions lingered, however, so it *had* to "end" somehow, lest too many people start asking too many awkward questions. Lest people look too closely, best to contrive the fiction that President Davis was apprehended wearing a woman's clothes. That will detract attention from what appears to be a large amount of missing money. Lest people look too closely, best to strangle questions by hanging a few of the assassination conspirators, and keeping a few others—Davis himself included, as we have seen—incommunicado, at least, for a while.

From the retrospective of nearly two centuries, however, there are as many deep and dark actors and connections behind the assassination of Abraham Lincoln as there are behind that of John F. Kennedy, and indeed, the types of players (and their motivations) are remarkably similar, for they have a lot to do with the Rialto in Richmond, the Weasels of Wall Street, and the Serpents of the City, that is, with *money*. To appreciate these types of players, their roles, their motivations, and their similarities to the Kennedy assassination, we must look closely at some of the known details of the Lincoln Assassination. Here, however, we are more fortunate than we are with the Kennedy Assassination, for in the case of the Lincoln assassination, rather than hundreds of books and articles spanning many decades with which to contend, there are surprisingly few "classic studies" with which an investigator must contend: Otto Eisenschiml's *Why Was Lincoln Murdered?*(1937), Theodore Roscoe's *The Web of Conspiracy: The Complete Story of the Men Who Murdered Abraham Lincoln* (1959), and David Balsiger's and Charles E. Sellier, Jr's *The Lincoln Conspiracy* (1977).

A. The Centrality of Otto Eisenschiml's Study: Anomalies Galore

Notwithstanding the fact of its publication in 1937, Otto Eisenschiml's *Why Was Lincoln Murdered?* remains perhaps the best single-volume investigation and catalogue of the anomalies surrounding the murder of President Abraham Lincoln that is more or less easily available to the public. The catalogue of anomalies surveyed in his study all point irresistibly to but one conclusion: that there was a massive conspiracy to murder not only the President but select members of his cabinet, and that the conspiracy could not have been organized, financed, nor accomplished without the aid and active participation of high members of his own government and political party. Like the equally infamous assassination of John F. Kennedy a little less than a century later, that of Lincoln was in reality a *coup d'etat* designed to bring about a wholesale change in the policy of the government *vis-à-vis* southern reconstruction, and to further enrich and empower the conspirators in the process.

But much more importantly, *it was also to ensure the death of the financial system(s) under which not only the Union, but the Confederacy, had prosecuted the war*, and it is that fact which suggests not only deep players, but the deepest, and very likely international, ones.

Eisenschiml's investigation consequently has the same relationship to the murder of Lincoln as the research and publications of attorney Mark Lane[3], researcher Harold Weisberg[4], New Orleans District Attorney Jim Garrison, forensic pathologist Dr. Cyril Wecht or other early J.F.K. researchers stand in relationship to that event: one simply cannot ignore it if one wishes to construct any revisionist history of the event, for just as those early J.F.K. researchers did, Eisenschiml erects the basic scaffolding for the revisionist view of the Lincoln murder that the subsequent studies, while contributing many important nuances and details, in the end merely elaborate. Similarly, while not nearly as detailed as Theodore Roscoe's *Web of Conspiracy* nor as up-to-date on more recently discovered anomalies and theories such as Balsiger's and Sellier's *Lincoln Conspiracy*,

---

[3] Lane, for those unaware, was a campaign volunteer for Mr. Kennedy's presidential campaign in New York, an early skeptic of the Warren Commission Report, and hired to represent Marguerite Oswald, Lee Harvey Oswald's mother, in an efforts to clear her son's name. Lane subsequently authored a number of books questioning the "lone nut" narrative, including *Plausible Deniability*.

[4] Harold Weisberg was yet another early skeptic of the Warren Report (in fact, one of the earliest). His two-volume study, *Whitewash* remains an early assassination revisionism classic, and outlines most of the prominent problems with the Warren Report. Subsequent authors and researchers would build on the profoundly robust scaffolding he constructed.

Eisenschiml's book has another distinct advantage in its topical, rather than chronological, arrangement. One never loses the thread of the argument, and by the end of the book, the reader is left with an all but overwhelming and compelling *prima facie* case that the assassination was, like that of Kennedy, the action of a desperate and greedy cabal of a military-industrial-intelligence complex and high international finance. We shall follow Eisenschiml's topical arrangement of the argument for a *coup d'etat* closely here, occasionally embellishing his presentation with our own references to the other studies. Indeed, even in the section headings which follow, the title of those sections are often deliberate paraphrases and summaries of Eisenschiml's own chapter titles, or actual quotations of those chapter headings from Eisenschiml's study, and are laid out as closely to the order that he presents it as possible, in the hope that this will allow the reader to see how carefully crafted and structured an argument his original work was. When necessary information from the other two studies will be added.

1. The First Ominous Parallel with J.F.K.:
Stripping the President of Security
a. Stanton's Five Telegrams of April 15, 1865, the Day After
the Assassination

Eisenschiml began his book by observing that Lincoln's assassination "has never been more concisely told than through the official telegrams in which Secretary of War Stanton informed the world of that tragedy."[5] For the most part, these five telegrams, all sent by Stanton during the small

---

[5] Otto Eisenschiml, *Why Was Lincoln Murdered?* (New York: Grosset and Dunlap, 1937, no ISBN), p. 6.

morning hours of April 15, 1865, as President Lincoln lay dying in a bedroom of the Petersen house near Ford's theater, were sent through Major General Dix in New York, as he was the established liaison with the Union press.[6] It is important to note that Secretary of War Edwin Stanton had virtually total control over the post-assassination investigation, press releases, and the military tribunal that eventually tried the conspirators. These five telegrams document Stanton's role in fashioning the narrative of the assassination; they are, so to speak, the Lincoln Assassination's version of the Warren Report. In the sections which now follow, I quote from these telegrams as they are given in Eisenschiml, with my commentary following.

Edwin Stanton,
Union Secretary of War

---

[6] Eisenschiml, op. cit., p. 6.

(1)The Telegram from Stanton to Major General Dix of April 15, 1865, 1:30 AM

WAR DEPARTMENT
April 15, 1865—1:30 A.M.
(Sent 2:14 A.M.)

Major-General Dix,
New York:

Last evening, about 10:30 P.M., at Ford's Theater, the President, while sitting in his private box with Mrs. Lincoln, Miss Harris, and Major Rathbone, was shot by an assassin, who suddenly entered the box and approached behind the President. The assassin then leaped upon the stage, brandishing a large dagger or knife, and made his escape in the rear of the theater. The pistol-ball entered the back of the President's head, and penetrated nearly through the head. The wound is mortal. The President has been insensible ever since it was inflicted, and is now dying.

About the same hour an assassin (whether the same or another) entered Mr. Seward's home, and, under pretense of having a prescription, was shown to the Secretary's sick chamber. The Secretary was in bed, a nurse and Miss Seward with him. The assassin immediately rushed to the bed, inflicted two or three stabs on the throat and two on the face. It is hoped the wounds may not be mortal; my apprehension is that they will prove fatal. The noise alarmed Mr. Frederick Seward, who was in an adjoining room, and hastened to the door of his father's room, where he met the assassin, who inflicted upon him one or more dangerous wounds. The recovery of Frederick Seward is doubtful.

It is not probable that the President will live through the night. *General Grant and wife were advertised to be at the theater this evening, but he started to Burlington at 6 o'clock this evening. At a Cabinet meeting yesterday, at which General Grant was present, the subject of the state*

82

*of the country and the prospects of speedy peace was
discussed.* **The President was very cheerful and hopeful;
spoke very kindly of General Lee and others of the
Confederacy**, *and the establishment of government in
Virginia. All the members of the Cabinet except Mr.
Seward are now in attendance upon the President.* I have
seen Mr. Seward, but he and Frederick were both
unconscious.

EDWIN M. STANTON,
Secretary of War[7]

(2) The Second Telegram from Stanton to Major General Dix of April 15, 1865, 3:00 AM

WASHINGTON CITY
No. 458 Tenth Street, April 15, 1865—3 A.M.
(Sent 3:20 A.M.)

Major-General Dix:
(Care Horner, New York.)

The President still breathes, but is quite insensible,
as he has been ever since he was shot. He evidently did not
see the person who shot him, but was looking on the stage
as he was approached behind.

Mr. Seward has rallied, and it is hoped he may live.
Frederick Seward's condition is very critical. The attendant
who was present was stabbed through the lungs, and is not
expected to live. The wounds of Major Seward are not
serious. *Investigation strongly indicated J. Wilkes Booth as
the assassin of the President. Whether it was the same or a
different person that attempted to murder Mr. Seward
remains in doubt.* Chief Justice Carter is engaged in taking
the evidence. *Every exertion has been made to prevent the
escape of the murderer.* His horse has been found on the
road, near Washington.

EDWIN M. STANTON,

---

[7] Otto Eisenschiml, op. cit., pp. 6-7, emphases added.

Secretary of War.[8]

(3) The Third Telegram from Stanton to Major General Dix of April 15, 1865, 4:10 AM

WASHINGTON CITY
No. 458 Tenth Street, April 15, 1865—4:10 A.M.
(Sent 4:44 A.M.)

Major-General Dix:

The President continues insensible and is sinking. Secretary Seward remains without change. Frederick Seward's skull is fractured in two places, besides a severe cut upon the head. The attendant is still alive but hopeless. Major Seward's wounds are not dangerous.

It is now ascertained with reasonable certainty that two assassins were engaged in the horrible crime, Wilkes Booth being the one that shot the President, the other a companion of his whose name is not known, but whose description is so clear that he can hardly escape. **It appears from a letter found in Booth's trunk that the murder was planned before the 4th of March, but fell through then because the accomplice backed out until "Richmond could be heard from."**

Booth and his accomplice were at the livery stable at 6 this evening, and left there with their horses about 10 o'clock, or shortly before that hour. It would seem that they had for several days been seeking their chance, but for some unknown reason it was not carried into effect until last night. One of them has evidently made his way to Baltimore, the other has not yet been traced.

EDWIN M. STANTON,
Secretary of War.[9]

---

[8] Otto Eisenschiml, op. cit., p. 7, emphases added.
[9] Otto Eisenschiml, op. cit., pp. 7-8, emphases added.

(4) The Fourth Telegram from Stanton to Major General Dix of April 15, 1865, No Time Stamp

This short telegram to Major-General Dix needs no commentary, for it is simply Secretary Stanton's announcement to the country, through the military liaison with the press, that President Lincoln had succumbed to his wound and died:

WASHINGTON CITY
April 15, 1865

Major-General Dix,
New York:
Abraham Lincoln died this morning at 22 minutes after 7 o'clock.

EDWIN M. STANTON,
Secretary of War.[10]

(5) The Fifth Installment of Stanton,
His Letter to the American Ambassador to the Court of St. James,
April 15, 1865, 11:40 AM

The final communication from Secretary of War Stanton that day was not in the form of a telegram, but rather an epistle written to the American ambassador to Great Britain. Eisenschiml quips that "considering the circumstances under which this communication was composed, it is a masterly effort."[11]

---

[10] Ibid., p. 8.
[11] Otto Eisnschiml, op. cit., p. 8.

85

WAR DEPARTMENT
Washington City, April 15, 1865—11:40 A.M.
HON. CHARLES FRANCIS ADAMS,
Minister of the United States to Her Britannic Majesty:

SIR: It has become my distressing duty to announce to you that last night His Excellency Abraham Lincoln, President of the United States, was assassinated about the hour of 10:30 o'clock in his private box at Ford's Theater in this city. The President about 8 o'clock accompanied Mrs. Lincoln to the theater. Another lady and gentleman were with them in the box. About 10:30, during a pause in the performance, the assassin entered the box, the door of which was unguarded, hastily approached the President from behind, and discharged a pistol at his head. The bullet entered the back of his head and penetrated nearly through. The assassin then leaped from the box upon the stage, brandishing a large knife or dagger and exclaiming "*Sic semper tyrannis*," and escaped in the rear of the theater. Immediately upon the discharge the President fell to the floor insensible, and continued in that state until 7:20 o'clock this morning, when he breathed his last.

About the same time this murder was being committed at the theater another assassin presented himself at the door of Mr. Seward's residence, gained admission by pretending he had a prescription from Mr. Seward's physician, which he was directed to see administered, hurried up to the third-story chamber, where Mr. Seward was lying. He here encountered Mr. Frederick Seward, struck him over the head, inflicting several wounds, and fracturing the skull in two places, inflicting, it is feared, mortal wounds. He then rushed into the room where Mr. Seward was in bed, attended by a young daughter and a male nurse. The male attendant was stabbed through the lungs, and it is believed will die. The assassin then struck Mr. Seward with a knife or dagger twice in the throat and twice in the face, inflicting terrible wounds. By this time

Major Seward, the eldest son of the Secretary, and another attendant reached the room, and rushed to the rescue of the Secretary. They were also wounded in the conflict, and the assassin escaped. No artery or important blood vessel was severed by any of the wounds inflicted upon him, but he was for a long time insensible from the loss of blood. Some hopes of his possible recovery are entertained.

Immediately upon the death of the President notice was given to Vice-President Johnson, who happened to be in the city, and upon whom the office of President now devolves. He will take the oath of office and assume the functions of President to-day. *The murderer of the President has been discovered, and evidence obtained that these horrible crimes were committed in execution of a conspiracy deliberately planned and set on foot by rebels, under pretense of avenging the South and aiding the rebel cause.* It is hoped that the immediate perpetrators will be caught. The felling occasioned by these atrocious crimes is so great, sudden, and overwhelming that I cannot at present do more than communicate them to you at the earliest moment.

Yesterday the President called a Cabinet meeting, at which General Grant was present. He was more cheerful and happy than I had ever seen, rejoiced at the near prospect of firm and durable peace at home and abroad, manifested in marked degree the kindness and humanity of his disposition, and the tender and forgiving spirit that so eminently distinguished him. *Public notice had been given that he and General Grant would be present at the theater, and the opportunity of adding the lieutenant-general to the number of victims to be murdered was no doubt seized for the fitting*
occasion *of executing plans that appear to have been in preparation for some weeks. But General Grant was compelled to be absent, and thus escaped the designs upon him.*

87

It is needless for me to say anything in regard to the influence which this atrocious murder of the President may exercise upon the affairs of this country, but I will only add that *horrible as are the atrocities that have been resorted to by the enemies of this country, they are not likely in any degree to impair that public spirit or postpone the complete and final overthrow of the rebellion.*

In profound grief for the events which it has become my duty to communicate to you, I have the honor to be, very respectfully, your obedient servant,

EDWIN M. STANTON[12]

The careful reader will have observed something in Secretary of War Stanton's missives; or rather, will *not* have observed something in those missives, because that "something" is not there; its omission is the clearest clue that there is something very wrong with President Lincoln's assassination. As we shall discover momentarily, Stanton, as Union Secretary of War, was responsible for Presidential security. Yet, in these earliest reports—most of them intended for the military liaison to the New York City press—there is *not one* mention of Mr. Lincoln's security, nor how an assassin managed to make his way into the Presidential box. Mr. Lincoln's security is, quite simply, not there in Stanton's reports. All that Stanton *does* say in this respect is that the door to the presidential box at the theater "had been left unguarded".[13] Nor is any mention made of *who* had left it unguarded, nor under what circumstances.

---

[12] Otto Eisenschiml, op. cit., pp. 8-10, emphases added.
[13] Ibid., p. 11.

b. Lincoln's Request for Particular Security Personnel & Stanton's Denial; Parker's Dereliction of Duty

Stanton's omission of any reference to Mr. Lincoln's security on the night of the assassination is most probably related to his peculiar and suspicious behavior in handling it prior to the event. President Lincoln's security on the night of the assassination was to have been provided by one John F. Parker, an officer of the Washington Metropolitan Police force, an officer who possessed, at best, a dubious record.[14] How he came to be assigned to duty at the White House is even stranger, for on April 3, 1865, Mrs. Mary Todd Lincoln, on White House stationary, personally wrote a certification assigning him to duty there. "This is to certify," it said, "that John F. Parker, a member of the Metropolitan Police has been detailed for duty at the Executive Mansion by order of Mrs. Lincoln."[15] Then and now, no one knows how Parker came to Mrs. Lincoln's attention, nor why she would have procured him a position in presidential security. This is not to suggest that the always mercurial and emotional Mrs. Lincoln had a hand in her husband's murder. It is, however, likely that Parker presented the conspirators with an opportunity, for during intermission he was apparently lured away from guarding the presidential box to have a drink with the President's valet and coachman.[16]

---

[14] See Eisenschiml, op. cit., pp. 11-13, for a review of Parker's record prior to being assigned to presidential security.

[15] Ibid., p. 14.

[16] Ibid., pp. 16-17.

*Mrs. Mary Todd Lincoln's Handwritten Note Certifying the
Appointment of Metropolitan Policeman John F. Parker to
the Executive Mansion Security*[17]

---

[17] Eisenschiml, op. cit., p. 15.

Needless to say, "Mrs. Lincoln herself believed that Parker was involved in the conspiracy to murder her husband."[18] Indeed, shortly after the assassination, Parker, still on guard duty at the White House, ran afoul of Mrs. Lincoln's notorious temper as she confronted the man for what she assumed was his alleged part in the murder, leaving Parker to protest meekly that at best he was guilty only of negligence, and that he had no part in any conspiracy.

But if Mrs. Lincoln's behavior in her grief was at least understandable, that of Secretary of War Stanton was downright suspicious and inexplicable:

> Even those only superficially acquainted with the history of the Civil War period would probably surmise that this policeman, guilty of criminal neglect while on important duty, was promptly court-martialed and executed. Stanton was in complete control of the situation and, without Lincoln's gentler hands to stay him, one would have expected the austere Secretary of War to make sure that the delinquent officer was summarily dealt with. Had not Stanton acquired a reputation for merciless severity toward poor country lads in uniform who had fallen asleep on sentry duty after long, weary marches? Had he not repeatedly and violently remonstrated with Lincoln for undermining the discipline of the army by letting clemency supersede justice? Now that he Chief was dead, murdered through the unbelievable carelessness of a special guard for whom no mitigating circumstances could be pleaded, one would certainly have expected that Stanton would have had Parker shot at dawn.
>
> But Stanton did exactly nothing. Parker was not shot; nor was he court-martialed. He not only kept his life, he also kept his position. He was not reprimanded, not

---

[18] Eisenschiml, op. cit., p. 18.

dismissed, not even immediately relieved of his White House appointment. This inexplicable failure on the part of the authorities to act brought forth no burst of indignation from the populace. It elicited no diligent research among questioning newspapermen. In short, it has remained one of the unexplained mysteries of those eventful days.[19]

Indeed, not only did Stanton make no reference to the President's security in any of his missives other than a brief reference to the presidential box's door being unguarded, but as Eisenschiml observed, Parker's name "does not appear in any official story of Lincoln's death. He was not called to the witness stand in the conspiracy trial nor in any subsequent investigation. Silence settled like a merciful fog around this unfortunate policeman..."[20]

Up to this point, the glimmer of suspicion has begun to fall upon Secretary of War Stanton, but now that glimmer becomes the glaring beam of a spotlight, for on the very afternoon of his assassination, President Lincoln personally visited his Secretary of War at the War Department for the express purpose of requesting Stanton's chief aide, Major Thomas T. Eckert(who was also the Assistant Secretary of War), to be the security guard for him and his guests. It is important to recall that at this juncture public notice had already been given that General and Mrs. Ulysses S. Grant

---

[19] Eisenschiml, op. cit., pp. 17-18. Eisenschiml goes on to observe that Parker was finally dismissed from the Metropolitan Police within mere weeks after Secretary of War Stanton "had finally been ousted from his position...", and that there was "no evidence that these two events were in any way related to each other; nor is there any proof that Stanton's protective hand had safeguarded Parker up to that time."(p. 19)

[20] Ibid., p. 20.

were to be the President's guests at the theater that evening, and thus the request for a military guard was a reasonable one.

Moreover, the President desired Major Eckert as a security guard because of his physical prowess. What this suggests is that the President "doubted the reliability of the new guard," Parker, who had just been acquired by Mrs. Lincoln, and who was to be the actual guard that night for the presidential theater-goers. Lincoln's request for Eckert was, however, flatly refused by his Secretary of War! Stanton maintained that Major Eckert could not be spared because of the workload in the telegraph and cipher room which Eckert ran. Undaunted, Lincoln entered "the cipher room" and personally and directly requested Eckert's presence, "coaxing him good-naturedly to come along, as both he and Mrs. Lincoln wanted him." Again the Commander-in-Chief of Union forces was rebuffed (by a mere major!).[21] This whole episode was first reported by another telegraph operator present that afternoon in the cipher room.[22]

As if this were not bad enough, Stanton's own subsequent account of this visit was completely different, with not the slightest suggestion of disagreement or friction between the President and his Secretary of War. On the contrary, it was, as we would now describe it, a "group hug moment":

The Secretary of War, in a detailed account he gave to General James B. Fry a few days after the tragedy, said,

---

[21] Eisenschiml, op. cit., p. 32.

[22] Ibid., p. 33. Eisenschiml, in recounting this episode, references a 1907 publication by David Homer Bates, *Lincoln in the Telegraph Office* (Century Co., (D. Appleton-Century Co.), New York, 1907).

"… that he had never felt so sensible of his deep affection for Lincoln as he did during their final interview. At last they could see the end of bloody fratricidal war…. As they exchanged congratulations, Lincoln, from his greater height, dropped his long arm upon Stanton's shoulders, and a hearty embrace terminated their rejoicings over the close of the mighty struggle. Stanton went home happy. That night Lincoln was assassinated…" This is Stanton's best recollection of what took place. Not a word about Lincoln's request for Eckert's services, nor about his obvious disappointment in having been refused to cavalierly. On the other hand, the (telegraph) operator, David Bates, who was such a keen observer, must have entirely missed the touching episode that filled Stanton's mind to the exclusion of everything else when he remembered Lincoln's call.[23]

Notice what all of this means: firstly, Mr. Lincoln has been denied the very security from military personnel that he, as the commander-in-chief of that military, had every reason he could expect, even if phrased in the form of good-natured requests. Secondly, it means that Eckert's presence in the telegraph room the night of the assassination allowed it to continue to function, in effect, giving Secretary of War Stanton complete control over the emerging narrative to be crafted around the facts he carefully doled out to the public.

---

[23] Eisenschiml, op. cit., p. 33, citing Allen R. Rice (Ed.,) *Reminiscences of Abraham Lincoln by Distinguished Men of His Time* (New York, 1886: North American Publishing Co.), p. 404. Eisenschiml, in his footnote, also states "see also note to chapter V, part II, *The Story Told by David Homer Bates.*"

c. The Calling Card, the Missing Dispatch, Premonitions, and Possible Narrative Preparation

Two of the strangest episodes on the day of the assassination was that of the calling card, and that of the missing dispatch. On the fateful night that President and Mrs. Lincoln attended Ford's Theater, two Union officers—a Captain McGowan and a Lieutenant Crawford—occupied chairs within a few feet of the door to the presidential box, when a man appeared during the third act of the play "who desired to pass up the aisle." At this time, Captain Parker was at his post, seated in a chair outside the door to Lincoln's box. The man, who was presumably John Wilkes Booth himself,

> ...drew a number of visiting cards from his pocket, from which, with some attention, he selected one. "These things,"—McGowan stresses the point—"I saw distinctly. I saw him stoop, and, I think descend to the level with the messenger... and as my attention was then more closely fixed upon the play, I do not know whether the card was carried in by the messenger, or his consent given to the entrance of the man who presented it."

> Captain McGowan repeated this tale on the witness stand during the conspiracy trial a few weeks later, so that the public was given two chances to hear it. Yet, no one sensed the unusual news value of his evidence or seemed anxious to ask him questions.

> Whose card was it that Booth handed to Parker? Was it that of some senator or other dignitary whose name might lull the suspicions of the guard? Or did Booth have enough bravado to produce a card of his own? And what became of it? Did Parker keep it or not? Was there any writing on this piece of pasteboard whereon the fate of a nation trembled for a fraction of a minute? Did Booth speak to the guard,

and f so, what did he say? These and other equally pertinent queries have never been answered.

Parker's name does not appear in any official story of Lincoln's death. He was not called to the witness stand in the conspiracy trial nor in any subsequent investigation. Silence settled like a merciful fog around the person of this unfortunate policeman who had so egregiously missed his opportunity to win eternal fame.[24]

Note that the man, according to McGowan, produced several visiting cards, examined them, and selected one. This suggests that the several cards were for different people or aliases, and that the man may have used them to present himself as different people, which an actor like Booth could certainly do.

But the man with the calling cards was not the only one to attempt access to the presidential box that night. A journalist for the Washington *National Republican* by the name of S.P. Hanscom also approached the presidential box. Herewith begins yet another strange episode, an episode indicating that there were deep eddies and currents flowing on the night of the assassination:

(Hanscom) went to the box, he said, for the purpose of delivering to the President a message which he was requested to convey from the White House. But who requested Hanscom to act as a messenger? What became of the letter? What could have been the contents of this document that was carried to Lincoln in such an unorthodox manner and under such unusual conditions?

It is difficult to envisage a trained news reporter, on the scene of a great national calamity, leaving these questions uninvestigated, unanswered. If Hanscom was any kind of

---

[24] Eisenschiml, op. cit., p. 20.

newspaperman, why did he not interview Forbes and Parker—not to mention himself—and thereby secure for his paper the great scoop of the century and for himself a prominent place in history?

There is no answer to all this. If a document was found on Lincoln's body, the story has never been told.... Thomas Pendel, the doorkeeper of the White House, who wrote in detail of the happenings at the Executive Mansion on the night of Lincoln's death, made no reference to Hanscom nor to any document that had to be delivered to the President while he was at the theater; least of all did he explain why such a message could not have been taken there through the ordinary channels.[25]

Perhaps the strangest indicator that the vultures of conspiracy were circling around the President is the fact that Mr. Lincoln himself appears to have had either a premonition of his impending death, or probable intelligence concerning it, or both. The President had confided to his friend Ward Lamon only a few days before the assassination that he had seen himself in a dream "on a bier in the East Room of the White House, the victim of an assassin."[26] While such dreams definitely fall under the "premonition" heading, what Lincoln said on the day of the assassination to his bodyguard, William Crook, may be more indicative of his possession of special intelligence, for Crook accompanied Lincoln on his visit to the War Department on the afternoon of the assassination, the very visit during which the President requested the presence of Eckert that evening at the theater to be his security. At some point during this trip, Crook reported that Lincoln "suddenly turned to him and said: 'Crook, do you know, I

---

[25] Eisenschiml, op. cit., p. 29.
[26] Ibid., p. 40.

believe there are men who want to take my life?' After a pause he added, as if to himself, 'And I have no doubt they will do it.'"[27] While neither Eisenschiml nor Crook clarify whether Mr. Lincoln made these remarks *before* or *after* this visit to the War Department and his request to Stanton and Eckert for Eckert's service as a bodyguard that evening, the President can hardly have been ignorant that his War Secretary and other members of his government, and the wider membership of his political party, were not completely supportive of his proposed policies toward the South upon conclusion of the war. His behavior upon Stanton's refusal of his request for Eckert's presence as security that night is one of acquiescence. It seems likely, therefore, that Mr. Lincoln may have made these remarks to Crook *after* their visit to the War Department, on their return trip to the Executive Mansion.

3. The Escape of the Conspirators and Managing the News: Secretary of War Edwin Stanton Takes Charge
a. When Did Stanton Know that Booth was the Assassin?

The Union Secretary of War, Edwin Stanton, exercised virtually total control over all official news appearing in the northern press via his control over the liaison between the War Department and the New York City press, and via is complete control over the telegraph service into and from Washington, D.C. Booth, who was a well-known and easily recognizable actor all over both North and South during the war, had been clearly seen by the audience at Ford's Theater and by the actors and actresses off the stage[28] to which he had

---

[27] Eisenschiml, op. cit., p. 43.

[28] Eisenschiml notes that at the exact moment that Booth shot Mr. Lincoln and leaped to the stage, there was only one actor

leaped down from the presidential box after shooting Lincoln. He had even stopped long enough to look at the stunned audience and shout his well-known declamation *Sic semper tyrranus!* Long enough for the audience to get a good look, before he limped off the stage to exit from the back of the theater and make his escape via a horse which had been previously placed there for the purpose. With such a bevy of witnesses who could identify the assassin, it was important for Secretary Stanton "to broadcast his name all over the country as soon as the actor's part in the crime had been ascertained. It is, therefore, of interest to determine just when the Secretary learned who had killed the President."[29]

It is known that Mr. Lincoln was moved from the presidential box at the theater to the Petersen house shortly after the assassination. What is now no longer remembered is that in the Petersen house's back parlor, Secretary of War Stanton and his close friend Justice Cartter had quickly established a "preliminary court of inquiry" and began to quickly interview "several persons, who had been either on stage or in the audience when the fatal shot was fired..." These, including the actor Harry Hawks who was actually on stage at the moment the sharp report from the shot was heard, all stated that they had seen a man who looked like Booth.[30] All this testimony was recorded by a Corporal James Tanner, who was present in the Petersen house parlor, taking the shorthand notes of the testimony. In an account of his experience written two days after the assassination, Corporal Tanner stated that he had begun taking transcriptions about midnight in the Petersen house. "In fifteen minutes I had

---

actually on the stage in front of the audience, the actor Henry Hawk. Q.v., p. 69.

[29] Eisenschiml, op. cit., p. 67.

[30] Ibid., p. 69.

testimony enough down to hang Wilkes Booth...higher than ever Haman hung."[31] Eisenschiml's comment on this leaves no doubt that he at least viewed Stanton as the master impresario of the conspiracy:

> In fifteen minutes, Tanner says. He had commenced writing about midnight, according to his own statement, so that it is safe to say that by twelve-fifteen, or by half past twelve at the latest, Stanton could have sounded the general alarm for Booth's capture. *Instead of doing this, he waited for three hours before disclosing the name of the assassin, and for two hours he did not send out any news at all.*[32]

The question inevitably occurs as to why, if Stanton was a deep member of a conspiracy to kill the President, he allowed Booth such a long time to escape, during which time, as is now known, Booth managed to slip through the ring of sentries around Washington, and escape into the Maryland countryside. Booth, if he *had* known of Stanton's involvement, could never be allowed to escape alive. Better to hunt him down and kill him, before he could ever talk about what he knew. And if he had *not* known of Stanton's involvement, he may have known enough information that investigation could lead to implication of Stanton. Had Booth been apprehended in Washington or elsewhere alive, there is little doubt that he would have met the same end as Lee Harvey Oswald.

Booth could conceivably have possessed information that could lead beyond his rag-tag band of conspirators to much deeper players. No loose ends could be tolerated. The delay also permitted something else; it permitted the basic

---

[31] Eisenschiml, op. cit., p. 71.
[32] Ibid., emphasis added.

outlines of a narrative to be conceived and promulgated, and a template for the control of information to be established.

It is important at this juncture *to view events "whole" and to understand exactly what is happening, for if the flight of Jefferson Davis is less a "flight" than it is a Continuity of Government operation, on the other side of the conflict, the assassination of President Lincoln is not a simple vengeance murder, as Booth's words "sic semper tyrranus" would suggest. It is, rather, a coup d'etat, a "deep event" brought about by the then extant Union "Deep State" to bring about a fundamental change of direction and policy.* Just why that fundamental change of direction and policy was thought to be necessary will be addressed in part two.

b. The Kidnapping Plot Article of 1864: Intelligence? Or Narrative Preparation?

Viewing events "whole" in this way also casts an intriguing interpretive light on a curious journalistic episode that appeared in the New York City press approximately one year and one month before the actual event. On March 19, 1864, the New York *Tribune* published an article purporting to be based on a letter smuggled out of the South and outlining a kidnapping plot on the Union President, and how it might be organized and executed:

> One hundred and fifty picked men were to go secretly North and take quarters in Washington, Georgetown, Baltimore and Alexandria, so as to be able to communicate daily with each other, and, upon a day fixed by their leader, were to assemble in Washington for the purpose of making the seizure. The President, it was claimed, could be easily seized at a private hour, at the White House, or in going to, or returning from church, or on some other favorable occasion, and thrust into a

101

carriage and driven off. The carriage was to be joined a few miles out of the city by twenty-five or thirty armed men on horseback. It was proposed to drive to Indian Point, about twenty-five miles south of Washington, on the Potomac— two or three relays of fleet horses being stationed along the way—where a boat was to be waiting to cross the river, and land the captive a few miles south of Occoquan, when it would be an easy matter for his captors to work their way with him through the woods by night into the Rebel lines. To prevent pursuit, every bridge between Washington and Indian Point was to be mined beforehand, and blown up as soon as the captive and his captors had crossed. Huge tress were also to be ready cut and thrown across the road in various places, as soon as they had passed, by mean stationed along for the purpose, who were afterward to separate and escape as best as they could....

But this is not the only scheme by any means that has been devised for kidnapping our President. Last summer a club or society of wealthy citizens of Richmond was formed for the purpose of raising a fund for this object. Circulars were send to trustworthy citizens in every other city and town in the Confederacy, inviting co-operation in the grand undertaking, and an immense sum of money was subscribed....

Whether these schemes have been abandoned, or whether the kidnappers are only awaiting a favorable opportunity to execute them, remains to be seen; but certain it is that too much caution can not (sic) be observed by the President, or the military commanders stationed at the capital.[33]

This article is notable not only for its accurate predictions of the basic operational plan actually followed by Booth and his

---

[33] Eisenschiml., op. cit., p. 41, citing *Assassination and History of the Conspiracy* (Cincinnati: J.W. Hawley and Company, no date), pp. 56-58.

fellow conspirators a year later, but also for the fact that it appeared in the tightly controlled Union press at all, for it must be remembered that Secretary of War Stanton exercised a near-dictatorial control over what could, and could not, appear in the press.

This fact has but two basic interpretations: (1) the story was complete fabrication, but was published to create a climate of opinion to prepare for the eventuality of a kidnapping or assassination attempt which would be blamed on the Confederacy, and thus to create a climate for vengeance; or (2) the story was based on actual intelligence but allowed to be published for the same purpose of narrative preparation.

c. An Ominous J.F.K. Parallel:
The Washington Telegraph Service Goes Down for Two
Hours

This near total control of the communications to and from Washington DC by Secretary of War Stanton is underscored by yet another incident, an incident sounding a great deal like the shutdown of telephone and telegraph communications in Washington on the day and hour of the John F. Kennedy assassination. Here we must cite Eisenschiml extensively:

> A bizarre incident on the night of April 14 was an interruption of all telegraphic communication between Washington and the outside world, lasting about two hours. "Within fifteen minutes after the murder," wrote Townsend in the New York *World* on May 2, "the wires were severed entirely around the city, excepting only a secret wire for government uses, which leads to Old Point. I am told that by this wire the government reached the fortifications around

103

Washington, first telegraphing all the way to Old Point, and then back to the outlying forts. This information comes to me from so many creditable channels that I must concede it."[34]

Townsend's story was not written on the spur of the moment, and is entitled to serious consideration. If the conspirators were able to isolate the Capital by cutting off its wire communications, there must have been many of them. But wire service was resumed early in the morning of the fifteenth, which would indicate that an actual severance of the wires, such as Townsend suspected, never took place; for the repair of the system, if actually destroyed, could not have been accomplished at night in so short a time. The impression the correspondent of the New York *World* leaves with the reader is, of course, that a cutting of the lines would have been of benefit to the conspirators by shielding them in their flight; "they had evaded the pursuit of lightning," he expressed it, "by snapping the telegraph wires." The inference, it must be admitted, is reasonable.

No official mention of this break in the wire system was ever made; yet the report would not down. Finally, during the so-called impeachment investigation of the House of Representatives' judiciary committee in 1867, this matter was brought to the fore, and Major Eckert, who by that time had resigned as assistant secretary of war, was put on the witness stand. The questions and answers that followed are not without interest:

Q: Did you have knowledge of the telegraph lines at or about the time of the assassination of President Lincoln?

A: I did.

Q: Was there any interruption of the lines that night?

A: Yes, sir.

Q: What was it?

---

[34] Eisenschiml, op. cit., p. 78, citing George Alfred Townsend, *Life, Crime, and Capture of John Wilkes Booth* (New York: Dick and Fitzgerald, 1865), p. 46.

A: It was my impression at the time they were cut, but we got circuit again very early the next morning. The manager of the Commercial office reported the cause to have been crossing of wired in main batteries. Throwing a ground wire over the main wires would have caused the same trouble, and taking it off would have put it in ordinary working condition.

Q: Was there an investigation into what was the real cause of the difficulty?

A: No, sir. It did not at the time seem to be sufficiently important, as the interruption only continued about two hours. I was so full of business of almost every character that I could not give it my personal attention. The interruption was only of a portion of the lines between Washington and Baltimore. We worked our City Point line all the time.

Q: Do you Know whether the Commercial lines were interrupted at that time?

A: Yes, sir. It was only the Commercial lines that were interrupted; it was in the Commercial office and not in the War Department office. I could not ascertain with certainty what the facts were without making a personal investigation, and I had not the time to do that.[35]

This matter should have been thoroughly looked into, in spite of Mr. Eckert's opinion to the contrary; the more so as, in the light of his disclosures, the interruption of the lines looked like and inside job. If an outsider had disrupted the telegraph service he would have cut the wires; but an outsider could not approach the main batteries undetected. Had he been able to do so, he would probably have destroyed them instead of causing a short circuit. The mere suspicion that there might be a traitor within the ranks of the telegraphic corps should have been enough to warrant a painstaking

---

[35] Eisenschiml, op. cit., p. 79, citing *Impeachment Investigation*, p. 673: no other publication data given.

inquiry. But evidently no alarm was felt by Eckert or by Stanton, and no investigation was ever made.

Once before Eckert had pleaded an excessive amount of work; that was when Lincoln had asked him to act as his protector on the night of the assassination. Now again Stanton's former confidant took this tack in disavowing responsibility....[36]

With these revelations we are now in a position to make a further conclusion as to the deepest foundations and layers of the conspiracy to murder Lincoln, for in the light of current and recent events, and in the light of the studies and books of well-known alternative researcher Peter Dale Scott, we know of the recurring connections between the "deep state," its "deep politics" and "deep events", and continuity of government operations and operators, i.e., the bureaucrats and department heads and managers who enable continuity of government plans, or conversely, enable such plans and infrastructure to be subverted to covert ends, such as *coups d'etat*.

Why are these contemporary considerations relevant to the Lincoln assassination? Because for one thing, such continuity of government plans *were clearly* maintained by the Union, because several tunnels had been deliberately constructed throughout Washington DC during the first Lincoln administration, many of these for the purpose of allowing Lincoln and members of his cabinet to escape the White House underground should the capital ever be invested by Confederate forces. Some of these tunnels, modernized and upgraded, are still in use today.

---

[36] The complete quotation with its own internal citations, appears in Eischenschiml, op. cit., pp. 78-80.

Viewing things in this way, the failure of the commercial telegraph service lines while the secret War Department lines were still able to communicate, and the particular *mode* of failure by shorting the circuit at the central point of failure, the batteries, indicates an inside job, as Eisenschiml correctly concludes. In other words, someone from within the War Department itself, someone familiar with telegraph operations, would have known that the system could be taken down, not by the clumsy and manpower-intensive method of cutting all the wires, but by the simple expedient of shorting the batteries that served specific lines. Someone, in other words, with specialized technical knowledge of how to short batteries *and with specialized knowledge of which batteries to short while leaving the secret government lines still operating*, and finally, with specific access to the batteries, had to have brought the Washington communications down.

Had Eisenschiml been alive, and known of Peter Dale Scott's research, he would have said that the "inside job" was an act of the Union's continuity of government infrastructure, which had been co-opted and subverted to enable the assassination.

It was, in other words, a *coup d'etat*.

Small wonder, then, that Mr. Stanton could not spare Major Eckert the night of the assassination, for he was needed not for security of the President, but quite the opposite, for the success of the plan.

4. Sub-Plots
a. A Faked Assassination against Vice President Andrew Johnson?

While space does not permit us to delve deeply and in detail into the immediate circle of conspirators surrounding

John Wilkes Booth, a few words about it are necessary in order to draw attention to aspects of the conspiracy that are typically not even addressed, even in the revisionist research on the Lincoln assassination.

In a nutshell, John Wilkes Booth did not act alone, nor was President Lincoln the only target on that Good Friday of 1865. As was seen, Booth and his fellow conspirators were shadowing Lincoln for weeks as a part of the kidnapping plan, and that plan—as was outlined in the New York *World* article—required the participation of others, as both armed guards had to be recruited, and fresh horses along the escape route had to be provisioned. Upon General Lee's surrender, that same network was activated, but now for assassination, not kidnapping.

In the previous chapter we noted that in the wake of the failed *Union* effort to kidnap or kill President Davis in the Dahlgren raid, that President Davis in response ordered an expansion of the Confederacy's secret service operations in Canada. Booth was a part of the networks that this Canadian Confederate cell established, for it is known that Booth travelled to Canada on more than one occasion. The links between this cell and Booth's circle of conspirators is thus clear and direct.[37] Like many such cells, it is likely that its day-to-day operational plans were never directly nor completely communicated to Davis or the Confederate leaders in Richmond. Again, the modern principle of intelligence operations, plausible deniability, was a factor in operational planning then as well as now. Booth, as an actor, is well suited for the role of spy and assassin, for his fame was spread on both sides of the lines, and he thus had reason

---

[37] Theodore Roscoe, *The Web of Conspiracy: The Complete Stry of the Men Who Murdered Abraham Lincoln*, pp. 42-43, 91-92. 449-453.

to travel both within the Confederacy and the Union. Such travel was, after all, how he plied his trade.

These considerations, and especially that of "plausible deniability," require a closer look into the nature of the conspiracy that was actually operating on Good Friday, 1865. In the previous chapter we noted that the Confederate leadership, including both General Joseph Johnston and President Davis himself were appalled and saddened when they heard the news of Lincoln's assassination. In other words, the Confederate leadership was well aware and apprised of the factions within Lincoln's administration, and of their intended post bellum policies toward the South, should it lose the war. Lincoln represented the moderating policy, whereas much of his government and of the Union Congress that of a much more radical and severe policy. This is significant, because by now it is clear that the fingers of suspicion are pointing to one of the highest ranking members of the "severe" party in Mr. Lincoln's administration: Secretary of War Edwin Stanton.

So why would the Confederate leadership have allowed the kidnapping operation to become an assassination operation? The answer is, that it is unlikely that it would, as it is also unlikely that it knew the details of Booth's assassination plan that day. *But we have seen evidence that Stanton suspected something might "happen" to President Lincoln at the theater, and we shall shortly encounter more evidence that he expected something to happen.* Indeed, the evidence suggests that and the faction he represented not only expected it, but was hoping for it. Thus, *Booth's conspiracy is the lowest level* of the operation, which had now, for the fanatical Southern partisan Booth, a vengeance operation. But at a much deeper level, it is a *penetrated* operation, one which Stanton and his deeper players whom we may designate as the "radical reconstuctionists" are willing to allow to proceed to enact their changes of policy. *Simply put, Booth's actions and the fanaticism of his associates are capable of explaining only the actions and motivations of the conspirators. They are utterly incapable of explaining or rationalizing the subsequent military tribunal, the Union's attitude to Jefferson Davis, the actions of Mr. Stanton, and so on.*

It is against this backdrop and context that the indications of a wider conspiracy in evidence that day should be viewed and assessed. For example, two days after the assassination, "the Washington *National Intelligencer* wrote: 'We can state on the highest authority that it has been ascertained that there was a regular conspiracy to assassinate every member of the Cabinet, together with the Vice President.'"[38] Whether this is true or not is a moot point, because the article itself indicates that its information came from "the highest authority," which could mean none other than Secretary of War Stanton, who exercised virtually complete control over the wires into and from Washington, and over the information being reported in the press. Adding to the plausibility of the story is the fact that an attempt on the life of Secretary of State Seward *was* indeed made on the day of Lincoln's assassination, and attempt which left him nearly fatally wounded, but which he managed to survive.[39]

But other than the attack on Seward, the rest of the Washington *National Intelligencer* article appears to be pure fabrication; "No traces," Eisenschiml writes, "of a plot

---

[38] Eisenschiml, op. cit., p. 162.

[39] Theodore Roscoe, op. cit., pp. 108-114, recount the attempt on Seward's life made by fellow Booth cell members Herrold and Payne. It is the attack on Seward and the clear association of Herold and Payne with Booth that clearly outlined a conspiracy.

against the lives of the other secretaries have ever been found, but the government prosecuted Michael O'Laughlin for attempted assassination of General Grant,[40] and George Atzerodt for planning the murder of Vice President Johnson."[41] If there *was* a wider plot against the Lincoln administration, then the strangeness of events surrounding Lincoln's Vice President, Andrew Johnson, merit closer attention.

b. The Strange Events Surrounding Vice President Johnson, and Eisenschiml's Assessment

On Maundy Thursday, the Christian Holy Day before Good Friday, and one day prior to the assassination of President Lincoln, Booth cell member Georg A. Atzerodt booked a room at the Kirkwood House, the same motel where Vice President Johnson maintained his lodgings.[42] On the day after the assassination, having brought suspicion upon himself, the authorities broke into Atzerodt's room and discovered a damning inventory, which included a revolver, a black coat that was discovered to belong to another Booth cell member, Herold. In the pockets of this coat a bank book apparently belonging to Booth was found, along with an envelope marked "Hon. John Conness." Conness was a U.S. Senator from California, and very definitely a member of the "radical reconstructionist" faction of Lincoln's Republican Party. This is an indicator, *perhaps*, that at some deep level

---

[40] The attempt on Grant was made on the train taking him and his wife to New Jersey to see their children. The attempt was unsuccessful because the door to the Grants' carriage was locked, and McLaughlin was unsuccessful in trying to open it.

[41] Eisenschiml, op. cit., p. 162.

[42] Ibid., p. 166.

there was direct contact between Booth's fanatics, and the fanatical reconstructionists. If so, then it is another indicator corroborating the view advocated previously that the *coup d'etat* against the Lincoln administration was also a Let It Happen On Purpose scenario. The presence of an envelope addressed to the California senator may even thus indicate a *Made It Happen On Purpose* (MIHOP) scenario.

All of this, however, seems a bit too convenient, and Eisenschiml himself raises questions about why the vacillating and cowardly Atzerodt would have been selected by Booth to be the assassin of the Vice President, as was being publicly maintained. The evidence in Atzerodt's hotel room seems more likely to have been salted.[43]

There is a much more direct and indisputable connection between the Booth conspiracy and Vice President Johnson, a connection so direct that it is for that reason all the more problematical. On the very afternoon of that Good Friday, John Wilkes Booth *himself* left the Vice President a calling card after having visited his hotel and being told by the front desk that the Vice President was not there. Booth wrote the message "Don't (sic) wish to disturb you Are you at home? J Wilkes Booth".[44] The card is a significant problem, for its easy, off-handed tone suggests some prior and friendly association between the two. Indeed,

> On the subject of Booth's card, Johnson seems to have shut his mouth like a trap. Most historians believe the leaving of the card was an evil trick to implicate the Vice President in the conspiracy. But could his refusal to discuss the card

---

[43] Eisenschiml, op. cit., p. 168.

[44] Ibid., p. 170. Eisenschiml simply cites "War Dept. Archives" here, without any further specific information. ,,,,,,,,,,,,,,,,,,,,,,,,,,,,,,,,,,,, ,

have rested on a former acquaintance with the actor? In 1867 detectives sent out to investigate Johnson's part reported that when he was governor of Tennessee he had met Booth in Nashville on a local level hardly recommended for a public official.[45]

But as Eisenschiml observes, Booth, who had shadowed Lincoln's movements around Washington for over a month since the latter's second inauguration, was unlikely not to have known of Johnson's movements. Additionally, why would Booth assign the timid and vacillating Atzerodt to assassinate the Vice President, and then compound matters by leaving a calling card?[46]

Yet another possibility presents itself: what if it was not Booth at all, but a look-alike, a body double, that left the card? What if, in other words, the alleged plots against Lincoln's cabinet members and the Vice President were all entirely fictitious? What if they were *faked* in order to aid the establishment of the new policy of radical reconstruction on the part of an angry North wanting to seek vengeance against the "scheming South"? With respect to these questions, Eisenschiml's speculations on the motivations of the deep level conspirators are worth citing, because they constitute the core thesis of the revisionist views of the assassination, and consequently a crucial component of the argument being advanced in this book:

> The faked attempt on Johnson's life calls for an explanation. Who profited by it? Certainly not the assassins. The fury against them could only be further intensified by the belief that they had intended to spread

---

[45] Roscoe, op. cit., p. 182.
[46] Eisenschiml, op. cit., p. 172.

terror in Washington by a carnival of murder. Then who could possibly wish to create the illusion of an organized wholesale massacre while singling out Lincoln and Seward as the only real victims?

The President and the Secretary of State were the two men in power whose program on reconstruction chiefly stressed conciliation. Lincoln especially was willing, nay anxious, to have the South resume, unpenalized, its former role in the concert of all the states. Stanton and Johnson, on the contrary, were at that time the South's worst enemies. They were not only in favor of treating the Confederacy as conquered territory but even vowed that a traitor's death awaited the leaders of their enemies. Had Lincoln and Seward alone been attacked, it could have been suspected that the plot had its origin in the minds of Radical Republicans who hated Lincoln and Seward and what they stood for; but if both friends and enemies of the Southern people were the apparent victims in the murder plot, then— so it would be reasoned—it was the product of brains that tried to rob the North of its entire government and thereby render it impotent. In other words, if Lincoln's assassination were only part of a plot to throw the North into anarchy, the inference would be justified that the murder was a last and despairing war move of the dying Confederacy. But if the existence of such a plot could not be proved, the South would be innocent, and suspicion would naturally fall on the Radicals of Lincoln's own party. They were the only ones who benefitted.[47]

We gain a final measure of how important it was to preserve this narrative of events, and to "prove" it by the military trial, conviction, and execution of some of the conspirators of Booth's cell by noting that the very same Major Eckert, whose protection Lincon had sought, and Stanton denied, was

---

[47] Eisenschiml, op. cit., pp. 173-174.

also charged with personally guarding the assassin who made the attempt on Secretary Seward's life, Lewis Payne. This is remarkable because Major Eckert happened to be *the Assistant Secretary of War to Secretary Stanton*. An assistant secretary, on guard duty?[48] It strains credulity to imagine that this bizarre posting was for any other purpose than to insure that Payne never be able to communicate any information to anyone outside the tribunal which would ultimately convict him. Stanton, and the radical reconstuctionists, made sure that whatever information they were afraid might get out, did not do so, dying in the strangled and broken neck of Lewis Payne when he was hung for his part in Booth's conspiracy.

c. The Strange Behavior of General and Mrs. Ulysses S. Grant, and More Evidence of Secretary Stanton's Foreknowledge of the Assassination

All of the previous considerations bring us at last to General and Mrs. Ulysses S. Grant. As was mentioned earlier, the General and his wife were initially to have attended the theater with President and Mrs. Lincoln. Indeed, it was the well-publicized fact that the General was to be present that night that assured that Ford's theater was sold out to a full crowd. As Eisenchiml observes, Lincoln was a fairly common site around Washington, often walking or riding around the city. Grant, on the other hand, was the hero who had captured Vicksburg, splitting the Confederacy, and who had finally defeated Lee. It was Grant's assumed presence at the theater that guaranteed a full house on what was under normal circumstances a "slow day" for theaters: Good Friday.[49]

---

[48] Eisenschiml, op. cit., p. 187.
[49] Eisenschiml., op. cit.., p. 61.

Grant and his wife had indeed been personally invited to attend the theater by the Lincolns themselves, and the Grants *had accepted* the invitation, hence, the publicity of their planned attendance. But they were *not* in attendance on the night of the assassination. At the last minute, they had suddenly cancelled their plans, and explained that they wanted to travel Burlington, New Jersey to visit their children. The Grants' sudden cancellation became the occasion for some of Otto Eisenschiml's most brilliant speculation on the nature of the conspiracy surrounding Lincoln's assassination. He began by noting:

> This discourteous conduct cannot be passed over lightly. It would have been doubtful etiquette to declare such an invitation in the first place; but to accept and then to leave town, especially after public notice had been given that Grant would attend the performance, looks like a colossal *faux pas*. Or has the incident a deeper significance than appears on the surface?
>
> Grant's life had been that of a soldier; strict obedience t the wishes of a superior must have been second nature to him. The invitation to a presidential party, given in honor to the victor of Appomattox Court House, implied a command.[50]

So what had happened between the Grants' initial acceptance of the Lincolns' invitation, and their quick departure from Washington, to change their mind? Eisenschiml speculates that, in part, it was due to an ugly contretemps between the mercurial Mrs. Lincoln and Mrs. Grant herself, whom just a

---

[50] Eisenschiml, op. cit., p. 54.

few days before the assassination, Mrs. Lincoln accused of having her own designs on the White House.[51]

More importantly, Mrs. Grant "had learned, about three o'clock in the afternoon, that Secretary and Mrs. Stanton, who were also to have been guests at the theater, had definitely refused the invitation, and thereupon she sent a note to her husband which was handed him at the White House."[52] Eisenschiml speculates that the note simply contained Mrs. Grant's announcement to her husband that she was not going to attend the theater and was leaving Washington to see her children.[53]

However, I do not believe this to be the most plausible explanation. Rather, I believe Mrs. Grant somehow learned that the Secretary of War had misgivings about attending the theater that night, and that she perhaps learned this from Mrs. Stanton, or from someone who had contact with her. The reason this seems to be a more plausible explanation is that General Grant departed the White House and went immediately to the War Department to confer with Secretary Stanton, who urged the general not to attend the theater because "the presence of both the President and the lieutenant general at a public function would invite disaster."[54] Notably, Stanton was willing to share such anxieties with his subordinate General Grant, while as we have seen he denied to President Lincoln the latter's request for his desired security guard!

This raises the question of why Stanton, if he was indeed involved in the conspiracy against the President at a deep level, wanted the Grants *not* to attend. Eisenschiml's

---

[51] Ibid., pp. 58-59.

[52] Ibid., p. 61.

[53] Ibid.

[54] Eisenschiml., op. cit., p. 61.

speculation is, again, a brilliant one condign and congruent to the salient data points reviewed thus far:

> If Grant had been in the theater that night, it is more than likely that the attempt on Lincoln's life would not have been made. Not that Grant was a dangerous antagonist in a physical encounter. The general was scarcely a match for the young and athletic Booth; nor was he particularly alert. It is quite possible that the assassin could have entered the loge unhindered and unobserved, so far as Grant was concerned. His presence would have been fatal to the plans of an assassin for quite a different reason. With Grant in the box, hundreds of eager eyes would have been turned in his direction every minute of the time, and Booth's entry and exit could not have escaped detection. His murderous bullet might not have been stopped, but he could not have escaped.
>
> *Moreover, it is almost a certainty that Grant's presence in the box would have led to a more efficient guarding of the door through which Booth entered with such ridiculous ease.* Even the neglectful Parker, who had once been a soldier, would have hesitated to leave his post when standing sentry for the lieutenant general....
>
> ...
>
> From the point of view of the assassin, it was absolutely essential to have Grant absent from the theater that night; and whoever induced the lieutenant general to turn his back on Washington, played—knowingly or unknowingly—straight into the hands of the conspirators.
>
> Verification of Bates' statement that it was Stanton who helped bring about Grant's departure is furnished by Samuel Beckwith, his cipher operator, who accompanied the general to Philadelphia on April 14. In an account written many years after the event, he stated that Stanton

had urged the general in chief not to accept Lincoln's invitation.[55]

There is one final, but very damning, tidbit that fastens Stanton at the center of any deeper players in the assassination than just Booth and his crew;

> Stanton seems to have taken it for granted that Lincoln had known of some definite threat against his life, for on the day after the tragedy he sent the following wire to General Sherman:
>
> ...I FIND EVIDENCE THAT AN ASSASSIN IS ALSO ON YOUR TRACK, AND I BESEECH YOU TO BE MORE HEEDFUL THAN MR. LINCOLN WAS OF SUCH KNOWLEDGE.[56]
>
> This tell-tale message conveys three distinct and separate allegations: first, that evidence on hand showed an assassin to be on Sherman's trail; second, that Lincoln had possessed actual knowledge of his impending assassination; third, that he had taken no head of this warning.[57]

But this accusation of Stanton is, as we have seen, complete codswallop, because President Lincoln *had* requested more intense security from Stanton in the form of Major Eckert, and both Stanton, and Eckert himself, had refused it!

All these facts argue that there was *some* degree of anxiety and foreknowledge that "something" was going to happen that evening at Ford's Theater. But there is one final anomaly surrounding the Lincoln assassination, and it is an

---

[55] Eisenschiml, op. cit., p. 63.

[56] Ibid., citing *Official Records*, I, vol 47, part 3, p. 221, no publication data given.

[57] Ibid., pp. 51-52,

anomaly springing from yet another; that "other" anomaly is a gaping one, one we have yet to encounter and deal with: Booth's Diary. Before the sleight-of-hand associated with the identification of Booth's corpse—another topic with which we have yet to deal—a small red notebook was found in Booth's clothing which he apparently had used for a diary. Colonel Lafayette C. Baker, the head of the Union Secret Service, was part of the party which searched for, and eventually cornered, Booth, and as such, Baker claimed to have read some of that diary.[58] For the present, however, we are concerned with the issue of *foreknowledge* of the assassination. In this regard, Baker writes in his post war memoirs that when he met the Secretary of War in his office after the assassination, that

> As I entered the Secretary's office, and he recognized me, he turned away to hide his tears.

(By this point it should be clear that these were probably crocodile's tears.)

> He (Stanton) remarked—"Well, Baker, they have now performed what they have long threatened to do; they have killed the President."
>
> Therewith one of Stanton's secrets was a secret no longer. Baker's indiscretion suddenly disclosed that Stanton had been aware of threats against Lincoln's life.[59]

---

[58] Q.v. Eisenschiml's discussion, op. cit., pp. 144-146.

[59] Ibid., p. 148. Eisenschiml adds that the post-assassination House investigating committee "could well have asked who 'they' were and what threats had come to the knowledge of the War Minister. It was fortunate for Stanton that they failed to do so." Was it fortunate, or a bit of very deliberate covert-up by way of intentional omission?

With this we now have yet another analogy to more recent and contemporary events, for with Stanton's complicity increasingly evident, and the motivation of profit for a change of policy via assassination, we see a nineteenth century version of the "military-industrial-media" complex in action.

5. The Torture, Trial, and Execution of "Agents of the Conspiracy"

Most revisionist approaches to the assassination of President Lincoln spend a great deal of time with the named and convicted conspirators of Booth's cell, and this is true of the classical and indispensable studies of Otto Eisenschiml and Theodore Roscoe. I have not done so because those studies are easily available, and to spend an inordinate amount of time on those matters would detract from the central theme of this review, that the Lincoln assassination was a carefully planned and penetrated operation that was allowed to happen (LIHOP) and perhaps was made to happen (MIHOP) for the purposes of a *coupd'etat* to implement a radical policy.

This theme is further corroborated by briefly noting the conditions under which Secretary Stanton ordered the conspirators to be incarcerated and tried. For one thing—and over strenuous objections raised at the time as to the propriety of the jurisdiction of the military over such individuals, much less its ability to conduct a trial, and paralleling more modern examples—Stanton arranged for a military tribunal to conduct a "trial." In what was truly unusual, he ordered *hoods* to be perpetually placed over the heads of the accused, hoods that were specially made to keep them in perpetual darkness, minimal external noise, and unable to talk beyond muffled speech. The only exception to this order was Mrs. Mary Surratt, whose boarding house had hosted some of the conspirators.[60] Additionally, all of the accused were shackled by "stiff shackles" which maintained their hands at a fixed distance from each other, and did not permit one hand or arm to be raised without raising the other in tandem. This, plus the hoods, made it difficult if not impossible to write legible messages.[61] Finally, the accused were all placed in cells that were isolated from, and not adjacent to, each other. Additionally, the physical layout of the room to hold the tribunal was such that the defendants were made to sit facing the tribunal, with their attorneys behind them.

The results of the tribunal are now well-known: Mrs. Surratt, Georg Atzerodt, Lewis Payne, and David Herold were all found guilty, sentenced to death, and hanged on July 7, 1865. The other four conspirators—Michael O'Loughlin, Samuel Arnold, Edward Spangler, and Dr. Samuel Mudd— were sentenced to several years' hard labor. Initially to have served this time at the New York State penitentiary at Albany, Stanton (!) persuaded President Andrew Johnson to order their penal incarceration to be served at the remote facility on dry Tortugas island in southern Florida.[62] The purpose was again clear, for try as the chief trial judge of the tribunal might to have all eight defendants sentenced to death, "the military commission balked at this wholesale hanging."[63] Indeed, the "peasants" were already restive, as numerous

---

[60] Eisenschiml, op. cit., p. 175. Eisenschiml observes that Stanton would no doubt have ordered the hooding of Mrs. Surratt as well if he had thought public opinion at the time would not have been outraged by the provision.

[61] Ibid., p. 177.

[62] Ibid., p. 180.

[63] Ibid.

public outcries and complaints about the whole procedure had been aired, and more professional voices questioned the whole legitimacy of the tribunal in the first place. Theodore Roscoe captures the mood in his celebrated study:

> Now that the trial was over, the public mind harbored a perceptive suspicion that the Army's Judge Advocate General, the Military Commission, the Bureau of Military Justice and the war lord behind the scene had been guilty of something worse than "petty tyranny." The frantic haste with which the defendants were placed on trial—the vaporous wording of the conspiracy indictment—the arbitrary rulings of the court wherein every objection made by the prosecution was sustained whereas all objections made by defense counsel were overruled—these and other manifestations of a witchcraft proceeding began to bite into the national consciousness.[64]

As for the matter of Secretary of War Stanton's foreknowledge of the event, there are a few final and highly suggestive points worth mentioning. At the very time that

---

[64] Roscoe, op. cit., p. 489. Eisenschimly refers briefly to these "vaporous" official indictments against the conspirators: "The charge against all prisoners was that of 'maliciously, unlawfully, and traitorously, and in aid of the existing armed rebellion against the United States of America... combining, confederating, and conspiring togetherwith... Jefferson Davis... and others unknown, to kill and murder, within the Military Department of Washington, and within the fortified and entrenched lines thereof, Abraham Lincoln... and lying in wait with intent... to kill... Andrew Johnson... and... Ulysses... Grant...'". (Eisenschiml, op. cit., p. 242.) It is to be noted that the basis of asserting military and not civilian jurisdiction was the commission of a crime within a military zone.

President and Mrs. Lincoln were leaving the White House that Good Friday evening to go to Ford's Theater, anomalies were appearing in, or had already appeared in, the press around the Union:

> About that time news was circulating through the streets and homes of St. Joseph, Minnesota, that the President had been murdered in Washington. St. Joseph was 40 miles from the nearest railroad and 80 miles from any telegraph communication.
>
> Also, at 10 o'clock *that morning*, residents of Booth's hometown, Manchester, New Hampshire, were speaking in the past tense of Lincoln's assassination, discussing the event as it if had already happened.
>
> By noon that day, a well-known surgeon of high standing in an unnamed New England town had been informed of the President's death.
>
> At 2:30 that Good Friday afternoon, a writer on the Middletown, New York *Whig Press* asserted that he had been informed that the President had been shot and, "it was currently so reported in the village of Pine Bush and in the town of Crawford before 12 o'clock of that day."
>
> The *Newburgh Journal* confirmed the reports in the *Whig Press*, but was more conservative in its editorial opinion.
>
> From 12 to 4 hours before the President was to sit in his box, hid death had been reported in half a dozen scattered parts of the country.[65]

---

[65] David Balsiger and Charles E. Sllier, Jr., *The Lincoln Conspiracy* (Los Angeles: Schick Sunn Classic Books, 1977, NO ISBN), pp. 152-153, citing Otto Eisenschiml, *In the Shadow of Lincoln's Death* (No publication data given, 1940, no page data given.

Was this merely a coincidence of the "yellow journalism" of the time? Or was it some psychic prescience in the aether? Or was it a collective speculation on the inevitable clash between Lincoln and his advisors? Or was it, again, the same sort of prescience that Stanton had exhibited elsewhere and under different circumstances, a prescience that had percolated through his carefully controlled press? We will perhaps never know.

In any case, we must now turn to the biggest anomaly in the Lincoln assassination of them all: the assassin himself, his death, and his diary... John Wilkes Booth. These matters, however, will require a chapter of their own.

Mary Eugenia Surratt,
Hanged, July 7, 1865

Lewis Payne, or Paine,
Hanged, July 7, 1865

David Herold, Hanged, July 7, 1865

Georg Andreas Atzerodt (George Andrew Atzerodt),
Hanged, July 7, 1865

Samuel Arnold, Imprisoned

Michael O'Loughlin, Imprisoned,
Note the "Stiff Shackles" on his wrists

Edward Spangler, Imprisoned,
Again, note the "stiff shackles" on his wrists

Dr. Samuel Mudd, here shown in his imprisonment at Dry Tortugas, where he continued to treat fellow inmates as their physician.

Vice President Andrew Johnson,
17th President of the United States of America;
Booth left a calling card at his hotel on the afternoon of the
assassination

William Seward, Lincoln's Secretary of State,
Survived an assassination attempt on his life by Lewis Payne

Edwin Stanton, Secretary of War under Lincoln and Briefly
under his successor, Andrew Johnson;
The One (of many others?) Who Got Away?

John Wilkes Booth,
Actor, Assassin, Amanuensis

3

THE DEATH AND DIARY OF JOHN WILKES BOOTH, ACTOR, ASSASSIN, AMANUENSIS

"Booth wrote a good deal in the little red book. If one takes his writing as that of confidante to diary, it stands as a masterpiece of self-pity, self-interest, self-glorification. He sees himself as a heroic figure abandoned by the Fates... But no thought for Lewis Paine, for John Surratt, for others who, if caught, would certainly face the gallows, or stand before the firing squad as his henchmen."
Theodore Roscoe[1]

JOHN WILKES BOOTH: HIS NAME IS CARVED In the hard, unfading, and unforgiving granite of history as the first and preeminent bust in a rogue's gallery of America assassins and murderers: Sirhan Sirhan, James Earl Ray, and, of course, Lee Harvey Oswald. The story of Booth's flight from Washington after the assassination is well-known. After fatally wounding President Lincoln, he leaps from the Presidential box to the theater's stage, wounding and twisting his foot in the process. He shouts *Sic semper tyranis* (Thus always to tyrants!) to the shocked audience and thespians, bolts from the stage and exits the building through the rear of the theater. There he mounts a horse which has been prepared, and makes his way from Washington into the Maryland countryside in the company of his fellow cell member and co-conspirator David Herold.[2] In yet *another*

---

[1] Ibid., p. 219.
[2] Herold had been assigned the task of conveying the slow-witted Lewis Paine to Secretary Seward's house. As he waited outside, when he heard the reports from inside the house, he

incredible incongruity in the parade suspicious facts surrounding the Lincoln assassination, the assassins manage to escape the environs of Washington because Secretary of War Stanton, who controlled the district's military sentries and outposts, never ordered the closure of the most likely route for Booth's escape, even though the route was well-known both to Confederate spies and smugglers, and to the Union officials![3] Rather, the routes to the north and northwest of the capital were closed first![4] "There is, apparently," writes Eisenschiml,

> only one theory that offers a plausible explanation for these vagaries.... Booth's escape from Washington under circumstances which justify the suspicion that some powerful influence was exerted to safeguard his flight. The assassin, of course, was fully aware of whatever secret arrangements may have been made in his behalf.[5]

It is not difficult to conclude who would have been in a position to ensure the assassin's escape, and then to put out a reward for his capture, dead or alive.[6]

In any case, in excruciating pain from his injury, Booth and Herold make their way eventually to Dr. Samuel Mudd's, where the latter—probably innocent of any real involvement

---

abandoned Paine's horse, and rode away from the scene. Roscoe believes that Booth might have ordered him to abandon Paine to his fate. (Q.v. Roscoe, op. cit., p. 149.)

[3] Eisenschiml, op. cit., pp. 97-99, 107.

[4] Ibid., p. 91.

[5] Ibid., p. 305.

[6] Eisenschiml observes that the orders—with but one exception—emanating from Stanton's War Department were to take Booth alive. But after the incident with Dr. Mudd setting his foot, one order was issued to kill Booth if he was ever found. Q.V. Eisenschink, op. cit., p. 185.

in the conspiracy—sets Booth's wound. After having his wound tended to by Dr. Mudd, Booth and Herold leave; pursued by Federal forces, Booth and Herold are finally surrounded at Garrett's farm where both men are trapped inside its tobacco barn. The Federals under the command of Colonel Everton Conger gather brush, stack it against the barn, and threaten to burn it—and the conspirators—down, unless they surrender. After some time with no adequate response, the fire is set, eventually driving David Herold from the barn, where he is apprehended by Lieutenant Edward Doherty. The accompanying Union soldiers tie the man to a tree, happily already spending the $25,000 bounty that had been posted for the capture of the conspirator.

But then the narrative begins to fray around the edges.

A. The Anomalies of the Death, Autopsy, and Identification of John Wilkes Booth

According to the account compiled by Colonel Conger afterward, Booth remained inside the burning barn, hobbling about amid the flames on a crutch. Colonel Conger's account would have posterity believe that, as the crippled Booth is hobbling about inside a burning barn, a sergeant drew aim on Booth, and fired a shot through the boards of the burning walls, a shot which severed Booth's spine at the neck. Later, Conger would "correct" this account, maintaining he had fired the shot.[7]

Within a matter of mere weeks, however, this version of events at Garrett's farm was contradicted by testimony given at the military trial of the conspirators, where it was maintained that after the shot rang out which felled Booth, the soldiers rushed the barn, where, mindful of the $100,000

---

[7] Roscoe, op. cit., pp. 388-389.

already placed on Booth's head, they carried the mortally wounded man out of the barn before the fire had a chance to consume him altogether, and laid him at the bottom of a locust tree. There the dying assassin gasped a request for water. Some Union soldiers and officers, able to closely observe him for the first time, maintained that his wound appeared self-inflicted.[8]

As Booth lay dying of a severed spine in the neck— and as Theodore Roscoe quips, incongruously making speeches in the best tradition of Victorian tragedy[9]— Colonel Conger "itched with impatience to get the dying over with" in order to "gallop off to Washington to report the big news to Headquarters."[10] There was, after all, the matter of the hundred-thousand dollar bounty. Before doing so, however, Colonel Conger searched the dying man (apparently oblivious to any discomfort it might have caused him):

> Conger…finds the captive's prolonged suffering most uncongenial. So, unwilling to wait for the captive's demise, Conger and Baker begin to search him…. Conger dutifully lists the items. A leather holster. A soldier's knife. A pipe. A nail file. Some cartridges. A spur. A Canadian bill of exchange. A pocket compass, smeared with candle drippings. A diamond pin. And a little red booklet—a diary![11]

---

[8] Ibid., pp. 390-391.

[9] Ibid., p. 392: "…a man agonized by a punctured spinal cord does not utter stilted speeches in the best tradition of Victorian literature."

[10] Ibid., p. 394.

[11] Roscoe, op. cit.., p. 395.

We shall have much more to say about the contents—and alleged contents—of this diary shortly, but for now we must remain focused on Booth's death.

What emerges from this story, if one pays close attention, is that there are really *no eyewitnesses* to the shooting of Booth.[12] More importantly, why was no attempt made to take the assassin alive? Or was the burning of Garrett's barn an attempt to flush the assassin out in order to do so?

The problems of Booth's death begin to multiply like rabbits, for at his autopsy, the caliber of the weapon which had caused the fatal wound was never estimated, nor was any attempt made to ascertain if any of Booth's inventoried weapons were missing a cartridge (or if it was, the result was never recorded). Thus, we do not know if Booth was shot, or if he attempted to take his own life. In either case, however, one is in the presence of a true "magic bullet" story, for the bullet's owner and origin is unknown to this day, thanks to yet another strange parallel with assassinations a century later: a botched autopsy.[13]

The strangeness of all of this is underscored by the next chapter of John Wilkes Booth, or rather, the next chapter of what remained of him, for his corpse was brought to the monitor *Montauk* which was anchored nearby, along with his accomplice, David Herold, who was incarcerated on the ship prior to being taken back to Washington for his appearance before the military tribunal with the rest of his fellow conspirators. This occurred on April 27, 1865. By this point, Booth's body had already begun to deteriorate rapidly.[14]

Stanton ordered that after the autopsy, Booth's body be placed in a strong box, sealed, and delivered to Colonel

---

[12] Eisenschiml, op. cit., p. 154.

[13] Ibid., pp. 156-157.

[14] Roscoe, op. cit., p. 413.

Lafayette Baker. But the intriguing point to observe is that of the autopsy party, which included the Surgeon General, the Judge Advocate General, and Stanton's code room assistant (and the man Lincoln had requested as security on the night of his assassination) Major Thomas T. Eckert! There is one thing all these men had in common (besides that of reporting ultimately to Stanton as the chief of the War Department): none of them had ever been "personally acquainted with John Wilkes Booth" and thus none of the observing autopsy part "was qualified to identify the body."[15] By this point, while the autopsy results were clear—the man before them was dead of a gunshot wound to the neck—the identification was not. By this point, someone in the autopsy party apparently raised doubts about the identity. "This contorted corpse with matted hair, blotched forehead, wild eyes and snarling teeth—could it really have belonged to the matinee idol, once the Apollo of the footlights and the glass of fashion?"[16]

Stanton was forced to issue orders to round up witnesses who were personally familiar with Booth and bring them to the *Montauk* to identify the corpse. These included the front desk clerk of Booth's hotel in Washington, a well-known Washington photographer and his assistant, a physician, Dr. May, who had removed a tumor from Booth's neck two years previously, and a local dentist.[17] The photohrapher—Alexander Gardner—was reported to have taken a photograph of the corpse on the monitor. Predictably, this photograph was quickly lost.[18]

There were other means, however, of identification. Booth, as an actor, had accumulated numerous scars on his body, mostly on the arms, from many mock combats on stage.

---

[15] Roscoe, op. cit., p. 414.
[16] Ibid.
[17] Ibid., pp. 414-415
[18] Ibid., p. 416.

Additionally, Booth's close friends all stated he had two small tattoos, one between the thumb and index finger of his right hand which was of the three initials of his name, J.W.B., and another of a small cross between the thumb and index finger of his left hand.[19] These facts were communicated to Secretary of Stanton, but again, another oddity: during the initial autopsy and "identification," no remarks noting the scars were ever recorded, and only one witness reportedly recorded any notice of the initials tattooed on Booth's right hand.[20]

But then there was the strangely ambivalent testimony of Dr. John F. May, the surgeon who had removed a small tumor from Booth's neck. Summoned to the monitor *Montauk* to identify Booth's corpse, the physician was led to the deck of the monitor with Surgeon General Barnes where the body was covered with a tarpaulin. The doctor's initial response was that "there was to me no resemblance to the man I had known in life!"[21] Later in a statement made to the Judge Advocate General, Brigadier Joseph Holt, in a series of questions and answers, the doctor gave what at first glance appears to be an irrefutable identification:

> A. ...I told the Surgeon General these facts this morning before I looked at the cicatrix at all, and said that he would probably find a large ugly looking Scar, instead of a neat line. He said it corresponded exactly with my description. The scar looks more [crossed out] as much like [the effect of] a burn [as the cicatrix from] a Surgical operation....

---

[19] Ibid., p. 417.

[20] Roscoe, op. cit., p. 419.

[21] Ibid., p. 421.

Q. Do you recognize the body as that of J. Wilkes Booth from its general appearance, and also from the particular appearance of the Scar?

A. I do recognize it, though it is very much altered since I saw Booth. It looks to me much older, and in appearance much more freckled than he was. I do not recollect that he was at all freckled. I have no doubt it is his body. I recognize the features. When he came to my office, he had no beard excepting a mustache.

Q. From the nature of this wound, even apart from the general appearance, you could not be mistaken as to the identity of the body?

A. From the wound [crossed out and written over] Scar, I think I could not be [cross out and written over] but I also recognize [crossed out and re-written] in connection with the recognition of the features, which though much changed and altered, still have the same appearance, (I think I cannot be mistaken). I recognize the likeness. I have no doubt that it is the person from whom I took the tumor, and that it is the body of J. Wilkes Booth.[22]

But when closely scrutinized, the doctor's testimony hardly yields the type of certainty one would hope for in such cases. Theodore Roscoe lists four glaring problems:

> (1) May says Booth's scar resembles the cicatrix *of a burn.*(2) The corpse is *freckled.* Dr. May does not recall (nor does anyone else) Booth being freckled. (3) In his later essay May states he could not recognize the body when he first saw it. In original testimony to Judge Holt he had *no doubt* it was Booth, although "very much altered." (4) Testifying, May declares that *he could not fail to recognize the body by the Scar.* This is crossed out, carefully re-worded. So is his next statement. The result is a garbled paragraph, as though May is sputtering uncertainly.

---

[22] Roscoe, op. cit., pp. 422-423.

(Incidentally, such erasure and re-wording constitutes a "palimpsest." Today such alteration, unless initialed by the deponent, would automatically invalidate a document.)[23]

In other words, the one most able to identify Booth, the surgeon who removed a tumor from his neck, ends up giving testimony that records a feature on the corpse—freckles—that *no* one who knew Booth ever maintained he had.

There is, in other words, reasonable doubt as to its identification. Who then, *did* die at Garrett's Farm? Balsiger and Sellier argue that it was a Booth body-double, James William Boyd. The one person who *could* have destroyed the whole substitution was David Herold, but he, like all the other conspirators, had been isolated on Stanton's orders, and thus the possible substitution of a body-double may have been the reason behind Stanton's draconian measures regarding the conspirators' incarceration.[24]

John Wilkes Booth, left, and James William Boyd, right. Was Boyd the man who died at Garrett's Farm and whom Dr. May "identified" to the Judge Advocate General?

---

[23] Ibid., p. 423.

[24] Balsiger and Sellier, op. cit., pp. 248-249. Balisger and Sellier also mention the strange cases of "real John Wilkes Booths" who died many years after the war.

All of this, however, is to suggest yet another strange analogy between Lincoln's assassination and that of John F. Kennedy only 98 years later, for the possibility exists of "more than one" John Wilkes Booth lurking in the shadows of President Lincoln's murder, just as there was more than one Lee Harvey Oswald.

But there is something even more problematical, for in addition to being an actor, and an assassin, Booth was also an amanuensis, dutifully recording things in the little red book that he kept as a diary.

B. The Diary
1. The Stunning Comment

Booth's diary contains a record, meticulously recorded, of his thoughts and feelings during his flight from Washington. As observed previously, Colonel Conger discovered it while going through the dying "Booth's" clothes. The diary eventually reached the Secretary of War, and eventually the museum at Ford's theater, where it is missing 18 pages! Those missing 18 pages will be treated momentarily, but there is an entry amid all the self-pity, grandiosity, self-glorification that comprises the bulk of the diary:

I have almost mind...

Booth writes

...to return to Washington and clear my name, which I feel I can do.[25]

---

[25] Roscoe, op. cit., p. 396.

Clear his name? How did Booth intend to do that, since he was clearly seen, heard, and recognized by the theater goers at Ford's Theater? More delusional ravings of self-pity?

Perhaps. Theodore Roscoe, however, points out that any good detective could not dismiss the line, but rather, would have immediately started asking questions. "No astute investigator," he states, "could have failed to read the implication behind that entry. No quick-thinking intelligence officer would have passed up a chance to interrogate a dying assassin on the meaning of such a notation."[26] But then there are the problems associated with the missing 18 pages, and with that, we are at last chin-to-chin with the nasty motivation at the heart of Jefferson Davis' Continuity of Government hopes, at the heart of Abraham Lincoln's murder, and at the center of the puppeteers pulling Booth's and the conspirators' strings: money.

2. The Problematical Missing 18 Pages of Booth's Diary

With the alleged missing eighteen pages of John Wilkes Booth's diary, we are confronted the central problem surrounding Booth, and indeed, the motivation for the whole assassination. The pages are either a complete fraud and hoax, and such conspiracy as there may have been is merely that sketched by Eisenschiml and Roscoe in their critical works, or there was a much deeper layer of players, and a much deeper conspiracy, than that of Booth, Herold, Paine, and Atzerodt. The choice is either between some version of "the standard narrative" with "revisionist embellishments", or a deep and wide conspiracy involving men in high and powerful positions in the Union, including in Mr. Lincoln's Administration. There is no middle ground, and the

---

[26] Ibid.

controversy surrounding the alleged eighteen missing (and rediscovered) pages continues to this day.

So convoluted is this story that before we can even review it, we must first record a few notices and caveats about the available sources. It is difficult to do, because in outlining the notices and caveats about the sources, one inevitably gets glimpses of the story, and vice versa, for the two things exist in a kind of "symbiotic" relationship.

When one searches high and low for the actual alleged text of the missing pages, one eventually discovers that there is but *one* printed source. This is a small octavo-sized paperback reprint titled simply *The Assassination of Abraham Lincoln: John Wilkes Booth's Diary, Excerpts from Newspapers and Other Sources*, part of the Classic Reprint Series published by Forgotten Books. As the title suggests and as quickly becomes apparent upon reading the work, the book consists of photocopies of articles from newspapers, and from articles from much smaller newsletters specializing in Lincoln assassination research and related matters. It is in these latter photocopies that the actual alleged *text* of the missing pages occurs. This caveat on the record, the small book is a goldmine of information, and the conspiracy recorded in the alleged text indeed reaches out to encompass and explain much of the *post bellum* financial history and government policy. The missing text makes it clear that the assassination was a fully fledged and carefully planned *coup d'etat*.[27] And Booth, no ordinary "lone nut" nor gullible conspirator, was a careful amanuensis of it all.

---

[27] *The Assassination of Abraham Lincoln: John Wilkes Booth's Diary, Excerpts from Newspapers and Other Sources* (London: Forgotten Books [Imprint of FB &Co, Ltd]: 2018. ISBN 978-0-282-85287-0. There is a problem for citation orthography that this work poses. Composed largely of photocopied articles from newspapers and small, specialized newsletters and journals,

The Rialto in Richmond

a. The Jack Anderson Column, August 3, 1977

The story that is told in the pages of the Booth diary's missing pages is as breathtaking as any of the revisionist literature concerning the assassination of President Kennedy. One of the photocopied articles is a column of the famous American columnist, Jack Anderson, in which one reads the following about the missing Booth diary pages:

> The pages are a fascinating account, presumably written by Booth, of his intrigues with Lincoln intimates shortly before the assassination. Some of the most prominent politicians of the period, including Stanton, are implicated.
>
> Referring to a plot perhaps unrelated to the murder, Booth allegedly writes that he may be working for the Secretary of War himself. At another point he declares: "I swear that I shall lay the body of this tyrant dead upon the altar of Mars." Apparently, Lincoln is the "tyrant," and "Mars," the god of war, could have been a code name for Stanton.
>
> …
>
> The FBI's findings may establish whether the 18 newly discovered pages are authentic. Lynch[28] gained considerable credibility by insisting that the missing pages

---

there is no pagination in the entire work. The pages numbers thus referred to in future footnotes citing this work have been added by me, beginning the numeration on the first page upon opening the paperback's cover. This page is actually an advertisement for Forgotten Books and its website. Continuing throughout the whole book, the page numbers end on the number 78, the blank page at the back of the book.

[28] Ed,: Lynch: the man who discovered the missing pages. More will be said about the actual circumstances of the discovery later.

were lined. Most experts had thought the diary was unlined. But the museum's curator, Michael Harman, has now inspected the diary more scientifically and has confirmed that its pages, like that of Lynch's discovery, are dimly lined.[29]

In other words, arguing for the credibility of the missing pages is the fact that their discoverer maintained that they were lined *when scholars and historians, based on the extant Booth diary on display at the museum, thought they were unlined.* When the authentic portion of the diary was scrutinized more closely and carefully, however, it too proved to be lined.

But what of the FBI examination? A comparison of the handwriting in the extant portion of the diary, which is known to be Booth's, with the handwriting of the allegedly recovered eighteen missing pages, would seal the case. This examination, however, has never been done (or, if it *was* done, it was done secretly, and its results were never published).

b. The Sunn Pictures' Transcript Problem

In their 1977 book, *The Lincoln Conspiracy*, authors David Balsiger and Charles E. Sellier, Jr., argue that the murder of President Lincoln was part of a deep and far-reaching conspiracy to change the *post bellum* policy of the government by removing Lincoln himself, and installing the presumably more pliant Vice President Andrew Johnson, a Northern Democrat. The book itself was based on the Sunn Pictures movie of the same name, starring the then-well-known actors Bradford Dillman as Booth, and John Dehner as

---

[29] Jack Anderson and Les Whitten, "FNI Probes Lincoln Assassination," *The Washington Post*, August 3, 1977, in *The Assassination of Abraham Lincoln*, p. 51.

Colonel Baker, the man who transmitted the diary to Stanton.[30]

This is where the story of the 18 pages becomes problematical, for no one has ever seen the actual pages, *only transcripts* of what they purportedly contain. A 1979 article in *The San Diego Union* explained the problem:

> Sunn Classic Pictures, in its publicity material, says the film is based in part on "many unpublished sources," among them "the purported missing pages" of a diary Booth kept and which was found and delivered intact to Stanton.
>
> From the condition of the diary, at least 18 pages are missing, with some scholars believing there were more.
>
> The diary, sans the pages, was introduced during the Andrew Johnson impeachment proceedings and the congressional inquiry into the assassination.
>
> The missing pages supposedly incriminate Stanton and other officials in the alleged plots against Lincoln, according to Sunn.
>
> ...
>
> *According to Sunn, a collector of Americana, Joseph Lynch of Worthington, Mass., found the missing pages when he was asked to appraise papers belonging to Stanton's heirs.*
>
> *The film company says its negotiations with the heirs "to acquire film rights to the actual pages: broke down for a number of reasons.*
>
> *However, it says, it "acquired transcripts of the missing pages."*
>
> ...
>
> *But the Sunn people admit they haven't seen the pages, or even allowed to have a sample page examined to*

---

[30] The paperback book itself is the 1977 publication of Schick Sunn Classic Books.

authenticate the handwriting. They are asking us to accept the document on faith.[31]

In other words, we have the following basic narrative concerning the missing pages of Booth's diary:

1) Stanton's heirs in Massachusetts found the missing 18 or so pages of Booth's diary;
2) Joseph Lynch, an Americana authority, was called in to authenticate the pages;
3) The pages came to the attention of Sunn Classic Pictures which negotiated for the rights for them to use them in its film about the assassination;
4) These negotiations broke down, and Sunn was allowed to see only transcripts of the contents of the alleged missing pages; and thus,
5) The handwriting of the missing pages was never authenticated, or, if it was, was done so secretly and privately.[32]

It will be recalled, however, that Joseph Lynch, who authenticated the pages, indicated that they were *lined*, and closer examination of the extant Booth diary did in fact reveal that the pages known to be authentic were dimly and faintly lined. Given this fact, I believe the preponderance of the facts argues that the missing pages are authentic.

---

[31] S.A. Desick, Staff Writer, "Lincoln Authority 'Outraged' By Movie; 'Conspiracy' Story Called Hoax," *The san Diego Union,* Sunday, October 30, 1979, in *The Assassination of Abraham Lincoln*, p. 55, emphasis added.

[32] Additionally, as of this writing, I have been unable to ascertain who allegedly has possession of the missing pages now. The following extensive excerpt details where the pages supposedly ended up.

This does not, however, mean that the contents of those missing pages as recorded in the alleged transcripts are authentic. Such an argument must be made on other bases, as will be shown below.

c. The Actual Transcript as Cited in "The Lincoln Log"

One of the photocopied sources in *The Assassination of Abraham Lincoln* is a small newsletter published in the 1970s in the State of New York called *The Lincoln Log*. This source contains the most detailed and complete version of the story of how the alleged missing pages of the Booth diary were found. It is cited extensively here. As it was initially a typed and presumably mimeographed article, I have attempted to preserve the underlining and capitalization of the original article:

> Back in November, 1975, antique firearms dealer Paul Weisberg of New York was trying to sell a polished wood case for $10,000 at the Potomac Arms & Gun Show in Lanham, Maryland. The case was unique because Weisberg claimed it had once belonged to Edwin M. Stanton. There was even a silver clasp, with his initials on it. Fitted inside the case were portions of the nooses that hung Mrs. Surratt and Lewis Paine, along with a section of the scaffold beam. Weisberg said he had no documents authenticating the case or its contents. Without them, he was having difficulty in selling it. (Those who examined it at the gun show thought it was certainly old enough to be genuine, but they were not able to pass any professional judgement (sic) as to its authenticity. Weisberg said the case belonged to a great-granddaughter of Stanton, who, according to a "Mr. X", from whom it came, also had missing pages of Booth's diary, among other items. We were neither able to learn who "Mr. X" was nor the identity of the Stanton heir, who, Weisberg said, did not want any notoriety. Therefore, our

efforts to follow up on the story of the "missing pages" were frustrated.

We had been led to believe that the Stantons still owned the case, and were trying to sell it through "Mr. X". but it now appears that "Mr. X" had bought the case from the Stanton family, and that Weisberg had, in turn, purchased it from him before he began exhibiting it.

Sunn Classic Pictures heard about the missing pages also, and wanted to see them for possible use in their film on Lincoln's murder. They finally tracked down "Mr. X", and a contract was eventually drawn up. Shortly after we had begun talking to Sunn, in an effort to learn something, anything, we received the first of a number of phone calls from none other than "Mr. X" himself. We spent hours on the phone with him, listening to some fascinating leading questions about the conspiracy and the missing pages, but he could not impart any information about the film's disclosures, due to his contract with Sunn Classic Pictures. We still know very little. Eventually, Mr. X" revealed his identity to us as Joseph Lynch, from Massachusetts. With his help, as well as the others involved, we related the follow story of the saga of the missing pages.

It was a mutual lawyer friend of his & Stanton's great-granddaughter who contacted Mr. Lynch, to appraise Stanton family material that had been passed down to her, and which lay dormant for many years. While examining this material, Mr. Lynch discovered what he believed to be the missing pages of Booth's diary, plus some other documents bearing on the Lincoln murder case. The material did not directly implicate Stanton, but, rather, those around him. Mr. Lynch theorized that Stanton had held onto this evidence as a sort of "insurance policy", in case any of the other implicated parties, ignorant of Stanton's cards, might someday be compelled to point their finger at him, to extricate themselves, or attempt to blackmail him.

The Rialto in Richmond

When Sunn Classic Pictures finally located Mr. Lynch, they contracted with him for movie rights to tape recorded transcripts he had made of the missing pages and the other documents—but not until Mr. Lynch had seen a scenario of the film and felt reasonably certain that the material would be presented in a scholarly rather than a sensational way. Additionally, the Stanton great-granddaughter (to whom the material still belongs), retained her anonymity.

Mr. Lynch had done a great deal of time-consuming research of his own after studying the material, and passed many of his findings and conclusions over to Sunn, who coordinated it with material they had also separately gathered, for use in the film.

Having studied the missing pages first hand (to our knowledge, only Lynch and the Stanton family have ever seen them), Mr. Lynch went to Washington to see the diary from which the pages had come, having already drawn some conclusions based on what he had seen in the missing leaves.

In Washington, Mr. Lynch found at least one blank page with writing—in invisible ink. The writing had begun to surface from exposure to heat over the years. The page (the ne dated July 18th, 19th, and 20th, 1864) apparently contained a list of names and numbers. The ones most readily visible with the naked eye are "White: and "Jenkins". Lynch also observed some faint writing in the front of the little book, which had also previously not been noted. The first name and the address are a little faint, but Mr. Lynch makes it out to be, without the slightest of doubt, the name and address of Frederick Douglass. This would be the famous black orator who fought for negro (sic., et passim.) rights and was a close advisor to Lincoln on negro problems. Lynch is sure it is written in Booth's hand. (If indeed it is Douglass, what in Heaven's name is it doing in John Wilkes Booth's diary???) Mr. Lynch also observed other bits of writing that have been victim of an attempt at defacing, through erasure.

155

Mr. Lynch then contacted the people at Sunn Classic Pictures and suggested that they arrange to have special light photographs (ultra-violet, infra-red, etc.) taken of the pages, to see what they might reveal. (He had in mind the National Archives.)

Mr. Ray Neff then appeared on the scene, with his own equipment, to take the pictures. Neff is an associate professor in the department of Health and Safety at Indiana State University, but back in 1961, when he was a research chemist in New Jersey, he discovered a coded message written by Secret Service Chief Lafayette Baker, in an old military journal.[33] (Baker had become embroiled in the controversy surrounding the missing pages of the diary, and testified at the Johnson Impeachment hearings on the subject.) The code was easy to decipher, and it implicates Baker, Stanton, and unnamed high government officials in a conspiracy to kill Lincoln. (The story, by editor Robert Fowler, appeared in the August, 1961 issue of his Civil War Times. Comments about it can be found in the October, 1961 issue.) Although the code implicates Stanton, historians questioned the veracity of baker, who was enough of a scoundrel to have fabricated the code, to embarrass his former boss. There is little doubt that the writing is Baker's, as far as we know.

(The other possibility, of course, is that the real conspirators behind Booth, to protect themselves, are each scrambling to gain whatever leverage they can over each other in order to prevent being framed. We continue with *The Lincoln Log's* account:)

David Balsiger, of Sunn Classic Pictures, explained to us that Neff took the pictures because he had seen some of his

---

[33] Ed.: Colonel Baker was one of the officers credited with bringing Booth's diary from Garrett's farm to Secretary of War Stanton.

photographic work, and felt that he was highly qualified to photograph the diary. As of this writing, Neff is still reviewing the results of the hundreds of sophisticated pictures he took, but at this time, he says he <u>doesn't</u> think the pages contain any material that is particularly revealing.

But what about Joseph Lynch's own examination of the diary? <u>Something</u> must be in those pages. Lynch told us that it was the nature of the <u>missing</u> pages that led him to <u>conclude</u> the sort of thing <u>he</u> says he found in the diary. We are merely reporting the story as we have received it, and will not draw <u>any</u> conclusions. But at this point, it is only important that we see for ourselves just what is on those pages. Now, Mr. Neff was placed under no obligation to turn any of his pictures over to the Park Service. But all parties agree on at least one thing, that being that Mr. Neff gave verbal assurance to Mr. Michael Harmon, the curator of Ford's Theatre, that he would donate copies of all the photos he took, and that Mr. Harman (sic., et passim.) would then make them available for research. Harman told us that he expects to receive them by mid-March.

Mr. Lynch protested to Mr. Harman that if photos were not taken by the government, as well as by Mr. Neff, the results of only one series of pictures, taken by a private individual, would be subject to speculation. At the time Neff's first series of pictures were taken (he returned at a later date for some more, the first series being a preliminary session), Mr. Lynch says that he asked for, and received, permission to take his own pictures, as well, to insure that at least two independent sets of pictures existed. (This is not meant to cast any shadows over Mr. Neff. We don't think there was anything wrong in the request, considering the circumstances.)

Researcher James O. Hall soon contacted Mr. Harman, asking him to arrange with the National Archives to take its own special light-photographs of the diary. The request was refused. Mr. Harman, in his position as Ford's Theatre's curator, is evidently interested more in preserving artifacts than in investigating Lincoln's murder. He told Mr. Hall that any more pictures would mean "unnecessary handling of a priceless artifact, and would pose a threat to its preservation, which would not be acceptable." He also explained, to THE LINCOLN LOG, that the pages were very fragile, having suffered from recent handling and the effects of aging—too fragile too (sic.) tamper with anymore. He therefore sent the diary off to the National Park Service Restoration Museum at Harper's Ferry, Virginian, where park Service consevators would "refurbish" the diary, whatever that means. "None of the work... would in any way alter, erase, or obscure any portions of the text or any part of the diary itself." After the diary is refurbished and sent back to Ford's Theater, Mr. Harman told us that he would not be likely to allow any more photographs of the diary, unless he thought that the condition of the pages permitted it. He admitted that this might mean weeks, months, or years. The issue here is not the fact that <u>Mr. Neff</u> took the pictures, It is that a <u>private citizen</u> took them, and that another branch of the Federal Government, such as the National Archives, which certainly knows how to handle fragile documents, was not given the opportunity to take pictures of a government artifact, pictures which might conceivably, shed additional light on Lincoln's murder. Mr. Neff's generosity in sharing his own pictures with researchers should not go unnoticed, and we would like to thank him for saying that he would make them available to researchers. We do not mean to insinuate that Mr. Neff's pictures would ne unreliable, either. But what could be more reliable than pictures taken by the National Archives?? It is to <u>our advantage</u> that Mr. Neff was about to take his. Now we think that the government should be impressed with the importance of taking a <u>second</u> set of photographs.

Just before "going to press", we learn that through the efforts of the editor of <u>Civil War Times Illustrated</u>, officials in the Interior Department have called the NPS[34] at Harper's Ferry and told them to hold up, for the time being, any work on the Booth diary, until they are further instructed. To be continued...[35]

From this lengthy excerpt, one learns the following:

1) That no originals of the 18 missing pages were ever seen; but that
2) infrared and ultra-violet photographs were made of the *entire* Booth diary by a private individual;
3) that the pages ironically ended up in the hands of the National Park Service in Harper's Ferry, Virginia, scene of the notorious radical abolitionist John Brown's murderous raid, and that the process of refurbishing Booth's diary, and taking more pictures, could be a matter of years, a convenient method of dealing with the Booth diary in order to not to have to deal with it!
4) The key figure in the whole story is Joseph Lynch, the only one who claims to have seen the missing pages; these pages, it must be recalled, he maintained were lined. At the time he stated this, the other portion of the Booth diary in the Ford's Theatre Museum was thought to be *unlined* by the vast majority of assassination researchers, until closer examination revealed that they, too, were lined.

---

[34] NPS: National Park Service.
[35] Richard Sloan, editor, *The Lincoln Log* (Volume II, No. 2, Feb-March, 1977, in *The Assassination of Abraham Lincoln*, pp. 18-21, underlined and capitalized emphases in the original, italicized emphases added.

But *The Lincoln Log* was not done reporting on the matter of the missing pages of Booth's diary.

In the following edition, *The Lincoln Log* published the actual alleged *transcripts* of the missing pages behind the following introduction:

When John Wilkes Booth was killed at Garrett's farm in Virginia twelve days after assassinating Lincoln at Ford's Theatre, a memorandum book was found in one of his pockets. Booth had confided his inner-most thoughts to this book in the course of his escape. Colonel Everton J. Conger, who had been given honorary command f the troopers that found Booth, personally took the book and handed it over to Secretary of War Edwin M. Stanton. The little book, or "diary", as it became known, was locked in a vault, and not made public until two years later, when word got around that Stanton's Secret Service Chief, Lafayette Baker, had mentioned it in his memoirs, which were about to be released. A furor was raised in Washington, and Congress clamored for the little book. At that time, hearings were being geld into charges of impeachment against President Johnson, and one of the accusations being made concerned the President's possible role in Lincoln's assassination. Stanton produced the diary, and its contents were made public by the press a few weeks later. But the controversy over the diary did not stem from the mere fact that the diary had been suppressed, but because when it was finally produced, it was claimed by those who had seen it before Stanton had that there were now about 18 pages missing, cut with a knife. Stanton testified at the House Judiciary Committee Hearing that the pages were missing when he received it. Just who was responsible for the pages being cut out remained a mystery. Were they cut out by Booth? Or by Stanton? If Stanton was responsible, it indicated that someone in the Government was trying to cover-up a conspiracy. Historians have argued for more than a century with each other, as to whether or not Stanton, or anyone for that matter, had engaged Booth in a plot to first kidnap

Lincoln or to assassinate him. All agreed upon one thing, however: If the missing pages were ever found, they would provide the answers to many of the questions that were still being asked.

The pages show that among those involved with Booth in plots against Lincoln were Senator John Conness of California, financier Jay Cook, Confederacy Secretary of State Judah Benjamin, political boss Thurlow Weed, Michigan Senator Zechariah Chandler, Confederacy Secret Service Chief Jacob Thompson, U.S. Secret Service Chief LaFayette Baker, Col. E.J. Conger, and others.

As with all of this material acquired by Sunn, we point out that only Sunn officials, their researchers, and the parties from which the material came, have ever seen it. We have Sunn's word that everything they show in their movie, when it is released in mid-June, is thoroughly documented. But Sunn realizes that many will ask to see these documents, and let outside experts pass judgement (sic., et passim.) on their authenticity. Until that is done, the public will have to consider Sunn's assurances for themselves, and use the (sic) own judgement as to whether or not the material is valid.

The pages delineate Booth's involvement in a conspiracy plot with Confederate leaders, some of Lincoln's own trusted friends, and N.Y. businessmen. Here are excerpts from the transcript as supplied to us by Sunn.[36]

At this juncture, an extensive excerpt from the alleged missing pages follows.

Again, we reproduce this exactly as it is given in *The Lincoln Log*, as photocopied in *The Assassination of Abraham Lincoln*. It is to be noted that, for transcripts from alleged missing pages in a diary, the absence of dates is perhaps telling, for in the authentic extant portions of the diary, Booth

---

[36] Richard Sloan, Editor, *The Lincoln Log* (Seaford, New York), Vol. II, No. 3, Mar-April, 1977, emphasis added, cited in *The Assassination of Abraham Lincoln*, pp. 22-23.

does make a point to record the dates of the entries. Whether on the original pages the dates are recorded, and then omitted by Lynch or Sunn in their transcripts, or whether the dates were faithfully recorded on the transcripts by Lynch and Sunn, and then omitted by the editor of *The Lincoln Log*, we will never know. It is my strong suspicion, however, that at least *some* dates appeared in the original, and that for whatever reason these were omitted in the transmission of the transcripts.

The transcripts also contain parenthetical remarks, and there is no indication if these are in the original, or if they were added as editorial clarifications by Lynch, or by Sunn Pictures, or by Sloan, the editor of *The Lincoln Log*. They are thus reproduced here with the exact punctuation with which they appear in the photocopied *Lincoln Log* article in *The Assassination of Abraham Lincoln*.

Here, then, are the only extant versions of the transcripts of the 18 missing pages of Booth's diary that I have been able to find:

At a party given by Eva's parents, I met Senator John Conness (California Senator). Conness says Eddie (Booth) and he are friends from says in California in '55 and '56.

In a private conversation he informed me that he could render some service to the South.

He suggests that I call on him tomorrow as we might have some common interests.

I saw him this morning and he produced documents which proved that he was not an enemy spy.

He gave me the name of a wholesale druggist who could be trusted and said the druggist would supply from 5,000 to 25,000 ounces of quinine.

I purchased a six-week list in advance of all the passwords which changed daily on the post roads for the sum of $3,000.

The Rialto in Richmond

He said that he would supply the new passwords every six weeks as they changed for as long as I wished, providing each time $3,000 would be forthcoming.

He said he was not a patriot for either North of South, but rather a man with a small pocket and a large need.

In Philadelphia today I met with Jay Cooke (Lincoln's Civil War financier).

Cooke brought his brother Henry (Washington banker)— greeted me warmly and said he thought most highly of Judah Benjamin (Confederate Secretary of State) and acknowledged that anyone who that wily fox, Benjamin, would send would be the best man available.

We had lunch, then went to a room where the people present were a number of speculators in both cotton and gold.

Present were *Thurlow Weed (Lincoln's campaign manager and loyal supporter)*, a person by the name of (Samuel) Noble *(New York cotton broker), a man by the name of (Zechariah) Chandler (Michigan Senator)*, A Mr. (Isaac) Bell (cotton merchant)—who said he was a friend of John Conness.

Each and every one asserted that he had had dealings with the Confederate States and they would continue, too, wherever possible.

Cooke said that they would continue to have dealings with the Confederacy, but not out of fear of betrayal, but because in peace and in war, a businessman must do business whatever the stakes.

Cooke gave me two letters—one to Beverly Tucker (Confederate diplomatic agent) and the other to Jacob Thompson (Confederate [PORTION MISSING]

At the St. Lawrence Motel in Montreal—

A half hour went by and Thompson arrived. I presented both gentlemen with the letters given me by Cooke. They read them and shortly we had dinner.

And after dinner, Thompson gave me $50,000 in bank notes with instructions to take $15,000 to Senator Conness and to leave in a sealed envelope $20,000 in notes and the home of Senator (Benjamin) Wade (Ohio Senator). The *balance of the money to be used to obtain recruits for our plan. The plan goes forward.*

Washington again at the National—

(John) Surratt[37] and I are to go south to reconnoiter the ground which we will cover. We have four routes and at least a hundred supporters along the way—most patriots, some who need money, but all loyal to the South.

We are ready at last. We waited all day—all six of us in the freezing rain and he did not come.

Answering a knock on my door this morning, I found LaFayette Backer (chief of the National Detective Police, a division of Stanton's War Department) on my doorstep. I thought the end had come.

But instead, he handed me letters from Jefferson Davis (President of the Confederate States of America), from Judah Benjamin, and from Clement Clay (Confederate States diplomat). I gave him the money and sent a message to Richmond.... I don't trust him. I wait for answer. I receive reply, my orders—trust him! I do not!

I went to Conness. He said to trust Baker—that he knew him in California in '55 and '56 and that Baker could be trusted because of that fact. I cannot. They believe in him. I cannot!

I purchased a carbine entirely covered in leather. I darken it with lamp black.

I took (Lewis) Paine and (John) Surratt with me and we waited on the road near the gardens.

In the late hours of the morning we heard a horse approaching. It was him. It was dark and I waited until he was 25 or 30 yards from me. I fired! I saw his hat fall.

Paine fired twice. He stayed in the saddle and galloped away. Within minutes they pursued us. Within two miles, we eluded them. Another failure!

---

[37] Ed: John Surratt, son of hung conspirator Mary Surratt. John escaped to Europe where, for a period, he was actually a solider in the Papal militia.

I met (Col. Everton) Conger (Baker's aide) at the Herndon House. He was in mufti (plain clothes) and warned no new attempts until we have a new plan.

If I try again without orders they will find me in the Potomac along with my friends.

No new orders come in the last ten days. I go to New York. I make it plain. I believe we have been betrayed and that I think the scoundrel responsible is Baker.

I believe that Baker and that (Maj. Thomas) Eckert (Stanton aide and chief of the War Department Telegraph Office) and the Secretary (Stanton) are in control of our activities and this frightens me.

There is great excitement tonight. Rumors say that (Robert E.) Lee has surrendered. If it is true, it means the end.

I believe that these politicians, these vipers and their cronies will strip the South bare.

It seems that all things we have planned and striven for have come to naught.

By the almighty God, I swear that I shall lay the body of this tyrant (Lincoln) dead upon the altar of Mars. ["Mars" was Lincoln's name for Stanton]. And if by this act, I am slain, they too shall be cast into Hell for I have given information to a friend who will have the nation know who the traitors are.[38]

And that is the only version—anywhere and in any sort of publicly accessible record—of the transcripts of the alleged missing pages of Booth's diary.

The question is, are there any *internal clues* that would indicate that the transcript is authentic? Consider firstly the list of names with whom "Booth" (as we shall designate the author of these transcripts) claims he had been in contact; it is

---

[38] Richard Sloan, Editor, *The Lincoln Log* (Seaford, New York), Vol. II, No. 3, Mar-April, 1977, emphasis added, cited in *The Assassination of Abraham Lincoln*, pp. 23-25.

a very curious and at first glance unlikely list for a "devoted son of the Confederacy":

1) The U.S. Senator from California, John Conness, whom "Booth" paid money for the passwords to get in and out of Washington's military cordon after hours or in cases of orders sealing off the city;

2) Jay Cook, a prominent financial backer of Lincoln;

3) President Lincoln's campaign manager Thurlow Weed(!);

4) The U.S. Senator from Michigan, Zechariah Chandler;

5) Colonel LaFayette Baker (who claimed to have seen the diary!);

6) Colonel Conger (who would remove the diary from Booth as he lay dying at Garrett's farm!). Conger allegedly informs "Booth" not to act without orders, or he ("Booth") and his recruits would end up dead; and finally,

7) Note that "Booth" suspects, on his trip to New York, that he is being manipulated by Stanton and his aide, the Assistant Secretary of War Eckert, whom Lincoln had requested as a bodyguard the night of the assassination! Note also that

8) "Booth" allegedly traveled to Montreal where he was given $50,000 in notes—presumably Union greenbacks—by Thompson, head of the Confederate secret service and the Confederate cell in Montreal, to recruit members for the "plan", with some of the money being directed. This no doubt was the "kidnapping" version of the plan, which changed to an assassination plot on the news of Lee's surrender.

Note that if all this *is* true, then "Booth" is taking orders both from the Confederacy *and* from the Union, and that the chain of command in *both* cases goes very high.

This is where the detail about the meeting between "Booth" and New York City commodities speculators becomes a crucial detail tending to authenticate the alleged missing pages, for this is a rather rarefied *conceptual* detail at odds with the rest of the transcript; it is the sort of detail an intelligent man, but someone unfamiliar with the day-to-day mechanics and importance of commodities speculation, might make, someone like Booth. The presence of speculators *in gold and cotton* in the North indicates that there were people making money speculating on commodities prices of the two things the Confederacy needed to conduct trade, to buy weapons on the international market, and to continue to prosecute the war: specie, and more specifically, gold, and cotton.

As we shall discover in Part Two of this book, this detail is also a strong indicator of a *third* level to the conspiracy, the most deeply hidden element, cloaking its actions behind the level of the Confederate conspirators, and the deeper level of the Northern financiers.

There is, however, a detail that must be mentioned here that tends to corroborate the version presented in *The Lincoln Log*. The articles and excerpts published in *The Lincoln Log* were published in the year 1977. In the same year, Sunn Classic Pictures released the *book* version of its movie by authors David Balsiger and Charles E. Sellier, Jr., to which we have previously made reference. In that book's presentation of the missing 18 pages, no portion of the transcript is ever cited, but it is summarized in a fictionalized meeting *between some of the same individuals mentioned in the excerpted transcript we have just quoted from The Lincoln Log.* Baker, Senator Conness of California, Senator Chandler of Michigan, Secretary Stanton and Major Eckert are all in attendance, discussing what to do about these incriminating 18 pages of Booth's diary. But also in attendance in this dramatized version of the diary's contents is Indiana representative George Washington Julian.

So the question arises, does the presence of these men in the transcript make *sense*? A glance at three of them is in order, for this glance will reveal nothing that would argue strongly against their involvement in such a conspiracy, and contains a clue as to why their presence in the alleged diary transcripts:

1) U.S. Senator John Conness was with fellow U.S. Senators William Stewart (Nevada) and Charles Sumner (Massachusetts) on the Good Friday night of the assassination. When they heard of the attempt on Secretary of State Seward's life, the three Senators hastened to Seward's house, and when learning of the Secretary's survival of the attempt, Conness declared that the events appeared to be a conspiracy to assassinate "the entire cabinet". Conness then ordered soldiers to protect Secretary of War Scranton![39]

2) Representative George Washington Julian of Indiana is a more telling alleged member of the plot A radical Republican, Julian was in favor of the harsh post bellum reconstructionist policies, and as such, was an opponent of Lincoln's successor, President Andrew Johnson, and assisting in

---

[39] "John Conness," *Wikipedia*, en.wikipedia.ord/wiki/John_Conness

drafting the articles of impeachment against Johnson.[40]

3) U.S. Senator Zechariah Chandler from Michigan, was a radical abolitionist and in favor of harsh reconstruction policies for the post bellum South. A senator from 1857-1875, he became Secretary of the Interior for President Ulysses S. Grant, and subsequently was chairman of the Republican National Committee, helping to elect President Rutherford B. Hayes.

When one considers these men with some of the others mentioned in the transcripts and in the book version of the Sunn Classics movie—people like Edwin Stanton himself, or his assistant secretary of War, Eckert, or Ohio Senator Benjamin Wade, and so on, *one very telling commonality emerges: all are opposed to Lincoln's more lenient policy to the South.* Each of these individuals, in turn, thus points to that much deeper layer of conspiracy, for each raises the question of why such a harsh reconstructionist policy should even be advocated to the degree is was. In this advocacy there was, if one wishes to read a bit between the lines, a bit of an hysterical element, and element that suggested that the policy was less a choice, and more of a requirement. The question is, if so, then a requirement from whom, and why? Again, we shall have to wait until part two before we will be in a position to answer that question.

For the present, we must return to the Continuity of Government operation surrounding President Davis with a necessary but short trip to the *goal* of that operation, the Confederate Trans-Mississippi Department of Louisiana,

---

[40] "George W. Julian," *Wikipedia*, en.wikipedia.org/wiki/George_W._Julian.

Arkansas, Texas, and the Indian Territories, a department and Confederacy unto itself, known by the nickname of its military governor, "Kirby Smithdom."

Indiana Representative George Washington Julian

U.S. Senator from Michigan, Zechariah Chandler, pre-war Chairman of the Republican National Committee, Secretary of the Interior under President Ulysses S Grant

U.S. Senator from California, John Conness

4

THE FORGOTTEN THEATER OF THE WAR: A VERY BRIEF DETOUR TO THE TRANS-MISSISSIPPI DEPARTMENT, OR "KIRBY SMITHDOM"

"...President Davis...was moving southwest through the Carolinas and Georgia in an effort to reach 'KirbySmithdom,' where Davis believed the war could be continued indefinitely with an alliance with Mexico."
Patricia G. McNeely[1]

"Grant wrote, 'For my own part, I think that Johnston's tactics were right. Anything that could have prolonged the war a year beyond the time that it finally did close, would probably have exhausted the North to such an extent that they might then have abandoned the contest and agreed to a settlement.'"
Patricia G. McNeely, citing General Ulysses S. Grant[2]

ONE OF THOSE OBVIOUS THINGS THAT NO ONE seems to notice, much less comprehend the significance of, is the fact that after General Ulysses S. Grant's successful campaign against the Confederate fortress of Vicksburg, Mississippi and its fall in 1863, the War Between the States, at least as far as standard historiography relates it, was something confined to the great campaigns and

---

[1] Patricia G. McNeely, *President Abraham Lincoln, General William T. Sherman, President Jefferson Davis, and the Lost Confederate Gold*, p. 138.
[2] Ibid., p.174, citing Ulysses S. Grant, *The Civil War Memoirs of Ulysses S. Grant* (New York: Charles Webster & Co. (No date nor ISBN given), p. 295.

battlefields east of that river. The names are well known to us: Fredericksburg, Chancellorsville, Cold Harbor, Hardin Pike, Murfreesboro, Chickamauga, Gettysburg, Spotsylvania, and a host of lesser battles and campaigns consume the pages of popular history books and preoccupy the imagination.

The result of this attention is that it is as if three whole states of the Confederacy, Louisiana, Arkansas, and Texas (not to mention the Confederacy's Indian allies in what would become Oklahoma, and its claimed territories in New Mexico and Arizona) suddenly ceased to exist. Dare one call this not merely inattention, but perhaps deliberate misdirection? Thomas W. Cutrer, who wrote probably the only detailed and recent study of the Civil War west of the Mississippi, put the problem in such a way as to at least allow the possibility that the inattention might be, to some degree, deliberately intended; the impression thereby created by this inattention is that the department and its states and territories had nothing of any consequence to contribute to the war effort of the Confederacy, and were nothing but a waste and drain on the precious military resources of the Union. Cutrer puts this perception this way in his excellent study of the theater:

> For nearly 150 years, historians tended to disregard what one called "the dark corner of the Confederacy." Early in the twentieth century, historian Nathaniel W. Stephenson wrote that "a great history of the time would have a special and thrilling story of the conduct of the detached western unit, the isolated world of Louisiana, Arkansas, and Texas – the 'Department of the Trans-Mississippi'—cut off from the main body of the Confederacy and hemmed in between the Federal army and the deep sea." But to the largest degree, this story has not yet been written. *The Annals of the Civil War: Written by Leading Participants, North and South,* one of the major collections of primary documents relating to the

Civil War, contains not a single article on the war west of the Mississippi. The classic *West Point Atlas of American Wars* contains not a single map of the trans-Mississippi.[3]

It was one giant undeveloped wasteland of distraction.

Yet, as we saw, it was precisely to this region of the Confederacy that Jefferson Davis hoped to flee to continue the war, and it was the mere *possibility* of that happening that both Union Generals Grant and Sherman, with more intelligence and foresight than the then or current public, feared. This, too, confronts us with a difficulty, for the impression created is that the war could be barely supported by the *developed* areas of the South. But the barren wastes of Texas? The swamps and plantations of Louisiana? The rural villages and small farms of Arkansas?

It was an absurd notion.

This is, however, largely a false impression, and to understand just how false it is, one has to understand Confederate Lieutenant General Edmund Kirby Smith, the military governor of the Confederacy's "Trans-Mississippi" department, its crucial role in sustaining the Confederacy's war effort, and Jefferson Davis's hopes.

Our purpose here, however, is not to give even the most cursory and rudimentary overview of either the Union's or the

---

[3] Thomas W. Cutrer, *Theater of a Separate War: The Civil War West of the Mississippi River 1861-1865* (Chapel Hill: The University of North Carolina Press, 2017 [ISBN 978-1-4696-3156-1]), p. xi. Cutrer's book is an indispensable and detailed one volume history of this forgotten theater. The other indispensable study of the Trans-Mississippi Department is William Royston Geise's *The Confederate Military Forces in the Trans-Mississippi West, 1861-1865: A Study in Command* (El Dorado Hills, California: Savas Beatie, 2022 [ISBN 978-1-61121-621-9]).

Confederacy's military operations or policies in the Trans-Mississippi. Our purpose is rather to briefly survey the infrastructure and resources of the Trans-Mississippi that may have enabled it to sustain military operations for a "rump Confederacy" and to fulfill Generals Grant's and Sherman's fears.

In short, was there sufficient industrial plant in the Trans-Mississippi to produce weapons, to maintain field armies, and were there other sources and avenues available to procure them, if not?

A. The Military and Trade Infrastructure of the Trans-Mississippi
1. Economic and Agricultural Self-Sufficiency

When the Trans-Mississippi Department is examined more closely, one soon discovers that President Davis had very good reason to assume that a Continuity of Government operation with the Department as its goal had a reasonable chance of success. For one thing, the shared international border with Mexico offered the Confederacy a direct means of relying upon a neutral and its ships and ports for the conduct of its vital international trade. Cotton and specie could flow out, and war material could flow in, uninhibited by the Union blockade.[4] Additionally, the Confederate fast ships of its own blockade running typically plied their trade from the Bahamas and Cuba, through the Caribbean and the Gulf of Mexico. In spite of the attention of history books on the Federal blockage and eventual occupation of the crucial

---

[4] Thomas W. Cutrer, *Theater of a Separate War: The Civil War West of the Mississippi River 1861-1865* (Chapel Hill" The University of North Carolina Press, 2017, ISBN 978-1-4696-3157-1), p. 2.

ports of Mobile, Savannah, Charleston, Wilmington, or Norfolk, these ports, while certainly vital ports of departure and destination for the blockade runners, diminished in importance as the war progressed.

From the standpoint of logistics, the region was more than capable of producing the food, fodder, and clothing to sustain field armies. Texas alone at the time possessed more than three and a half million head of cattle. Sugar and molasses production in Louisiana "was by far the largest on the North American mainland," [5] and the region produced enough grain and hogs – not to mention cotton – to not only feed and clothe its own population, but a substantial portion of the rest of the Confederacy as well. Indeed, as the war progressed and production in the eastern portion of the Confederacy fell dramatically, the Trans-Mississippi remained the Confederacy's only productive region. Food and other supplies continued to flow from west to east across the porous Union patrols on the Mississippi.

The free population of the three Confederate States comprising the Trans-Mississippi Department was approximately one million two hundred thousand people, a population sufficient to support medium-sized field armies.[6] This population the Trans-Mississippi was more than capable of sustaining and supporting agriculturally:

> When it came to matters of subsistence the Trans-Mississippi was more self-sufficient than most other Confederate military departments because beef, pork, and bacon were generally plentiful in Texas, wheat and corn were grown in quantity along the Red River, salt was

---

[5] Cutrer, op cit.., p. 1.

[6] Cutrer gives the population of Louisiana as 375,000, Arkansas as 324,000, and Texas as 420,000. (Q.v. p. 1)

available, and sorghum, beans, potatoes, sugar and other crops were all produced within the limits of the department.[7]

Besides being fed, populations and field armies also need to be clothed.

In this respect, again, the Trans-Mississippi was in a better situation than the rest of the Confederacy, for not only could it trade its cotton and specie for finished textile products from Europe and neighboring Mexico, it had a limited textile manufacturing capability of its own at the Texas State Penitenatiary in Huntsville. Additionally, there was a much more *dispersed* textile manufacturing capability as many of the farms of the region maintained their own family looms which could contract for small deliveries of clothing.[8]

2. Financial Policy of "Kirby Smithdom"

In February 1863, President Davis appointed Lieutenant General Edmund Kirby Smith to head the Trans-Mississippi Department[9] that would soon acquire the name "Kirby Smithdom" in recognition for the general's effective administration of the department. President Davis authorized General Smith to assume civil and military authority within the department, effectively making the general a kind of

---

[7] William Royston Geise, *The Confederate Military Forces in the Trans-Mississippi West, 1861-1865: A Study in Command* (El Dorado Hills, California: Savas Beatie: 2022 ISBN978-1-61121-621-9), p. 126.

[8] Ibid., p. 116.

[9] McNeely, op. cit., p. 131.

Viceroy of the region.[10] It was an appointment that played to General Smith's strengths, for while he was but a mediocre tactician and strategist, he more than made up for these deficiencies as a policy-maker and administrator.

Confederate Lieutenant General Edmund Kirby Smith,
Military Governor of the "Trans-Mississippi Department" of the
Confederacy, or "Kirby Smithdom"

---

[10] Ibid., p. 132.

Fearing the revival of sectionalism after the fall of Vicksburg, President Davis urged the general to call a conference of the Department's civil officials.[11] The President need not have bothered, for General Smith anticipated the same difficulties and called for such a conference in Marshall, Texas, on August 15' 1863. The conference was attended by Texas Governor Lubbock, the Texas Governor-elect Pendleton Murrah, C.S. Senator Williamson Oldham, Louisiana Governor Moore and Louisiana Supreme Court Justices Edwin Merrick and Albert Voorhies, Arkansas C.S. Senators Robert Johnson and Charles Mitchell, both representing the state's governor, Harris Flanagan, and Missouri Governor Reynolds, among others. Governor Lubbock of Texas was elected chairman of the conference.[12]

This conference ratified a number of important policies proposed by General Smith under President Davis' broad authorization to Smith to run the military and civil affairs of the Department as a kind of "viceroy" of the Confederate executive branch of government. Following Davis' own suggestions, it authorized Smith to appoint commissioners directly representing the Trans-Mississippi to Mexico and France.

Additionally the conference, recognizing that there were too few Confederate Treasury notes in circulation within the Department to buy cotton for sale abroad to purchase supplies for the army, and being unwilling to depreciate the currency further by purchases in the notes, a plan was adopted to issue six percent specie bonds for the cotton. These plans were adopted, with the exception of the bonds in specie.

---

[11] Geise, op. cit., p. 107.
[12] Ibid.

Finally, the conference agreed that General Smith should assume the powers of the Confederate presidency within the department. General Smith was now, effectively, President Jefferson Davis' viceroy within the department.[13]

"Kirby Smithdom" had been born.

The failure to endorse the six percent specie bonds deserves further comment. It will be apparent that the concern of the conference was to avoid further depreciation of the Confederate currency within the department. By the same token, however, the Department had to maintain its silver and gold specie reserves because this was absolutely vital to maintain its ability to finance purchases in foreign markets. In this respect, gold was absolutely vital, since the Department's ultimate primary trading partner was Great Britain, as it was the rest of the Confederacy's. And Britain was on the gold standard. Accordingly, the Department could ill-afford to dilute its specie holdings in interest pledges to cotton-bond holders. This reasoning is reflected in the fact that General Smith was using the Cotton Bureau of the Department to purchase "cotton at three and four cents a pound" which he would then sell for "fifty cents a pound in gold."[14] General Smith also did something else to stabilize prices: the monetary value of the cotton purchased and sold by the Cotton Bureaus of the Department we measure in pence sterling per pound.[15]

The above details are significant, for they are an indicator of the financial system that will be explored in more detail in part two, but suffice it to note that the Confederacy, and particularly the Trans-Mississippi department, is functioning with basically a two-tiered financial system, one

---

[13] Geise, op. cit., p. 108.

[14] McNeely, op. cit., p. 136.

[15] Geise, op. cit., p. 109.

which involves the printing and circulation of paper money notes within the country, and another based on the use of specie, and especially gold, as a reserve and medium of international exchange, or to put it differently, in international trade the Confederacy is operating a commodity barter system of cotton for gold, and gold for finished goods.

The Trans-Mississippi Department's General Smith has added one more feature to this system: the stabilization of the circulating paper on the basis of the commodities—both cotton and specie—on which its international trade is conducted. This is also an important consideration, for it is an indicator that the Union blockade is not as effective against the Trans-Mississippi as it was elsewhere in the Confederacy. Had it been so, such a means of stabilization would not have been effective.

This consideration also permits us to properly understand a curious event that occurred during President Davis flight. During this episode, it is recorded that eventually Davis' party, which had brought with it a considerable sum of Confederate paper money notes, burned much of these. Most individuals understand this as an act of desperation and futility, as it was realized "the cause was lost" and there was no point in lugging around paper currency of a country that soon would no longer exist. This is, of course, one possible way to interpret the event. The other, however, is suggested by the monetary policies of "Kirby Smithdom," for if the Trans-Mississippi Department was the ultimate goal of Jefferson Davis' Continuity of Government flight operation, a sudden influx of paper money could easily have upset the economy of the Department. Accordingly, the decision was taken to burn the notes and remove the possibility. In support of this interpretation of this episode, after the August 1863 conference, General Smith had requested that Richmond supply his department with fifty to one hundred million in bonds to "soak up the surplus currency in the hands of the public, and to curb depreciation.... What Smith emphatically did not want from the Confederate Treasury was a large shipment of Confederate notes to depreciate the currency further."[16] If one compares this policy to the rest of the Confederacy east of the Mississippi, it is as if one is dealing with a whole different policy and even a wholly separate Treasury.

3. The Manufacture of Weapons and Heavy Ordnance

A final requirement for sustaining field armies at the time is the ability to provision troops with weapons, both in terms of firearms and heavy ordnance, and the ammunition for both. This means that one must have supplies or sources for iron, wood, and so on, but foundries and forges for manufacture, and the skilled labor for all of it.

In this respect the Trans-Mississippi, whose resources in this respect were small, were again not completely lacking. In addition to a foundry at Shreveport – eventual headquarters for "Kirby Smithdom"—which was capable of a small production of heavy ordnance,[17] the department had undertaken to make itself self-sufficient in this respect as well, even before the fall of Vicksburg and the arrival of General Smith as the department's head.[18] There were also arsenals within the department capable of supplying the small arms ammunition at San Antonio and Houston, with that at San Antonio capable of a small manufacture of heavy

---

[16] Geise, op. cit., p. 112.

[17] Ibid., p. 99.

[18] Ibid., p. 98.

ordnance.[19] Finally, the Texas state foundry at Austin was also capable of the manufacture of heavy ordnance.[20] All in all, while the Department's capabilities in the crucial area of weapons and ammunition manufacture was small, it was nonetheless capable of the manufacture of weapons, up to and including smaller cannon.

4. The "Military Topography" of the Trans-Mississippi

There is one final and crucial reason that the Trans-Mississippi Department could have functioned as a foundation for a Continuity of Government operation, and this has to do with what may be called its "military topography." Thomas W. Cutrer puts it this way in his excellent and comprehensive study:

> One reason that the theater failed to establish a hold on either the political, military, or popular imagination in the South was that it lacked a strategic focal point. In the East, military operations were dominated by the battle cry of "Onward to Richmond"; in the West, the war was defined by the reopening of the Mississippi River and the drive into the vital Confederate heartland. While the cockpit of the war in the East was largely defined by a ninety-mile axis running from Washington, D.C., to Richmond, Virginian, and even the more fluid "Western" theater was largely confined to a line running from Nashville to Chattanooga to Atlanta to Savannah, in the trans-Mississippi no such

---

[19] Ibid., p. 123. Geise observes that small arms ammunition was always in short supply within the Department, but attributes this more to the poor fire discipline of its troops than to an inability to keep pace with the supply needs of disciplined units.

[20] Geise, op. cit., p. 124.

strategies were possible because no such vital objectives existed.[21]

This crucial fact is buttressed by yet another, for lacking the critical communications infrastructure of roads, railroads and telegraph lines in the density they occurred east of the Mississippi, even in the more rural and agrarian eastern Confederacy the infrastructure could supply and support the troop concentrations of the large field armies that both the Union and the Confederacy fielded in that theater, armies that numbered in their tens of thousands.

No such parallel existed in the Trans-Mississippi; railroad mileage was much less dense, as were roads and telegraph lines. Thus, while the Trans-Mississippi could and did at various times field as many as 60,000 men-at-arms, these were much more widely dispersed because large concentrations simply could not be logistically sustained (as the Union would discover in its various attempts at invasions). The Trans-Mississippi was much more suited to smaller types of operations, and its widely dispersed manufacturing centers offered no concentrations of strategically viable targets.

Small wonder, then, that Union generals Grant and Sherman feared the possibility of the remaining Confederate field armies of 1865 making their way, with President Davis, to the Trans-Mississippi, and continuing the war.

B. The Implications

So what does all of this amount to? What are the implications of this (regrettably) short detour to the Trans-Mississippi Department? In 1863, in his letter to Lieutenant

---

[21] Thomas W. Cutrer, op. cit., pp. 6-6.

General Smith appointing him to command the department and conveying to him the sweeping "vice-regal" powers that he did, President Davis observed

> That the department contained great mineral resources and that its commander should "get iron, test its qualities, combine it into the best gun-metal, and cast ordnance"....
> Davis also pointed out that Smith would also be responsible for the manufacture of gun carriages and army wagons, the construction of a powder mill, the tanning of leather for shoes and harnesses, the domestic manufacture of clothes and blankets, and the production of food. The president even went so far as to suggest that the department establish a rolling mill for the construction of gunboats on the Arkansas and Red Rivers.[22]

In other words, whatever the practicality of such measures during the war, the Confederate President had taken an accurate measure of the potentials of the region, no doubt formed during his tenure as U.S. Secretary of War, and advocate of a southern route for a trans-continental railroad. As such, he had a no doubt accurate understanding of the region's existing infrastructure, and that it was already minimally self-sufficient in the ability to equip, supply, and sustain military field units.

With the military reversals the Confederacy had experienced and would experience up to that point in early 1863, it takes little imagination to see that perhaps, already, Jefferson Davis was thinking of long term plans for a successful continuity of government. If one looks at just what has been reviewed here concerning the department, it becomes abundantly clear that it is a "confederacy within the

---

[22] Cutrer, op. cit., p. 260.

Confederacy," with its own Department of War, of the Treasury, and with its commissioners to Mexico and France, its own diplomacy and Department of State. "Taken together," writes William Geise, "the bureaus and other agencies under Kirby Smith amounted to a kind of War Department for the Trans-Mississippi."[23] Indeed, Geise perhaps saw all of these implications some years ago when he began his critical study of the department with the following observation:

> The range of authority the confederate government in Richmond bestowed upon the department had no precedent in the war. For a country so sensitive to states; rights, the authority vested in the department is truly remarkable. What is even more astounding is that the Southern governors west of the Mississippi accepted this authority. At an August 1863 conference at Marshall, Texas, the governors of Texas, Arkansas, Louisiana, and Missouri endorsed the military's assumption of administrative powers *to ensure continuity of confederate authority west of the river.* Because of this compact accepting military leadership, the Department of the Trans-Mississippi assumed responsibility for virtually every function of the central government, including regulation of foreign trade and the issuance of sovereign debt.[24]

The department was the perfect and moreover *essential* place for a successful Confederate Continuity of Government operation.

Small wonder, then, that Confederate President Davis was trying to get there, and that Union Secretary of War Stanton was bending every effort to prevent him.

---

[23] Geisde, op. cit., p. 130.
[24] Ibid., p. ix, emphasis added.

*Confederate Fifty Dollar Note, Obverse,
with Jefferson Davis, 1864 Issue
Black and Tan Colors predominated*

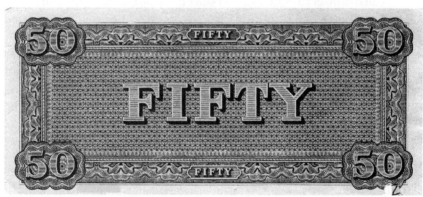

*1864 Issue Confederate Fifty Dollar Bill,
Original Blueback Reverse*

5
CONCLUSIONS TO PART ONE

"Gloss over the Stanton-Eckert episode, veil Mrs. Lincoln's involvement with Parker, secrete evidence concerning Jefferson Davis, bury two hours in the life of Andrew Johnson, and a vast cover-up is under way. Attribute the purest motives to this official censorship, and it still amounts to the concealment of facts."
Theodore Roscoe[1]

W HAT EMERGES FROM THE PREVIOUS PAGES is a radically different version of the end of the War Between the States than the romanticized version that often plays in the mental theater of the public imagination, the narrative of cordial surrender conversations between Lee and Grant, or that of a fanatical Jefferson Davis frantically galloping to and fro across the Carolinas trying to evade Federal forces, or that of a crazed John Wilkes Booth assassinating the one Union leader who might have prevented the post bellum rape of the South. A review of the some of the salient features of this scenario reveals that there are deep players involved in shady conspiracies on both sides, and there are hints and suggestions, the faint whispers, of ever deeper players.

Here is what we have encountered, and these facts are by no means an exhaustive catalogue:

---

[1] Theodore Roscoe, op. cit., p. 27.

189

A. Considerations involving President Davis

1) In February of 1863, Jefferson Davis appoints Lieutenant General Edmund Kirby Smith to head the Confederacy's Trans-Mississippi Department, and gives him sweeping powers to make the department as financially, diplomatically, economically, militarily, and agriculturally self-sustaining as possible. It was posited that this may have been a deliberate continuity of government policy—albeit a very secret one—from the outset. General Smith does so, and conducts as vigorous a financial policy as possible, restricting the flood of Treasury, and selling cotton for gold at tremendous profit.

2) President Davis, in response to the Union's Dahlgren raid which had orders to kidnap or kill him and his entire cabinet, authorizes an expansion of the Confederate secret service, which establishes strong cells in Canada.

3) President Davis' flight from Richmond is to be understood as a continuity of government operation, for in the trains accompanying him, or departing prior to his own departure from the Confederate capital, the following items accompany him:

    a) the Confederate treasury and the deposits of the Richmond banks, which include much gold and silver specie;

    b) the archives of the Confederacy, including the all-important archives of the Confederate Treasury with account, agents, and contact information, the *real* "missing Confederate treasure";

   c) the various departmental seals of the Confederate
federal governmental departments, and the Great
Seal of the Confederacy itself, one of which, as
was learned, Davis ordered an aide to hide
permanently. Additionally, there was a Great
Seal made of silver, apparently engraved in
London, which, we suggested, may have been a
gift from a group or groups within Great Britain,
a seal, moreover, that may have been engraved
with information leading to the identity of that
group or groups which were best hidden;

   d) a considerable supply of Confederate treasury
notes which are burned during the course of the
flight, which, it was argued, was mostly because
General Smith's policy within the Trans-
Mississippi department was to prevent
depreciation of the currency through inflationary
increases of its supply;

   e) Both Davis, and Union Generals Grant and
Sherman, made it clear that a continuation of
hostilities was possible from the Trans-Mississippi Department;

4) The real end of these hopes comes not with the
surrender of General Lee, but the surrender of
General Joseph Johnston to General Sherman;

5) Davis himself, originally publically implicated and
decried for alleged involvement in the assassination
of his opposite number, is the subject of a $100,000
bounty placed on his head by the successor of
Lincoln, President Andrew Johnson. Convicted by
Stanton's military tribunal *in absentia*, Davis never
publicly stands trial. Kept in prison for two years,
he is actually released, never stands trial, writes his

memoir which manages to almost completely avoid the subject of Confederate finances and Lincoln's assassination. Eventually, his citizenship is post-humously restored by an act of Congress which is signed into law by President Carter. As was noted, this event was either designed to prevent something from being known, or its exact opposite, was designed to draw attention to something by the sheer enormity of the incongruity. The question is, what could that "something" be?

B. Considerations involving President Abraham Lincoln, His Cabinet, Officers, and Assassination

5) There is a definite conspiracy around President Lincoln's murder, consisting minimally of two layers:
  a) The layer comprising John Wilkes Booth and his pro-Southern partisans, David Herold, Georg Atzerodt, and Mary Surratt via her son, John, and,
  b) a deeper layer, involving three centers and groups with each of which Booth has been in contact:
    i) a group in Montreal consisting of members of the Confederate Secret Service, a part of the expansion of the service ordered by President Davis in the wake of the failed Union Dahlgren raid on Richmond. This group supplies Booth with money for the plan to kidnap Lincoln, a plan which is revised to be an assassination plan after the surrender of General Lee;
    ii) a group of New York speculators in gold and cotton;

iii) a group of Radical Republicans in Washington DC opposed to Lincoln's more lenient reconstruction policies. This group, as was seen, includes US Senators Conness (California), Chandler (Michigan), and Wade (Ohio), and Indiana Representative George Julian. According to Booth's diary, Conness supplied Booth with the passwords necessary to get through the Union sentry lines around Washington.

iv) Yet another group which includes Stanton and his Assistant Secretary of War, Thomas Eckert, are *directly* involved in the security stripping of President Lincoln on the day of the assassination, in spite of Mr. Lincoln's specific requests for Eckert's presence as a guard. Suspiciously, General Grant and Mrs. Grant, who had been publicized as attending the theater with the Lincolns that night, under urging from Stanton, change their plans at the last minute.

An unusual fact emerges from a consideration of this brief Lincoln assassination inventory, namely, that Booth himself appears to inhabit two worlds with an ease normally attributed to that of a double agent. On the one hand, one has Booth, the rabid, self-important and self-pitying Southern partisan, shooting Lincoln with the shout *sic semper tyrannis!* On the other, Booth the actor, consorting with radical Republicans, conveying money to them and receiving information from them, the very worst enemies of the South! Two possible interpretations of this curious fact present themselves:

1) Either Booth's radical and fanatical southern sympathies are sincere, in which case the Radical Republicans are feigning friendship with him and his cause in order to pin the blame on Davis and the South (as was actually done); or,
2) Booth may in fact be acting as an agent for neither side in the war, but as an agent for interested "third parties" which need Lincoln dead for deeper reasons.

Boiling all of this down to its alchemical quintessence, what is one left with? Four things:

1) A Confederate Continuity of Government Operation;
2) A Union faction anxious to see the end of the war and the non-implementation of Lincoln's lenient post bellum reconstruction policy and a much more draconian policy of reconstruction that amounts to the rape of the South[2];
3) An assassination conspiracy with elements, layers, and players on both sides of the war, which suggests that there might be a hidden *third* layer straddling both sides and perhaps assisting the assassination at a very deep level; and finally,
4) Lots of money in all of the previous three things, including some missing money, and state seals...

Sequire pecunia... follow the money. To that task, we now turn.

---

[2] Booth's ability to travel more or less freely throughout the North and South during the war is a factor in this possibility.

PART TWO:
THE TWO SYSTEMS OF FINANCE

"The proposition to make the notes a legal tender, which was to be a contention in vain for four years, was early discussed. In its third session Congress had referred the matter to its finance committee on the motion of A.H. Garland, of Arkansas; and two weeks later on the motion of James A Seddon, of Virginia to make the Treasury notes receivable in payment of any debt due corporations or individuals, the vote was adverse."
Ernest Ashton Smith,
The History of the Confederate Treasury
p. 17.

A Union "Lincoln Greenback"
One Dollar Bill, Obverse

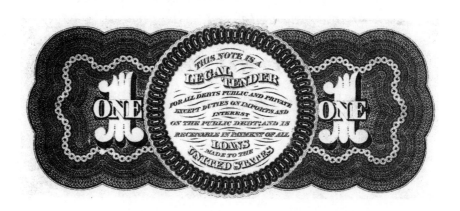

The Reverse of the Union One Dollar
"Lincoln Greenback" Bill

6
THE TWO CURRENCIES
AND THE UNDERLYING PHILOSOPHIES OF MONEY

*"The Southern Confederacy was rapidly organized; its
Constitution was adopted, and the machinery of its
government was in full working order, before the North had
been aroused to the meaning of the movement, and before the
(thirty-seventh) Federal Congress had met and taken any
measures in view of the impending conflict."*
John Christopher Schwab[1]

*"The Confederate government had it well within its power to
prolong its resistance to a point where independence or at
least a compromise peace might have been achieved."*
Douglas B. Ball[2]

F INANCIAL AND ECONOMIC POLICIES are never
formulated in a vacuum nor, unless one is a Marxist,
are they deduced from first principles. They are means
to ends and thus they are always formulated with specific
ends and outcomes in view, and are consequently also the
products of the histories and cultural circumstances that lead
to their formation. This is especially true of the plans and
policies of governments at the end of the eighteenth and the
beginning of the nineteenth centuries, for the American and
French revolutions, and especially the latter's introduction of

---

[1] John Christopher Schwab, A.M., Ph.D., *The Confederate
States of America, 1861-1865: A Financial and Industrial History
of the South During the Civil War* (New York, Burt Franklin: 1968
reprint of the 1901 edition, No ISBN), p. 3.
[2] Douglas B. Ball, *Financial Failure and Confederate
Defeat* (Urbana, Illinois: The University of Illinois Press, 1991,
ISBN0-252-01755-2), p. 17.

industrial scale standardization of weapons and the *levee en masse*, made it necessary from that point onward to include financial and economic policy in their strategic and even military planning.

A. Currency and War Aims

The American War Between the States becomes an especially convenient laboratory for the study of this phenomenon, for in this case, beneath the surface and superficial resemblances of the systems of money and finance between the Union and the Confederacy—they did after all up to the point of the Southern secession share a common history, financial, and banking policy and institutions – there are clear differences caused by the contradictory war aims of the two combatants.

These aims are, fortunately, easily enough stated and require no great subtlety nor nuanced formulation to understand: the financial policy of the Confederacy is aimed to defend itself and preserve its recently asserted independence, while that of the Union is to deny all of that to the Confederacy, and to force it back into the Union. By the nature of the case, then, the Union must (and did) fight a much more aggressive war, and that required a much more aggressive approach to money. The South, after all, had to be invaded, occupied, and conquered. There was no "maneuvering room". And that required lots of money.

Prior to the southern secession, however, each combatant had virtually separate developments, cultural histories, and institutions. The South's was an agrarian and slave-based economy. There was little industrialization, and that economy depending on the export of its most valuable and profitable economy to the hungry textile factories of Europe: cotton. By contrast, the North's economy, while agrarian, was much more industrial. As a result of this, the financial and economic policies favored and promoted by each region were diametrically the opposite: the South favored international free trade since it was a commodities driven economy. The North favored tariffs to protect its industry. In short, the pre bellum United States was in effect two countries and cultures held together by a common government.

So why have I characterized the southern system as "The Rialto in Richmond"? The answer, as will be elaborated in this and the next chapter, is rather simple: as an agrarian-based economy advocating free international trade, the South, and its national capital in Richmond, resembled the banks of the Venetian rialto in significant ways, for like those banks, and Venetian trading practices in general, the South's trade had to be commodities-based, reliant upon bullion and specie, and reliant on international speculative financial instruments and sovereign securities in a way that the Union did not. This will assume particular importance in the next chapter when we consider some of that speculation in international financial instruments and sovereign securities from the point of view of the Continuity of Government operation that the flight of Jefferson Davis must be viewed in.

With this stated, however, we must begin with the similarities of the Union and Confederate currencies, for both combatants realized early and clearly that the coming war would require massive financing, and that their respective reserves of specie were woefully inadequate to the task ahead. They turned to an old "tried and true" method within their histories, the method of the American and French revolutions: fiat paper money.[3] An actual look at some of the paper currencies of the two combatants will show those surface

---

[3] Q.v. Schwab, op. cit., pp. 5, 11.

similarities and deeper differences very clearly. These paper currency issues are noteworthy not only for their elegance, attractiveness, and visually appealing nature, but also for the declarations they contain, as will be seen shortly:

Union Five Dollar Greenback,
Act of Feb 25, 1862,
Obverse

Union Five Dollar Greenback,
Act of Feb 25, 1862
Reverse

Union Ten Dollar Greenback,
Act of March 3, 1863
Obverse

Union Ten Dollar Greenback,
Act of March 3, 1863,
Reverse

Union Five Hundred Dollar Greenback,
Act of March 3, 1863.
Notably, this bill is dated March 10, 1862,
Obverse

Union Five Hundred Dollar Greenback,
Act of March 3, 1863
Reverse

Union One Thousand Dollar Greenback,
Act of March 3, 1863
Obverse

Union One Thousand Dollar Greenback,
Act of March 3, 1863
Reverse

The beautiful obverses of these bills is what gives them their characteristic name, for they are printed with a deep rich emerald green ink, a color which has characterized American currency ever since, and which has become the subject of much literary allegory as we shall see in the final chapter. With the spread of the American dollar in the 20th century as the world's reserve currency, the idea that "green is the color of money" has become more or less a global phenomenon.

But much more important than the color are the declarations, for these bills contain several declarations of a formulaic nature. On the obverse, the declaration states:

> The United States promise to pay X dollars; payable at the Treasury of the United States at New York.

In some cases this formula is expanded to include the bearer:

> The United States promise to pay X dollars to the bearer; payable at the Treasury of the United States at New York.

On the reverse is an even more specific, and much more important, declaration:

> This note is a legal tender for all debts public and private, except duties on imports and interest on the public debt, and is receivable in payment of all loans made to the United States.

On the fifty dollar greenback of the 1862 currency act, the declaration on the reverse reads slightly differently:

> This note is a legal tender tor all debts public and private, except duties on imports and interest on public debt, and is exchangeable for U.S. six percent twenty years' bonds,

redeemable at the pleasure of the United States after five years.

Two notable things spring out from this cursory examination of the actual greenbacks. Firstly, each greenback explicitly states that it is "a legal tender for all debts public and private" with the exception of interest on the public debt, and duties on imports, and secondly, that each is payable at the United States Treasury in New York.

In the case of the fifty dollar greenback, the note was exchangeable for a six per cent twenty year bond "redeemable after five years at the pleasure of the United States", and this is a profound clue as to what the Lincoln greenbacks *actually* were, as opposed to what the popular imagination—particularly in "alternative research circles"—imagines them to be. To put it succinctly, the Union was not functioning and did not function with only one type of money or currency. More than one type of currency was in circulation.

When one turns to consider the "Davis blueback" currency of the Confederacy, one encounters remarkably similar declarations, with some new qualifiers.

Confederate One Dollar Blueback,
1864

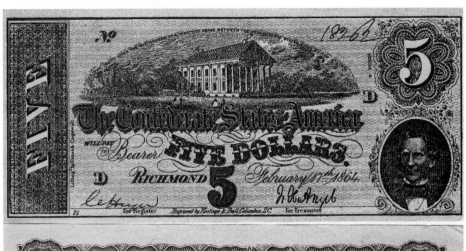

Confederate Five Dollar Blueback
1864

Confederate Ten Dollar Blueback
1864

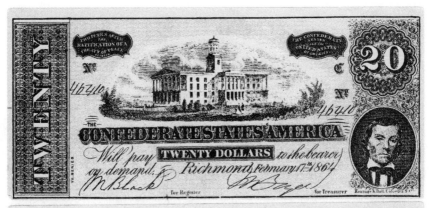

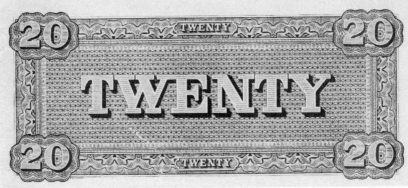

Confederate Twenty Dollar Blueback
Confederate Vice President Stephens is Pictured in the oval,
And beneath that the imprint of Keating & Ball Engravers of
Columbia, South Carolina, who minted most Confederate
paper currency. After the capture of the Keating and Ball
facility by Union Troops, the quality of Confederate paper
notes declined dramatically

Confederate Blueback One Hundred Dollar Interest Bearing
Money Bill of 1862

Confederate One Hundred Dollar Blueback (Facsimile)
Late 1864 Issue;
The decline in the quality of the reverse after the loss of the
Keating and Ball Engravers in Columbia, South Carolina, is
evident.

There is a feature on the obverse of all these paper notes that must be mentioned, for it is a distinguishing feature not only of Confederate money, but it is an actual monetary declaration of the Confederacy's war aims. This feature consists either of the two small shields that appear on the obverse, each of which contains one half of the declaration, or in other cases, the declaration is inscribed elsewhere and in some other manner. In the case of the five dollar note, the declaration is faintly visible in small print above the oval. In the case of the one hundred dollar 1862 blueback, the declaration simply appears on the obverse without any other distinguishing features.

A closer view of these is in order:

The Declaration Shields on the Confederate Ten Dollar Blueback, 1864 to the right and left of the picture oval

The Small Print Declaratio at the top of the Five Dollar Confederate Blueback Obverse Oval, 1864

*The Confederate One Hundred Dollar Blueback 1862
Obverse with its Declaration to each side of the picture oval
and its grim depiction of chattel slavery.*

A glance of the declarations on these bills is also in order.

While the bills depicted above show Confederate currency issues authorized by various acts of the Confederate Congress from 1862 to 1864, these declarations follow a standardized and uniform formula; from the 1864 ten dollar blueback, this reads:

> (On the left side): Two years after the ratification of a
> treaty of peace between
> (And on the right side): The Confederate States and the
> United States of America

and then the rest of the declaration follows:

> the Confederate States will pay to Bearer Ten Dollars.

On the 1864 five dollar blueback the formula is the same.

On the earlier issues, however, and particularly on large denomination bills, the declaration is slightly different, with the addition of an unusual clause. On the 1862 one hundred dollar blueback, the declarations read:

(On the left side): Six months after the ratification of a
    treaty of peace between
(And on the right side): The Confederate States and the
    United States of America

and as with the later 1864 issues, the declaration continues:

The Confederate States of America will pay to the bearer
on demand one hundred dollars...

And then two additional declarations immediately follow in
small print:

...with interest at two cents per day; Receivable in Payment
of All Dues except Export Dues.

These declarations are important clues to the nature of the
monetary and fiscal policy problems faced by the
Confederacy, and how it sought currency solutions to those
problems.

As noted above, the first component of the declarations
is that the Confederacy undertakes to pay to the bearer a
certain sum of money at a certain period after the end of the
war is formally ratified by a treaty of peace between the two
combatants. As the war progressed and the financial demands
increased, these times increased, from six months at the
beginning of the war, to two years, and finally, in the very last
currency issues, sometimes to ten years.

But in the case of the 1862 one hundred dollar
blueback (and the larger five hundred and one thousand dollar
denominations), the declarations include a statement of
interest, and that the note is receivable for all dues (and
therefore debts) except export dues. In short, the 1862 issue
of currency (as some of the 1861 issue which preceded it) was

an interest-bearing money. This expedient was the brainchild of the first Confederate Secretary of the Treasury, Christopher Gustav Memminger.

The First Confederate Secretary of the Treasury,
C.G. Memminger,
In office February 25, 1861-July 18, 1864.

Memminger was inspired to this idea by similar precedents of financing that had been undertaken by the Continental Congress during the American Revolution, and my the French experiments with interest-bearing *assignats* during the late French revolution.

So exactly *what* was to be "paid to the bearer in demand" within the six months, two or ten years after the ratification of a treaty of peace between the Confederate States and the United States of America? To answer this question it is necessary to recall that at the provisional congress in Montgomery, Alabama to organize a Confederate government and draft its constitution, one of the first orders of business was to settle the matter of legal precedent or *stare decisis* by legislating that all laws and court decisions of the United States prior to the secession were the law of the land of the Confederate States. In this respect the Confederacy was little different than the original colonies after their secession from Great Britain, accepting all laws and crown and county court decisions up to the point of break as having full legal weight and precedent in law:

> The fundamental law of the Southern Confederacy differed slightly from that of the North. In regard to the issue of legal tender paper money, the Constitutions of both sections were practically identical. These granted both governments the right to borrow money on their credit, to coin money, regulate the value thereof and of foreign coin, and fix the standard of weights and measures; they also granted the identical war powers.
>
> In framing legal tender laws to apply to coin, and especially foreign coin, the Confederate Congress followed the well-worn path indicated by previous Federal legislation. The act of March 14, 1861, continued the

Federal mint laws, including presumably the legal tender laws, and accepted them as the laws of the Confederacy.[4]

This is a crucial point, for it means effectively that the Confederacy is operating—at least *initially*—with a *de jure* "bi-metallic" definition of the meaning of "dollar" in terms of so many grains of silver or gold. Moreover, the relationship of these two metals *to each other* was pegged at roughly a 16-to-1 ratio of silver to gold ounces. This is the clue one needs not only to understand the fiscal and monetary policies of Memminger throughout his tenure as Confederate Treasury Secretary, but also the *initial* policies of his opposite number, Salmon chase, in the Union.

To understand this clue, one must look again at the initial 1861 and 1862 Confederate currency acts and the issues that resulted. In the 1862 issue, what we see is *interest bearing notes* that are circulating—or at least, *intended* to circulate—as money, for the large one hundred dollar denominations of that issue bore a two cents per day interest. This currency was for all practical purposes a bond that was a bearer bond circulated as currency. Indeed, in the original 1862 act, the Confederate congress stipulated that the large denominations could indeed circulate, but that their transfer had to be endorsed, a stipulation rarely followed in practice. (One will observe, for example, that there is *no place* for such endorsement on the obverse or reverse of the note.)[5]

In practice, of course, what this meant was that the interest-bearing notes of these early issues were hoarded, but

---

[4] Schwab, *The Confederate States of America, 1861-1865: A Financial and Industrial History of the South During the Civil War*, p. 84.

[5] Q.v. the discussion of the Confederate currency recommendations of Memminger and the acts adopted by the Confederate Congress, Schwab, op. cit., pp. 10-12.

the ultimate purpose was served, for they were a means for the government to soak up gold and silver specie which the Confederacy needed for its foreign trade in order to purchase the supplies and weapons it would need for its war effort. Accordingly in addition to these interest-bearing notes, the Confederacy seized all Federal specie held in Federal mints in Louisiana and elsewhere. But there is something else: as soon as these measures were taken, the Confederacy also realized that the only method of sustaining further needed currency issues was by hypothecation of commodities, and in this case that meant its most valuable commodity: cotton.

Thus, the 1862 one hundred dollar note also indicates that the notes could not be used for export duties: *specie alone or hypothecated cotton alone* sufficed for that.

What emerges from this is that the Confederacy's monetary system is effectively a *two-tiered system*: one for international trade based on specie and commodity hypothecation (largely cotton) and the bonds and bills of exchange generated by this means which in turn function as an analogue of a "fractional reserve" for a dramatic expansion of circulating paper currency. As a result of this thinking, the Confederacy was "irretrievably committed to a paper money policy".[6] *Within* this circulating paper currency, *some* was interest bearing, as in the large 1862 denominations, and some was not.

However, this was a paper money policy that was constantly tied both to *interest* and *future redemption in specie*, as is evident from Memminger's proposals to consolidate the Confederate debt—which had mushroomed to approximately 990 million dollars by 1863—with yet another new bond issue of one billion dollars of twenty year bonds at 6 percent. The Confederate congress, which had debating the

---

[6] Schwab, op. cit., p. 18.

matter of making paper money a legal tender by law, never was able to pass any such legislation, and thus the Confederate currency issues remained ultimately wedded to debt and the necessity of commodity and specie.

At this juncture, Memminger's close association with South Carolina businessman and importer-exporter, George Alfred Trenholm, must be mentioned, for Trenholm not only succeeded Memminger as the second Confederate Treasury Secretary, but he was the crucial corporate lynchpin to the Confederacy's financial agents in Europe, and particularly in the crucial trade with Great Britain. We have already noted his part in the Continuity of Government flight of President Jefferson Davis. His importance to the Confederacy and its war effort can scarcely be over-estimated, for it was the ships of his company that constituted the bulk of the Confederacy's blockade-running foreign trade, and it was the Liverpool branch of his company that was the Confederacy's agent of accounts in Great Britain.

If we now compare the Confederate and Union systems, one very important, and crucial difference emerges, for the Union too, and as is very well known, had its own interest-bearing paper money issues early in the war. But as it became apparent that the war would be long and costly, the Union likewise determined on a paper money policy, but with one huge and crucial difference: while traditional bonds would continue to be sold, this was not to be the principal method of funding. Rather, interest-free treasury notes— Lincoln's "greenbacks"—were circulated. These notes, as we have already seen, were declared legal tender for all debts "public and private," were "redeemable" by the bearer on presentation at the New York treasury, a declaration which implies, like its Confederate counterpart, an underlying legal and financial history of the definition of a "dollar" in terms of a certain amount of grains of silver or gold. In other words,

Lincoln's greenbacks were simply declared to be "convertible," but that convertability could only be exercised at a certain place, thus permitting a "fractional reserve" of specie to back a paper money supply much larger than the specie reserve. And the same sort of two-tiered system is again in evidence, for the Union currency is *not* receivable for export or import dues, for which specie alone would suffice.

In effect, this means that both systems are inflationary, but it means also that the Confederate system adds debt interest more quickly, and as debt is added, more bonds must be created to allow more currency, and thus one is quickly in a hyper-inflationary cycle. The Union system adds the paper money, but not the interest, after 1863. And both systems are implying a *future redemption in specie or hard assets*, a fact that will become crucial in the post-war decades, as the effort is made to straighten out the financial wreckage left in the wake of the war. Finally, all of these considerations highlight one more thing about such fiat currency systems, whether they be a mixed system of some interest-bearing currency and predominantly interest free currency as in the Union, or a mixed system of predominantly interest-bearing currency but also some interest-free currency as in the Confederacy: both require strong militaries to back the currency, and thus successful prosecution of war aims becomes existentially necessary to the survival of the financial system and its currency. In the Confederacy's case, independence, and in the Union's, total and complete victory, and absolute surrender of an opponent.

One oft-overlooked episode that illustrates and underscores Trenholm's and his company's vital importance to the Confederacy occurred shortly after the secession, and the original seceding states' meeting in Montgomery, Alabama, to form a provisional government and draft the Confederate constitution. The British East India Company approached the new government, offering to sell ten of its largest and fastest ships for the price of £2,000,000, or approximately 40,000 bales of cotton. At the time, the Confederacy had available between 3 and 4 hundred thousand bales in storage, and could easily have afforded the ships. The ships were built so as to be capable of being armed and were, of course, capable of carrying substantial cargo. Lieutenant General P.G.T. Beauregard was approached by William Trenholm (George Alfred Trenholm's son) who told him to urge President Davis to "snap up the colossal bargain." Beauregard did so. Trenholm also offered "half of his own fleet of ships to the Confederate government on condition that they agree to put their strength in building a navy, rather than an army, and attempt to blockade all northern ports."[7]

George Alfred Trenholm,
Second Confederate Secretary of the Treasury, 1864-1865.

---

[7] Ethel Trenholm Seabrook Nepveux, *George A. Trenholm, Financial Genius of the Confederacy: His Associates and His Ships that Ran the Blockade* (Anderson, South Carolina: The Electric City Printing Company, ISBN 0-9668843-1-0), p. 38.

*Confederate General Pierre Gustave Toutant-Beauregard,
victor of the First Battle of Manasses Junction (Bull Run);
Beauregard's heavy artillery would reduce the Federal forts
in Charleston to rubble, opening the port and clearing the
way for Trenholm's ships, lighting the fuse of
The War Between the States*

B. Greenbacks and Post-Bellum Policy:
Compensated Emancipation, or a Rape Disguised as
"Reconstruction"?
The Relationship of Lincoln's Financial Policy to the
Reconstruction Policies of the Radical Abolitionists

As was seen previously, it is now a common component of the revisionist narrative of the Lincoln assassination that the motivations for the deed was a coalescence of interests:

1) *at the most visible level that of rabid southern partisans seeking revenge* for the surrender of General Lee's Army of Northern Virginia and the impending complete defeat of the Confederacy;

2) *at a deeper level that of John Wilkes Booth,* an actor and spy operating on both sides (and thus, perhaps also as a "deep" player representing even deeper interests), but minimally representing not only the rabid southern partisans, but *the radical Republican reconstructionists* seeking a reconstruction policy in the south designed to punish it and strip it of its remaining economic wealth and strength; and finally,

3) *a possibly "deepest" player seeking a similar reconstruction policy* for reasons presently unknown, whose presence is suggested by Booth himself, and his ability and willingness to operate on both sides of the lines.

Mr. Lincoln himself strongly hinted at the relatively soft nature of his intentions for the south in his 1862 Annual Message to the Union Congress, a speech made *after* the

Federal stalemate of Lee's invasion of Maryland at the Battle of Antietam (to this day the single bloodiest day of combat American forces ever suffered) and the Emancipation Proclamation that the battle permitted Lincoln to make.

It is a common criticism that Mr. Lincoln's proclamation was so much hot air, that it only manumitted slaves within the Confederacy, i.e., in states over which he had neither jurisdiction nor ability to enforce the decree, while he left the slaves within the slave states that had remained within the Union – Missouri, Kentucky, and Maryland – without any manumission whatsoever. Lincoln was not so naïve nor unintelligent, however, to believe that the issue could be addressed simply by a decree, without a corresponding economic plan. During that address to Congress, however, Lincoln explicitly proposed the following:

> .... I recommend the adoption of the following resolution and articles amendatory to the Constitution of the United States:
>
> Resolved by the Senate and House of Representatives of the United States of America in Congress assembled (two-thirds of both Houses concurring), That the following articles be proposed to the legislatures (or conventions) of the several states as amendments to the Constitution of the United States, all or any of which articles when ratified by three-fourths of the said legislatures (or conventions), to be valid as part or parts of the said Constitutions, viz:
>
> ART. – Every state wherein slavery now exists which shall abolish the same therein at any time or times before the first day of January, a.d. 1900, shall receive compensation from the United States as follows, to wit:
>
> The President of the United States shall deliver to every state bonds of the United States bearing interest at the rate of per cent (sic) per annum to an amount equal to the aggregate sum of ___ for each slave shown to have therein

by the Eighth Census of the United States, said bonds to be delivered to such state by installments or in one parcel at the completion of the abolishment, accordingly as the same shall have been gradual or at one time within such state; and interest shall begin to run upon any such bond only from the proper time of its delivery as aforesaid. Any state having received bonds as aforesaid and afterward reintroducing or tolerating slavery therein shall refund to the United States the bonds so received, or the value thereof, and all interest paid thereon.

ART. —All slaves who shall have enjoyed actual freedom by the chances of the war at any time before the end of the rebellion shall be forever free; but all owners of such who shall not have been disloyal shall be compensated for them at the same rates as is provided for states adopting abolishment of slavery, but in such way that no slave shall be twice accounted for.

ART. —Congress may appropriate money and otherwise provide for colonizing free colored persons with their own consent at any place or places without the United States.

I beg indulgence to discuss these proposed articles at some length. Without slavery the rebellion could never have existed; without slavery it could not continue.

Among the friends of the Union there is great diversity of sentiment and of policy in regard to slavery and the African race amongst us. Some would perpetuate slavery; some would abolish it suddenly and without compensation; some would abolish it gradually and with compensation; some would remove the freed people from us, and some would retain them with us; and there are yet other minor diversities. Because of these diversities we waste much strength in struggles among ourselves. By mutual concession we should harmonize and act together. This would be compromise, but it would be compromise among the friends and not with the enemies of the Union. These articles are intended to embody a plan of such mutual concessions, if the plan shall be adopted, it is assumed that emancipation will follow, at least in several of the states.

As to the first article, the main points are, first, the emancipation; secondly, the length of time for consummating it (thirty-seven years); and, thirdly, the compensation.

The emancipation will be unsatisfactory to the advocates of perpetual slavery, but the length of time should greatly mitigate their dissatisfaction. The time spares both races from the evils of sudden derangement—in fact, from the necessity of any derangement—while most of those whose habitual course of thought will be disturbed by the measure will have passed away before its consummation. They will never see it. Another class will hail the prospect of emancipation but will deprecate the length of time. They will feel that it gives too little to the now living slaves. But it really gives them much. It saves them from the vagrant destitution which must largely attend immediate emancipation in localities where their numbers are very great, and it gives the inspiring assurance that their posterity shall be free forever. The plan leaves to each state choosing to act under it to abolish slavery now or at the end of the century, or at any intermediate time, or by degrees extending over the whole or any part of the period, and it obliges no to states to proceed alike. It also provides for compensation, and generally the mode of making it.... In a certain sense the liberation of slaves is the destruction of property—property acquired by descent or by purchase, the same as any other property. It is no less true for having been often said that the people of the South are not more responsible for the original introduction of this property than are the people of the North; and when it is remembered how unhesitatingly we all use cotton and sugar and share the profits of dealing in them, it may not be quite safe to say that the South has been more responsible than the North for its continuance. If, then, for a common object

225

this property is to be sacrificed, is it not just that it be done at a common charge?

And if with less money, or money more easily paid, we can preserve the benefits of the Union by this means than we can by the war alone, is it not also economical to do it? Let us consider it, then. Let us ascertain the sum we have expended in the war since compensated emancipation was proposed last March, and consider whether if that measure had been promptly accepted by even some of the slave states the same sum would not have done more to close the war than had been otherwise done. If so, the measure would save money, and in that view would be a prudent and economical measure. Certainly it is not so easy to pay something as it is to pay nothing, but it is easier to pay a large sum than it is to pay a larger one. And it is easier to pay any sum when we are able than it is to pay it before we are able. The war requires large sums, and requires them at once. The aggregate sum necessary for compensated emancipation of course would be large. But it would require no ready cash, not the bonds even any faster than the emancipation progresses. This might not, and probably would not, closer before the end of the thirty-seven years. At that time we shall probably have a hundred million of people to share the burden, instead of thirty-one million as now.

The proposed emancipation would shorten the war, perpetuate peace, ensure this increase of population, and proportionally the wealth of the country. With these we should pay al the emancipation would cost, together with our other debt, easier than we should pay our other debt without it....

The plan would, I am confident, secure peace more speedily and maintain it more permanently than can be done by force along, while all it would cost, considering amounts and manner of payment and times of payment, would be easier paid than will be the additional cost of the war if we rely solely upon force. It is much, very much, that it would cost no blood at all.

The plan is proposed as permanent constitutional law. It cannot become such without the concurrence of, first, two-thirds of Congress, and afterward three-fourths of the states. The requisite three-fourths of the states will necessarily include seven of the slave states....[8]

It is to be noted that the implication of the very last remark cited is made without any provision nor discussion of how those seven slave states, which perforce included some of the seceded southern states, could give such assent without secession from the Confederacy, and a mechanism for their government's return to the Union.

But whatever one makes of Lincoln's remarks, it is clear that he has understood that economic compensation had, somehow, to be involved in any plan of genuine emancipation. Additionally, he recognized that a sudden manumission could be economically devastating to the slaves thus manumitted. He stops short, however, from including the manumitted them-selves from the plan of compensation. It was possible, however, that under his proposals individual states themselves may have undertaken such compensation to the manumitted slaves, recognizing that they too lost the economic provisions—food, shelter, clothing—that was provided by their owners. Under such circumstances, all it would have taken was for one state to recognize the need to such an addition to Lincoln's plan, and to enact it at a state level, in order to force other states to do so as well under the pressure the example would have provided.

---

[8] Abraham Lincoln, "Second Annual Address to Congress, December 1862," httpis://teachingamericanhistory.org/document/annual-message-to-congress-1862/

There is, however, an even more important point to take from Lincoln's remarks. In his speech he clearly ties the financing of a compensated emancipation to the debt being incurred as a result of the war, and therefore *to the means of financing that debt.* With the adoption of interest-free fiat greenbacks as legal tender to finance the Union war effort, the implication is that a compensated emancipation program might have been funded by a similar means.

For those on both sides of the war this was an intolerable situation. For those in the slave states that had remained in the Union, it meant the loss of hard tangible assets (the slaves), in return for green pieces of paper. For the northern industrialists and financiers, it meant the payment of their bonds and financial instruments with the very same green pieces of paper and not the hard tangible assets of specie. And for those on the other side of the war or overseas who held bluebacks or Confederate bonds, it meant that with the failure of the Confederacy a way had to be found to recoup losses, again in hard assets. Moreover, both currency systems had relied on their common historical basis in gold and silver bi-metallism, and *thus both currency systems, and the demands to recoup losses in tangible assets, set up the post-war monetary debates that will persist until the administration of Woodrow Wilson* in the next century. A way around Mr. Lincoln's inclinations and attitudes had to be found to rape and plunder the South, including the emancipated slaves.

The method would prove to be simple: (1) remove as much currency from circulation as possible, (2) thus deflating prices, which falls hardest upon (3) farmers and anyone working land, tying them more firmly to the land their working, and thus (4) converting former chattel slaves into uncompensated impoverished wage slaves, while (5) buying up land and other hard assets for pennies on the (greenback) dollar.

In order to see why this became the post bellum strategy, and in order to see who those deepest hidden players in Jefferson Davis' Continuity of Government hopes, and who those deepest players in the murderous schemes of the radical reconstructionist Republicans were, we must paradoxically look not at the *Union's* foreign operations and relations during the war, but once again at the foreign operations and diplomacy of the Rialto in Richmond.

Confederate Financial Agent in Europe,
John Slidell

Baron Frederic Emile d'Erlanger
(Friedrich Emil von Erlanger)
The German-French Banker
at the heart of the Erlanger Loan Affair.

7

THE CONFEDERACY IN EUROPE:
CORPORATE AND OTHER AGENTS, AND
THE MYSTERY OF THE CONFEDERATE "GOLD"

*"It was realized that the Confederacy must have obtained a
great deal of money, for such a war as it was waging could
not be sustained without capital, but exactly how great its
resources were nobody in Europe seemed to know. It was
generally felt that the South should be congratulated on
having made war not only with considerable success but very
cheaply."*
Richard I. Lester[1]

EVER SINCE THE END OF THE WAR BETWEEN THE
STATES and the assassination of Mr. Lincoln,
revisionist historians have pointed out the similarities
of Mr. Lincoln's currency policy to that of President John F.
Kennedy. Lincoln, by financing the war with debt-free fiat
money certificates, the so-called Lincoln Greenbacks, ran
afoul of the Wall Street financiers and the international
central bankers and merchant banks who were thus not able to
charge any interest on loans made to the government in the
form of monetized debt. Kennedy, similarly, and as is widely
known, issued an executive order in June of 1963 for the
Treasury to issue four billion dollars' worth of United States
Notes, and by-passing the Federal Reserve entirely; it was
four billion dollars' worth of debt free money. Many if not

---

[1] Richard I. Lester, *Confederate Finance and Purchasing in
Great Britain* (Charlottesville: The University Press of Virginia:
1975, ISBN 0-8139-0513-3), pp. 17-18.

231

most revisionist historians of the two most famous assassinations in American history agree that the two presidents' currency policies centered them in the crosshairs of the international bankers.

If there are "hidden players" in the Lincoln assassination, the argument runs, then by analogy to the Kennedy assassination and Kennedy's interest-free money policy, they must be the same players active in pulling the deep strings behind the Lincoln assassination as well. This way of thinking is reasonable, but when pressed beyond the parallels in motivations behind the putative deep players, it breaks down, for in the case of the Kennedy assassination there are two things that indicate such players with such motivations. Firstly, there is President Kennedy's executive order of June 1963 ordering the treasure to issue four billion dollars of interest-free paper notes, bypassing the Federal Reserve Bank and its private shareholders and investors completely. Secondly, there was Kennedy's Secretary of the Treasury, C. Douglas Dillon, himself, scion of the Wall Street investment firm of Dillon and Reed. Secretary Dillon not only represented the "money power", having personal contact with most of its members whose names are recognizable to us, but he also had one foot in the corridors of power in Washington, being a member of Kennedy's cabinet. Dillon made no secret of his opposition to the scheme, voicing his concerns privately—but vociferously—while maintaining a public posture of support for the President. In the case of the Lincoln assassination, however, we have no such indications of "insider" opposition, at least, not any that are well known today, unless if course, one is familiar with the sort of details presented in the second chapter of this book. Most people are not familiar with those details, however, so the question remains: is there an "insider" of similar stature to Kennedy's

232

Treasury Secretary who voiced opposition to his currency policy.

A. The Question of the Apocryphal Quotation from Prussian Chancellor Otto von Bismarck

In answer to this question and in support of the argument that the international financial community had a guiding and planning hand in Lincoln's murder, two quotations are often cited which are alleged to have been made by the then Prussian, and later Imperial German, Chancellor Otto von Bismarck. Note that it is stated that he is *alleged* to have made it, because there is some question as to whether or not he did. The statements appear to have surfaced first in the early 1920s, as we shall see, and then later reappeared in Ellen Hodgson Brown's 2007 book, *Web of Debt*, which was reprinted and updated in 2008:

> I know of absolute certainty, that the division of the United States into federations of equal force was decided long before the Civil War by the high financial powers of Europe. These bankers were afraid that the United States, if they remained in one block and as one nation, would attain economic and financial independence, which would upset their financial domination over Europe and the world. Of course, in the "inner circle" of finance, the voice of the Rothschilds prevailed. They saw an opportunity for prodigious booty if they could substitute two feeble democracies, burdened with debt to the financiers.... In place of a vigorous Republic sufficient unto herself. Therefore, they sent their emissaries into the field to exploit the question of slavery and to drive a wedge between the two parts of the Union.... *The rupture between the North and the South became inevitable; the masters of European*

finance employed all their forces to bring it about and to turn it to their advantage.[2]

Brown also references a second alleged quotation from the "Iron Chancellor":

The government and the nation escaped the plots of the foreign financiers. They understood at once, that the United States would escape their grip. The death of Lincoln was resolved upon.[3]

These two quotations have since been widely circulated on the internet after the appearance of Brown's book, but as a glance at the footnotes discloses, her source is a secondary source; there is no citation of a source originating with Chancellor von Bismarck himself.

The quotations have thus become the center of a controversy as to whether the wily Prussian Chancellor ever said or wrote such statements at all. Indeed, in a short internet article on the subject, author Gary North raises this very issue, and a few others: to whom were these statements made? And under what circumstances? And when?

---

[2] Ellen Hodgson Brown, J.D., *The Web of Debt: The Shocking Truth about our Money System and How We Can Break Free* (Baton Rouge: Third Millennium Press, 2007 Third Expanded and Updated edition, ISBN 978-0-9795608-2-8), pp. 89-90, citing Conrad Siem, *La Vieille France* (March 17-24, 1921), 216: pp 13-16. (It is unclear from Brown's citation orthography whether she has added the emphasis, or whether Siem or even von Bismarck did. Additionally, there is no indication from her citation if there was any citation for the original source of the quotation.)

[3] Ibid., p. 91, again citing Conrad Siem, *La Vielle France* (March 17-24, 1921).

Moreover, North correctly observes that "we are asked to believe that the Chancellor of what was about to become Germany (1871), or maybe after it had become Germany, would say such a thing about the Rothschilds and the other bankers, who helped fund his government. Ellen Brown seems never to have asked herself why a senior politician would say such a thing. It would be political suicide."[4] Perhaps, perhaps not; that would all depend, once again, on the person or persons to whom Bismarck was allegedly speaking or writing, and the circumstances under which such remarks were made. But again, we do not know, for there is no primary source, the quotations just appear, from thin air as it were, in an early 20th century French source.

However, do these apocryphal quotations from Chancellor von Bismarck make any sense in a wider context? Could they, in other words, have been uttered by him or someone in a similar position of power, influence, and knowledge, as a mid-nineteenth century Prusso-German chancellor?

Brown cites the quotations in the context of two other quotations, the first from the so-called Hazard Circular of 1862, and a later opinion editorial published in *The London Times* in early 1865. Of the Hazard circular, Brown writes: "The bankers preferred 'the European plan'—*capital could exploit labor by controlling the money supply, while letting the laborers feed themselves.* In July 1862, this ploy was revealed in a notorious document called the Hazard Circular, which was circulated by British banking interests among their American banking counterparts."[5] The citation quoted by

---

[4] Gary North, "Historical Error #18: Two Bogus Quotations from Bismarck on How European Bankers Planned the Civil War and Lincoln's Assassination."

[5] Brown, op. cit., p. 90, emphasis in the original.

Brown begins by predicting the end of chattel slavery as a result of the war. It then continues:

> This (the abolition of slavery) I, and my European friends are glad of, for *slavery is but the owning of labor and carries with it the care of the laborers, while the European plan, led by England, is that capital shall control labor by controlling wages. This can be done by controlling the money.* The great debt that capitalists will see too it is made out of the war, must be used as a means to control the volume of money. To accomplish this, *the bonds must be used as a banking basis.... It will not do to allow the greenback, as it is called, to circulate as money any length of time, as we cannot control that.*[6]

The second alleged quotation from *London Times* targets Lincoln's greenback currency policy even more specifically:

> (If) that mischievous financial policy, which had its origin in the North American Republic, should become indurated down to a fixture, then *that government will furnish its own money without cost.* It will pay off debts and be without a debt. It will have all the money necessary to carry on its commerce. It will become prosperous beyond precedent in the history of the civilized governments of the world. The brains and the wealth of all countries will go to North

---

[6] Brown, op. cit., p. 90, citing Charles Lindburgh, *Banking and Currency and the Money Trust* (Washington, DC: National Capital Press, 1913), p. 102. Again, it is unclear from Brown's citation orthography if she or Lindburgh has added the emphasis.

America. That government must be destroyed, or it will destroy every monarchy on the globe.[7]

The alleged *London Times* article might also have mentioned, as another potential danger in its list of concerns, that the northern Lincoln greenback system, far from draining Europe of its brains and talent, bight have spread *to* its principal powers who might have realized that if they wished to stay competitive, they would have to adopt a similar system.

In either case, the end result was the same: the "inter - national money power" would lose its power. Lincoln's government, its currency policy, and its advocates had to go, and another government, one more amenable to those international financial interests, had to be installed.

However, again, we have no primary sources that either directly and explicitly state these things, and thus indicate the high possibility of a very deep international finance connection to Lincoln's murder; we have only alleged quotations that might indicate the possibility. What we have are *apocrypha*, statements alleged to have been made at times, under circumstances, and to individuals unknown, with no clear provenance of how the allegations contained within them entered into the public record. As anyone who has dealt with apocrypha knows, they often contain valuable information and concepts, yet, without clear provenance, those concepts and information should be corroborated by other means, which means more often than not include actual facts that can be *interpreted* in the way suggested by the apocrypha.

---

[7] Brown, op. cit., p. 90, citing Rob Kirby, "Dead Presidents' Society," financialsense.com (February 6, 2007), "and many other sources" (Brown, p. 495, n. 3.)

Joseph P. Farrell

B. The Conspiratorial Elements as Indicated by the
Apocryphal Quotations

So let us stipulate that all these quotations and statements are apocrypha and treat them as such, *even if a cache of previously unknown documents should suddenly be discovered—a diary or bundle of papers titled "Letters and Correspondences of Bismarck and the Bankers" and written in the Chancellor's and bankers' own hands let us say—that are unquestionably authentic, and vindicating the quotations word for word.*

What, then, are the *outlines and salient features* of that international bankers' conspiracy that emerge from the quotations Brown has cited? Any such *real* evidence would have to be able to rationalize or account for the following elements:

1) The group is of international character, comprising European bankers, by which the context implies the major powers and banking centers of Europe; at that period of history contemporaneous with the American War Between the States, this would mean primarily Great Britain and France;

2) There is some sort of *Prussian* or *German* connection, as implied by the presence of apocryphal statements of Chancellor Otto von Bismarck;

3) The center of gravity of this group appears to be in England, with elements of the financial community associated with the Rothschild interest;

4) These international financial interests are intent upon splitting the Union by exacerbating sectional

and cultural tensions, presumably in order to indebt both sides;

5) After a certain point, the northern section ceases issuing a monetized debt fiat currency, and simply issues notes debt free, while the other side continues its own monetized debt fiat currency. Both sides suffer inflation as a result, but that in the southern section occurs with much more extremity and rapidity because the fiat notes are mostly monetized debt.

6) Because of this, the Lincoln government will have to be removed, and a government more amenable to this European currency policy will have to be installed, which will require *post bellum* policies to be of an extreme nature to allow the financiers to recoup investments.

We also observe that North's criticism that von Bismarck would never have publicly spoken about such a conspiracy is itself not strictly speaking true, for if the twentieth and twenty-first century practice of such bankers and their think tanks are any indicator, they do so often, publicly, and with such low regard for any reaction or discovery that their bulletins and papers almost approach the level of reckless abandon. The above outline is clear, and one that is moreover in line with their stated objectives in the century following.

Viewed in this way, we may thus return to points already mentioned in the very first chapter, and to our interpretation of Jefferson Davis' and his cabinet's flight from Richmond in April 1865 as a Continuity of Government operation, for it will be recalled he took with him two very important items, in addition to a few hundreds of thousands of dollars of specie:

(1) the Confederate archives, which would have included the real Confederate "lost gold", the foreign accounts, agents, contracts and contacts, and

(2) the executive department *seals* of the Confederate government.

From the standpoint of a Continuity of Government operation, then, all of this indicates something else, something equally important for the scenario that is emerging: *Davis and his cabinet intended to continue servicing, as best as they could, the debt of the Confederate government from the Trans-Mississippi department, the goal of their flight.* In this flight there were present *two **further** elements, also mentioned in the first chapter, that would have been indispensable in such a continuity of government continuing to service its debt:*

(3) *the Confederate Great Seal itself, which, it will be recalled, had been **engraved in London and smuggled into the Confederacy**, and*

(4) *an amount of British pound sterling notes, a vital currency reserve for such payments.*

With these elements we have the first indicators based in real fact that the *concepts* in Brown's quotations are not so far removed from fact. And they have led us to the heart of international finance in that century, Great Britain, and to the most unusual and little understood episode in Confederate financial history, the Erlanger loan.

C. The Erlanger Loan

If there is one aspect of Confederate finances that deserves closer scrutiny vis-à-vis the twin scenarios of a Confederate Continuity of Government operation in 1865, and a vast international bankers' conspiracy at work prior to, during, and in the final years or the American War Between the States, it is the Erlanger Loan, so some initial words must be put on the record here before we proceed to an examination of certain little known or featured details of that loan. Every fact mentioned below has been publicly known for some time. *However*, some of these facts—the "details" that suggest a potentially damning corroboration of a deep and hidden third player behind the events of 1865—appear only in older sources. More recent scholarly research on Confederate finances overlooks these details altogether. The sources that *do* mention these details offer no attempt to deduce their potential implications nor to place them into a wider speculative scenario of deep events, deep politics, Continuity of Government operations,[8] or of the *coup d'etat* that was the Lincoln assassination. So while these facts are on the record, our interpretation below is uniquely our own.

---

[8] The concepts of "Deep politics," "deep events", hidden States, and the role of continuity of government planning and operations are those which recur in the works of political analysis of Professor Peter Dale Scott. I would add only that one aspect that needs to be incorporated into such analysis as Scott's is the idea of the continuity of ideology by means of an extra-territorial, or underground, "state," a functional government, but one without a territorial base.

Joseph P. Farrell

1. King Cotton and Cotton Hypothecation

When the War Between the States began, cotton was the most valuable export of the Southern Confederacy, to the extent that all of its war aims, and its hopes even to be able to prosecute a war of the size and expense it was involved in, depended on its ability to supply its cotton to hungry markets, gaining enough revenue by which to buy the supplies and arms with which to equip its field armies. The relatively small manufacturing capability of the South, particularly for heavy ordnance, was simply inadequate to keep pace with the foundries of the North, which could just as easily turn out cannon as steam locomotives.

Our contemporary perceptions of the war tend to downplay the importance of cotton as a commodity in the financial and economic world of the mid-nineteenth century, so it is important to recall that cotton formed the absolutely necessary basis of virtually *all* clothing manufacture in the industrialized nations of Europe and North and South America, and Southern cotton constituted the bulk of that world market. It was thus, by the standards of that day, an *essential* and *life-sustaining* commodity. Everyone needed clothes, and cotton was the means to it.

At the beginning of the war, and in the weeks prior to the Union blockade clamping down on the South, the Confederate government possessed an inventory of between three and five million bales of cotton. It therefore faced a fateful decision: it could ship the bulk of that cotton to Europe, sell it, and use the proceeds to purchase arms and much needed supplies, including ships to run the blockage it knew was coming, *or* it could withhold its cotton, driving the

242

price of cotton up (the only other large source being in India),[9] and use its cotton as collateral to issue bonds against which to generate a currency. While the first course of action was urged to President Davis early in 1861 by the Trenholm company of Charleston, South Carolina, and by General P.G.T. Beauregard, with the proceeds to be used to create a small navy of fast ships to outrun the Union blockade,[10] it was thought at the time that the second course of action would enable the creation of a domestic currency of sufficient value to enable foreign trade of that cotton at increased prices. The problem, of course, was getting enough of it to market through the Union blockade.

2. Slidell Meets Emile Erlanger and the Loan Begins to Take Shape

Against this backdrop, a Confederate financial agent on the Continent, John Slidell net and befriended the German-French banker Emile d'Erlanger (Emil von Erlangen), a Frankfurter who had moved to Paris. During their discussions, d'Erlanger proposed a large loan, based on hypothecated cotton, with interest to be paid in specie, of £ 3,000, 000, or approximate CS$15,000,000. D'Erlanger even proposed increasing this amount, but Confederate Treasury Secretary Memminger demurred.[11] D'Erlanger himself actually travelled to the Rialto in Richmond, negotiated

---

[9] Schwab records that the cotton prices in Britain went from 7p (pence) to nearly 26p per pound of cotton by the end of 1862: op. cit., p. 30. This, of course, triggered a vigorous market for the commodities speculators all over Europe, and particularly in Great Britain and the Second Empire in France.

[10] Ethel Trenholm Seabrook Nepveux, op. cit., p. 38.

[11] Schwab, op. cit., p. 30.

directly and secretly with Memminger, and a contract was signed, and passed in secret (executive) session of the Confederate Congress on January 29, 1863.[12]

Confederate Financial Agent on the Continent John Slidell; he initiated the contact with Emile d'Erlanger that would lead to the Erlanger loan.

---

[12] Schwab, op. cit., pp. 30-31. I find it disturbingly ironic that the scholar who provides so much information about this loan to the slave-based economy of the Confederacy should share a surname with the founder of the so-called "World Economic Forum," and that the economic and financial policies advocated by the shared surname should be so similar.

Baron Frederic Emile d'Erlanger (Friedrich Emil Erlanger), The Franco-German Frankfurt-Parisian Banker who negotiated the Erlanger Loan with Confederate Treasury Secretary Memminger

The terms of the loan agreed to by Memminger and d'Erlanger was straightforward enough, and also upon closer examination, clearly onerous:

> The Secretary of the Treasury agreed to secure the necessary authority for an issue of 75 millions of francs of 3 millions of pounds sterling in 20-year bonds. They were to bear 7% interest, *payable semi-annually on March and September 1 in gold or its equivalent.*

We must pause here to explain what this semi-annual payment really represents. These payments the Confederacy scrupulously attempted to make, and did so, thus maintaining to the very end of the war enough credit in Europe's financial markets to be able to secure further loans, as we shall discover momentarily. But it *also* meant that, with gold "or its equivalent"—by which is meant a payment in silver specie at a bi-metallic ratio of approximately 16-1, or an equivalent commodity of cotton—that specie began to leave the Confederacy in regular and semi-annual increments, *further inflating its already wobbly and inflated currency which was issued domestically by similar types of bonds!* In addition to this semi-annual payment of interest on the principal,

> Half-yearly redemptions of one-fortieth of the face value of the principal (£ 150,000 annually), commencing on March 1, 1864, were provided for, the government agreeing to remit the amount necessary to meet the charges for interest and redemption to Erlanger and Company two months before they fell due, the bankers agreeing to disburse the amounts, charging a commission of 1 % thereon. Each bond was made exchangeable at its face value for New Orleans middling cotton at the rate of 6 pence a pound, and at any time not later than six months after the ratification of

a treaty of peace with the North. Two months' notice of such a proposed exchange was to be given to the Confederate agents in London or Paris. If such exchange of the bonds for cotton was desired during the war, the cotton was to be delivered at points within the Confederate States not more than ten miles from a railway or navigable stream, and was to be exported by the bondholders subject to no government charge except the usual export duty of one-eighth of one cent a pound. If the exchange was postponed till the establishment of peace, the cotton was to be delivered to the bondholders in Charleston, Mobile, or New Orleans. In case cotton of a higher grade than New Orleans middling was offered, the ratio of exchange was to be determined by a board of arbitration.

Erlanger and Company guaranteed the subscription to the loan at 77% of its face value; in fact, they purchased the bonds from the government at that figure. They were allowed a commission of 5% on the amount of the loan placed, and any difference between 77 and the actual price received, agreeing to open subscriptions in London, Paris, Amsterdam, and Frankfurt. At the opening of the subscription they were to pay to the government 750,000 francs, and the same amount 15 days later; 2 ¼ millions one month, 7 ½ millions two months; 9 millions three months; 11 ¼ millions four months; 13 1/8 millions five months; and 13 1/8 millions six months after the first payment,—a total of 57,750,000 francs.... If they had not succeeded in placing the entire loan, the installments, as stated above, were to be reduced in proportion...

The bonds were at once put upon the market on March 19, 1863, by Erlanger and Company in Paris and Frankfurt, by J.H. Schroeder and Company in London and Amsterdam, and by Fraser, Trenholm, and Company in Liverpool.[13]

---

[13] Schwab, op. cit., pp. 31-32.

The firm of Fraser, trenhom, and Company of Liverpool is the Liverpool branch of the same Trenholm firm of Charleston, South Carolina, and the same family of the Second Confederate Secretary of the Treasury, George Trenholm, who was part of President Davis' Continuity of Government flight from Richmond, and yet another indicator that the intention was to continue service on the Confederate debt.

The Erlanger bonds were, initially at least, well-subscribed and managed to sell at or just slightly below par. One factor contributing to this was that

> The Confederate government was known to hold in its possession over 350,000 bales of cotton, of which 333,000 bales at about £9 a bale—or 6 pence a pound—would suffice to cancel the entire loan. Such considerations led to the favorable reception of the bonds. In two days the loan was reported to have been over0scubscribed three times in London alone; and the total subscriptions were said to have amounted to 15 millions of pounds sterling, five times the face value of the loan.[14]

But soon reality set in, and trading in the bonds came increasingly to possess a speculative character, not the least of which was because Erlanger and Company began speculating in its own bonds, and with Union financial agents in Europe trying to bear the markets, a fact indicating that there was a full-scale "money war" between the North and the South in the bond markets of Europe,[15] because the Confederacy, in response to the northern efforts to bear the

---

[14] Schwab, op. cit., p. 33.
[15] Ibid., pp. 33-34.

market, attempted to *bull* it by pouring their precious specie, to the tune of CS $6,000,000, to no effect on the bonds, a disastrous course of action in any case, after the Union victories at Vicksburg and Gettysburg added their own bearing effect on the bonds.[16] This Union bearing policy on the European markets for Confederate bonds was in itself no small component of the result of Lincoln's greenback policy, for the greenbacks freed up Northern specie for such efforts while the Confederacy's specie was tied up in interest payments, and what little reserves were left we consumed trying to "bull" the bonds.[17]

The speculation that emerged was not because of any doubts

> ...of the good faith of the Confederate government, or that it held enough cotton to meet the demands of the loan. How

---

[16] Schwab, op. cit., p. 35.

[17] Secretary Memminger in his address to the Confederate Congress at the beginning of 1864 admitted "that the voluntary exchange of notes for bonds, from which so much had been expected, had proved a failure. He claimed that the plan would have worked well and the redundancy of the notes been prevented by their being funded in bonds, if the interest on these bonds could have been paid in specie. But the supply of specie had been cut off by the blockade, and to provide specie, he might have added, no adequate revenue system had been invented." (Schwab, ibid., p. 57) Strictly speaking, this statement epitomizes the "eastern focus only" of so much scholarship on Confederate Civil War finances, for it does *not* account for the Trans-Mississippi department, its common border with Mexico, and thus the fact that Mexico could, and did, function as a source of specie for the Confederacy. From chapter one, it will be recalled, President Davis's Continuity of Government operation and flight included not only English pound sterling notes, but a cache of Mexican silver specie.

to get the cotton out of the Confederate States to the foreign markets was quite another matter. It was evident at the outset that during the continuance of the war any attempt to do so would be futile. *Small amounts of cotton evaded the blockage or reached Europe by way of Mexico*, but the Federal fleet prevented any general exportation. What might happen when peace was established, or whether the Confederate government would then be in a position to redeem its pledge, was not seriously considered.[18]

One cannot ponder this statement too long, for it is yet another indicator of the importance of the Trans-Mississippi Department, of "Kirby Smithdom," to the ability of the Confederacy to service its debt and redeem its pledges; with this statement, the continuity of government hopes of Jefferson Davis, the taking of the executive seals and archives of the Confederate government departments with him, the Trans-Mississippi Department, and the Erlanger loan all coalesce.

---

[18] Schwab, op. cit., p. 34, emphasis added. Q.v. note 17, p. 245. With respect to the growing importance of the Trans-Mississippi and its common international border with Mexico and the trans-shipment opportunities it provided, Richard I. Lester observes that "Bonds, certificates, loans—all had been tried. Now, in the cold dawn of 1864, the Confederates had to resort to the systematic shipment of cotton to finance their foreign purchases. As they had begun to realize in 1863, it was the only course left; all else had failed. Now was the time to act. Before the war a bale of cotton cost about £11; now the price was £40." (Richard I. Lester, op. cit., p. 48.) To this effort the Trans-Mississippi, "Kirby Smithdom," was absolutely essential. Lester also observes that by March of 1865, the Confederate "blueback" had been so disastrously inflated that it was paying CS$60 for one gold dollar. (Lester, op. cit., p. 54).

Moreover, one important point has thus far emerged from this glance at the Erlanger loan, and that is that we are now in the possession of actual financial details trying the international banking centers of Europe—London, Paris, Amsterdam, and Frankfurt—with both Union and Confederate activities on their bond markets, and these, as our outline of the conceptual scaffolding implied in Ellen Brown's quotations, are centered upon Great Britain.

3. When it comes to the Erlanger Bonds, the Rothschilds'
Economist Magazine Flops around like a Mackerel on a
Moonlit Beach

Yet another indicator of high international financial shenanigans with respect to the Erlanger Loan is the attitude of the famous (or depending on one's lights, infamous) Rothschild magazine *The Economist*, for its attitudes to the loan appear to have shifted dramatically, for initially

> The *Economist* did not like the loan. It claimed that if a Confederate loan were allowed to draw bullion out of the country, an unfavorable balance of trade and payments would be created since cotton did not have the substance of bullion transactions. It pointed out, as it had so often before, that bullion drawn out of the country in this manner would raise the rate of interest in England and make money tight. The *Economist* desired to bring money home and to balance the operation as nearly as possible.[19]

But if this was actually the opinion of the Rothschild magazine, then it was an outright lie, for the provisions of the

---

[19] Richard I. Lester, op. cit., p. 34, referencing *The Economist*, 17 January, 1863.

loan, as we have seen, required the payments on the interest to be made in gold "or some equivalent," clearly implying either silver or cotton at acceptable exchange rates.

Once the subscriptions opened on the markets in London, Paris, Amsterdam, and Frankfurt, however, the Rothschilds' mighty Wurlitzer changed its tune, for while it was clear to many "from the outset that the loan was looked upon as a wild cotton speculation," *The Economist* suddenly was belting out a new march, for it now rated the Erlanger bonds "higher than the Federal securities on the English market" and *The London Times* while not rating the bonds held a favorable view of them![20]

These are important facts, for they indicate a vitally important point in the data supporting an international financial conspiracy at work, for this is a media campaign, led by the most respected voices in the British print media at the time, one that is trying to "bull" the market for the Erlanger bonds with full scale financial propaganda.

4. *Who is Lying, the Bank of England, or Confederate Secretary of State Judah Benjamin?*

As if all of this were not bad enough, the Confederate bonds continued to exercise a hold on post bellum financial and political policy after the war was over, and from here to the end of this book, we enter upon a minefield of speculation, and in this case, the speculation is based upon more rumor, and predictably, involves the "lost Confederate treasure," only as was pointed out at the beginning of this book, this is not treasure cached beneath some rock in New

---

[20] Schwab, op. cit., p. 3.

Mexico or Kentucky, but is the type of treasure that exists in entries in ledger books, secret or otherwise.

In 1865, after the war had sputtered to a halt with the surrenders of the last Confederate field armies and of "Kirby Smithdom,"

> The unlucky bondholders met in London in the fall…, and appointed a committee to look into their rights and take the necessary steps to enforce them. The question of the liability of the considered, and some urged approaching the United States government with their claims. *A report that the bankers who had placed the loan in 1863 still held some funds to the credit of the Confederate government roused the bondholders' hopes of recovering something, but these were soon dispelled by a statement of Erlanger and Company.* **Sixteen years later similar unfounded rumors that foreign banks, among them the Bank of England…**

(Editorial comment: **"!"**)

> **…among them the Bank of England, held large sums to the credit of the Confederate government** *aroused a temporary interest in the Erlanger bonds, and there was an active demand for them on the London market…*

(In 1879?!? That's some continuity of government operation!)

> *…on the London market which continued for some time,* **notwithstanding the statement by Judah P. Benjamin— then living in England, and formerly member of the Confederate Cabinet—that the Confederate government**

had exhausted their funds abroad before the end of the war.[21]

Please note what we have here:

1) A group of Erlanger bondholders meet in London after the war, to compare notes, and to figure out how they might recoup their losses. By what is no doubt mutual discussion and comparison of records, they prepare a *report* which concludes that there are still funds in the banks that *placed the loans*, i.e., the banks in Paris, London, Amsterdam, and Frankfurt, and that these banks possessed funds to the credit of the Confederacy. In other words, *the implication is that there is much more than mere **rumor** driving the report. Reports are not records of rumors unsubstantiated by any facts.*

2) This reports is then denied by the very banking house that initiated the loan, *and then in blatant insider trading style, then speculated in its own bonds*, hardly an example, one would think, of trustworthiness.

3) Then, even more glaringly, "unfounded" rumors emerge once again about "*large* sums to the credit of the Confederacy" are still held by various banks, but this time, the "unfounded rumors" include the Old Lady of Threadneedle Street herself, The Bank of England! Again, the plausible explanation for the origin of these rumors are the original bondholders that prepared the "report", who've probably continued their investigations. But now

---

[21] Schwab, op. cit., p. 38, all emphases and open-mouthed jaw-dropping expostulations added.

the amounts of the funds credited to the no-longer existent Confederacy are said to be "large." If true, does this in turn mean that other central banks also contain accounts containing such funds? If so, then we are *looking at stolen and disappeared money, a source of hidden reserves and liquidity which— since some of that is bound to be in the form of specie—may be secretly re-hypothecated.* To put this very differently, we may be looking at the nineteenth century proto-type of the hidden system of finance that I have hypothesized in some of my other books. Like that later hidden system, this one is based upon commodities backed bonds, a hidden and grossly re-hypothecated reserve, massive amounts of liquidity, and the physical possession and transfer of bullion for clearing.[22]

---

[22] For this hidden system of finance, see. my *Covert Wars and Breakaway Civilizations: UFOs, Oligarchs, and Space Secrecy* (Kempton, Illinois: Adventures Unlimited Press, 2013, ISBN 978-1-939149-04-6); *Covert Wars and Breakaway Civilizations: The Secret Space Program, Celestial Psyops, and Hidden Conflicts* (Adventures Unlimited Press, 2012, ISBN 978-1-935487-83-8); *Hidden Finance, Rogue Networks, and Secret Sorcery: The Fascist International and Penetrated Operations* (Adventures Unlimited Press, 2016, ISBN 978-939149-63-3); *Babylon's Banksters: the Alchemy of Deep Physics, High Finance, and Ancient Religion* (Port Townsend, Washington: Feral House, 2010, ISBN 978-1-932595-79-6); and *The Financial Vipers of Venice: Alchemical Money, Magical Physics, and Banking in the Middle Ages and Renaissance* (Feral House, 2010), 978-1-936239-73-3).

4) But all of this, says Judah P. Benjamin,[23] former Confederate Secretary of State, and in exile in England, is simply not true, because the Confederacy had no genuine money left. So, one or the other, either Benjamin is lying, or simply is reporting things to the best of his knowledge, but things which, ultimately he may not have known, or the hidden origins of "the rumor" of "large sums" credited to Confederate accounts in the Bank of England—a bullion reserve and clearing bank— are lying. As for the trade in Erlanger bonds, these continue until 1884.[24]

5. Who were some of the Subscribers to the Erlanger Bonds?
a. The Questions

The above points raise two very important and significant questions:

1) Since the rumors concerning the funds in European banks credited to the Confederacy could only have come from bondholders themselves, who, on the basis of careful comparison of the amounts of their subscriptions, then *who **are** some of these bondholders, and are the amounts of their subscriptions large enough to support the rumors concerning the Bank of England (and therefore, to imply that Judah Benjamin is either lying, or merely stating facts as best as he knew them;* and,
2) *do they tend to support or deny the involvement of "the high financial powers" of Europe, as stated in*

---

[23] In answer to the unspoken question in the reader's mind, Yes, he is.

[24] Schwab, op. cit., p. 39.

*the apocryphal Bismarck quotation? Could they or
do they exhibit connection to the Bank of England?*

b. The Bomb Drops

In searching for the answer to those two questions, I
discovered that virtually no one covers the subject, or
possibly that no one wants to talk about it, if they *do* know.

But there is one source that does, and some of the
bondholders are—to put it *very* mildly—very highly placed in
British financial, noble, and political circles. Richard I.
Lester, to whose work we have referred in this chapter, gives
a list of the names of the British subscribers to the loan in
Appendix III of his crucial and important work *Confederate
Finance and Purchasing in Great Britain*. The number of
subscribers listed by Lester is twenty-eight.

Of these, the following names detonate the bomb, and
vindicate the scenario outlined in the apocryphal Bismarck
quotation, for we encounter the following well-known, or not-
so-well-known, but powerful people and the amounts of their
Erlanger bond subscriptions:

1) Fleetwood, Pattern, Wilson, L. Schuster, directors
   of Union Bank, London, for £20,000;
2) *J.S. Gilliat, director of the Bank of England, for
   £10,000;*
3) Lord Campbell, for £1,000;
4) Lord Richard Grosvenor, for £1,000;
5) *Hon. Evelyn Ashley, son of Lord Shaftesnury, and
   private secretary to Lord Palmerston, for £500;*

6) *Right Hon. William Ewart Gladstone, for £2,000.*[25]

The figure of Prime Minister Gladstone is well known, and indicates that, without question, the very uppermost reaches of the British oligarchy are involved in the Erlanger loan. During the War Between the States, however, Gladstone was *the Chancellor of the Exchequer* in Prime Minister, the Lord Palmerston's, cabinet! Thus, we have one clear, and very powerful, connection to the British world of high finance, and to the Bank of England, in addition to a member *director* of said bank in J.S. Gilliat, a £10,000 subscriber to the bonds.

That's not all, however, because yet another subscribed is the personal secretary to Prime Minister Palmerston himself, Evelyn Ashley.

What of the other subscribers mentioned above? Richard Grosvenor was the 2nd Marquess of Westminster, a member of the Order of the Garter, and a member of the Queen's Privy council!

Then there is Lord Campbell, or John Campbell, the 1st Baron Campbell, who in spite of being apparently opposed to slavery, nonetheless was a subscriber to the loan. When the American Civil War was breaking out, however, he was Lord High Chancellor of Great Britain (from June 18th, 1859 to June 23rd, 1861), and as such, as part of his ceremonial duties, was keeper of the Great Seal of Great Britain itself, the seal that must be affixed to all royal promulgations of Parliamentary laws at the time. He had also been the Lord Chief Justice.

That these men are not the run-of-the-mill ordinary politician or even financial speculators should be abundantly

---

[25] Lester, op. cit, p. 209, emphasis added, citing John Brigelow, *Gladstone and the Confederate Loan of 1863* (New York: De Vinne Press, 1905), p. 8.

obvious. They form the very uppermost reaches of British political, financial, and judicial power, and two of them— Gilliat and Gladstone himself—are directly connected with the Bank of England.

We must therefore perforce conclude that whether or not Chancellor Otto von Bismarck ever really made the statements attributed to him, the core concept of those statements, that there was a high circle of financial power, behind the scenes, is true. Would that circle of people have had motive to ensure the demise of Mr. Lincoln, in order to recoup their losses through a policy of "reconstruction" of the South through pennies-on-the-dollar purchase of post bellum Southern assets? The answer to that is obvious too.[26]

But that hidden system of finance, I have argued in other books, was for the purpose of supporting a secret technological research, and the infrastructure needed to sustain it.

Are there any indicators of such a thing, hovering uneasily on the edges of the times and places of the War Between the States, having connections to British oligarchs and Prussian statecraft and American—Union or Confederate—shenanigans?

Hang on, because we're not quite done speculating just yet...

---

[26] Hmmm... you just *have* to wonder: "Erlanger in Chattanooga asks for $370 Million in Bonds to Pay debts, expand services," https://newschannel9.com/news/local/erlanger-in-chattanooga-asks-for-370-million-in-bonds-to-pay-debts-expand-services.

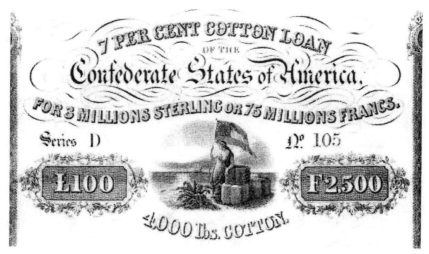

Top Portion of the One Hundred Pound/Two Thousand Five Hundred Francs Erlanger Bond

Top Portion of an Erlanger Five Hundred Pounds/Twelve Thousand Five Hundred Francs bond

PART THREE:
WILD, PURE, AND UNADULTERATED SPECULATION, *OR* ASKING SOME ESSENTIAL AND CRITICAL QUESTIONS

"...the Trans-Mississippi was never a drain on the eastern Confederate military resources. Rather, in almost every way, it bolstered eastern resources. Whenever it was possible for men, lead, grain, cattle, horses, clothing, and imported goods to flow, they almost always flowed east across the Mississippi."
William Royston Geise,
The Confederate Military Forces in the Trans-Mississippi West, 1861-1865: A Study in Command, pp. 189-190.

"...(We) are told Andrews met with tepid response from the War Department, but then we learn his request to meet personally with President Lincoln is honored. The result of that meeting, we are told, is that Lincoln ordered the War Department and Congress to provide details on acquiring Andrew's airship technology and bring it into the arsenal. Congress recommended immediate acquisition by the War Department, but a funny thing happened. It took until the spring of 1865 before Secretary Stanton informed Andrews... of the War Department's alleged rejection of the airship development project..."
Walter Bosley, *Origin: The Nineteenth Century Emergence of the 20th Century Breakaway Civilizations,* pp. 172-173.

"I learned that Mr. Wilson...formerly lived in Fort Worth."
Dr. D.H. Tucker, cited in Michael Busby *Solving the Great Airship Mystery,* p. 175.

261

The Wicked Witch of the West (played by Margaret Hamilton), gives orders to one of her flying monkeys to capture Dorothy, visible in the "crystal ball" with the other Oz pilgrims, from MGM's classic 1939 production of Baum's "The Wizard of Oz"

8

WE'RE OFF TO SEE THE WIZARD:
THE *POST BELLUM* MONEY DEBATES, THE WIZARD OF OZ, THE WONDERFUL WORLD OF AIRSHIPS, AND YET ANOTHER ALLEGORICAL INTERPRETATION OF FRANK BAUM'S CLASSIC

"When I get those ruby slippers, my power will be the greatest in Oz. And now, my beauties, something with poison in it, I think, with poison in it, but attractive to the eye, and soothing to the smell... poppies, poppies... poppies will put them to sleep... now they'll sleep."
The Wicked Witch of the West, played by Margaret Hamilton, *The Wizard of Oz* (1939 movie)

D EBATES OVER THE NATURES AND TYPES, of currency that were to be used in *post bellum* America consumed the decades following the end of the War Between the States all the way to the turn of the century. The difficulties and subtleties of those debates seem a world away from today, but perhaps those subtleties can be conveyed by a comparison of wartime, and *post bellum*, cultural, political, and financial thinking. If as some have argued the pre-war Union was a case of two very different cultures and countries sharing a common government, then the wartime condition might be construed as two governments with their own financial and economic policies trying to govern one country. The post-war situation returns to the pre-war condition as far as the government was concerned, but the economic and cultural sectionalism has now been exacerbated by the presence of new economic classes and new sections. To the old divisions of North and South and their industrial versus agricultural economies were now added the plains states and territories with a new farming class, and the western coastal states, with each region and class favoring its own kind of money.

A. A Necessary and Lengthy Trip Around Harvey's Barn

The farmers of the plains and old South favored a return to pre-war "bi-metallism", of the monetary use of gold *and silver* which, due to the exigencies of the war, had forced both North and South to favor gold specie as the favored medium for their international trade. Silver gradually was demonetized, even though still accepted as money in place of gold. This is for a very simple reason: with several ounces of silver equaling one ounce of gold, gold was much easier and cheaper *to ship* when clearing accounts; $20,000 in gold took up a lot less space than $20,000 in silver. The result was predictable, silver was *de facto* de-monetized.

The industrialists, bankers, and financiers of the northeast naturally favored a stable money for conduct of trade, and especially international trade, for the war had taught them well that as far as international trade went, the European bankers favored gold over all other commodities.

Then there were the paper money—"Greenbackers"— of the late nineteenth century populists. We've seen that both the Union and the Confederacy attempted to finance their war efforts with fiat currencies and paper money. There all resemblance stopped, for in most cases the Confederacy's paper money represented a currency issued off of bonds, and hence the Confederate "blueback" was monetized debt. As a result, it ended in extreme inflation and depreciation. The Union currency, the more well-known "greenback", was simply debt-free. It too was inflated during the war, and with the depreciation of purchasing power, prices increased, but at a much slow rate than in the South. The lesson, as we saw in the last chapter, was clear to everyone who looked, including the European bankers, who raised not a peep in protest at the South's paper money—there was not one opinion editorial in any major European newspaper raging against the Confederate currency—but who raised howls of protests over the North's greenbacks.

With the deflation that reigned in *post bellum* America from 1865 to 1900, the hardest hit parts of the country were, of course, the more agricultural areas of the South and plains, the farmers and middle classes of the small cities in those regions; farmers would have to finance the planting of their crops, which, by the time the crops were grown, harvested, and sold, they were sold at lower prices than when they were planted, and loans would have to be repaid with dollars that had gained in their intrinsic value, but which were in shorter supply. These areas were the biggest supporters of the re-monetization of silver in these decades, and eventually gave rise to the candidacy of William Jennings Bryan, whose famous "Cross of Gold" speech in 1892 elevated him to the Democratic Party's nomination for President.

But what had happened to create this deflation in the first place? How does one go from the extreme inflation in the South, and the strong inflation in the North, to decades of *deflation*, and thus of a smaller money supply, after the war? The question is an important one, because during the war neither the North nor the South operated with a central bank. There was no "Federal Reserve" to step in and raise interest rates to restrict the money supply. Both sides controlled money supply *directly through currency acts of their Congresses.*

But the Union Congress had approved of the greenbacks, so what happened after the war to create the deflation?

1. The Union's 1863-1864 National Banking Act: The First Step to a Central Bank

The answer was the national banking act of the Union Congress. "The Act," writes Ellen Brown, "looked good on its face." She continues:

> It established a Comptroller of the Currency, whose authority was required before a National Banking Association could start business. It laid down regulations covering minimum capitalization, reserve requirements, bad debts, and reporting. The Comptroller could at any time appoint investigators to look into the affairs of any national bank. Every bank director had to be an American citizen, and three-quarters of the directors of a bank had to be residents of the State in which the bank did business. Interest rates were limited by State usury laws; and if no laws were in effect, then to 7 percent. Banks could not hold real estate for more than five years, except for bank buildings. *National banks were not allowed to circulate notes they printed themselves. Instead, they had to deposit U.S. bonds with the Treasury in a sum equal to at least one-third of their capital. They got government-printed notes in return.*
> So what was the problem? Although the new national banknotes were technically issued by the Comptroller of the Currency, this was just a formality, like the printing of Federal Reserve Notes by the

Bureau of Engraving and Printing today. The currency bore the name of the bank posting the bonds, and it was issued at the bank's request. In effect, the National Banking Act authorized the bankers to issue and lend their own paper money. The banks deposited bonds with the Treasury, but they still own the bonds; and they immediately got their money back in the form of their own banknotes. Topping it off, the National Banking Act effectively removed the competition to these banknotes. It imposed a heavy tax on the notes of the state-chartered banks, essentially abolishing them. *It also curtailed competition from the Greenbacks, which were limited to specific issues while the bankers' notes could be issued at will. Treasury Secretary Salmon P. Chase and others complained that the bankers were buying up the Greenbacks with their own banknotes.*[1]

Notice that the effect of the National Banking Act is essentially to place the Union, if only partially, on the same sort of currency system as its rival, the Rialto in Richmond, for the currency issued under its aegis is almost exactly the same kind of currency (and therefore, subject to the same kind of dangers). Note also that the strategy also entailed the limitation of the Congressional issue of Greenbacks, which could only be authorized by law; the banknotes, however, as Brown notes, could be issued almost at will. A century later, around the time of the Kennedy assassination, this problem, too, would be solved in a much more efficient way, for any of his debt-free, red-shielded United States' Notes, when

---

[1] Ellen Hodgson Brown, op. cit., pp. 91-92, emphases added.

entering the Federal Reserve System, would simply be removed from circulation altogether, and physically destroyed.

2. The Resumption Act of 1875:
Specie Redemption and Stability,
And the First Steps to a Hidden System of Finance

Then came the final blow against the post-war economy, the Resumption Act of 1875, which called for the redemption of outstanding Greenbacks in specie.[2] While there is some debate over the effect of this act—some maintaining that it helped to stabilize the greenback, others maintaining that what acted to stabilize it was a rise in production, particularly in the South—the overall effect was deflationary, and it poses *a problem of missing money.*

By 1874, out of an estimated $450 million of authorized greenbacks, some $382 million was still in circulation, and of this, following the Resumption Act's passage, $300 million remained in circulation.[3]

At this juncture, a question occurs. Let us assume, for the sake of argument and in order to outline the conceptual problem at the heart of this widely speculative scenario, that the difference—$82 million in greenbacks—was redeemed for specie, most of which under the circumstances, would have been gold. The question is, did the postwar Federal government have enough gold in its reserves to do so? The problem occurs because during the panic of 1893, the

---

[2] Brown, op. cit., p. 94.
[3] "Specire Payment Resumption Act," *Wikipedia,* https://en.wikipedia.org/Specie_Payment_Resumption_Act.

government's reserves were only about $100,000,000, a figure that is down from the $192,000,000 of just three years previously.[4] We also saw that the Union supported a financial warfare effort against Confederate bonds in the European markets by trying to bear those markets, an effort that required not only lots of money, but most probably in the form of specie. So it is reasonable to assume that the Resumption Act may have severely depleted gold reserves at the same time it was constricting the money supply. Most of that specie payment is likely to have gone to the northern financiers and industrials who held the paper in large amounts and denominations. They had, after all, been issued to assist in funding the war effort.

Another, much more important, question now occurs: what happened *to the actual physical greenbacks thus redeemed themselves*? Conventional wisdom would have it that they were burned or otherwise destroyed, perhaps by bleaching the paper, re-pulping it, and reusing it for other purposes. ***But there is nothing whatsoever preventing the re-***

---

[4] Gary Richardson and Tim Sablik, "Banking Panics of the Gilded Age, 1863-1913: The Late 19th Century saw the expansion of the U.S. Financial System but was also beset by banking panics" (Federal Reserve History: https://www.federalreserve history. org/essays/banking-panics-of-the-gilded-age), p. 4. It is interesting to note that this article lists both authors as being at the Federal Reserve Bank of Richmond. So another question that occurs is: was Richmond chosen as a location for a branch of the Federal Reserve System *because of* its role as the Confederate Capital, and because the Confederate monetary system so closely resembles that of the Federal Reserve system, sans the central bank itself? Is this a mechanism chosen in part to recoup the losses European financiers incurred in the Erlanger loan and other support for the Confederacy? All my instincts say yes.

use—the effective re-hypothecation—of that paper money for other and covert purposes. After all, the paper still retained some value simply by virtue of having been declared legal tender. Such a practice continues to this day with worn-out Federal Reserve notes which are slated for destruction; these are diverted for use in covert operations, and so on.

While this is entirely hypothetical and there is no direct evidence to support it, I now assume that *one hidden cause of the post-war decades of deflation is the syphoning off of a supply of circulating paper money generated by the war for covert purposes, those purposes being to create and control an exotic technology (by the standards of the day), and thereby for foreign financiers to recoup losses incurred by their wartime investments.*

With that very high octane speculative thesis stated, we must now look closely at

3. Walter Bosley's NYMZA Hypothesis, To Which We Now Add Re-hypothecated Greenbacks

In 2015 my friend and colleague Walter Bosley published a most intriguing and unusual book about the 19th century airship mystery, titled *Origin: The Nineteenth Century Emergence of the 20th Century Breakaway Civilizations.*[5] While any attempt to outline here all the nuances of the complex hypothesis detailed in his book, we must deal with some of its core concepts because, in a certain sense, the Rialto in Richmond and the *post bellum* financial and technological developments are not understandable without it. Indeed, as I shall argue momentarily, even the

[5] Walter Bosley, *Origin: the Nineteenth Century Emergence of the 20th Century Breakaway Civilizations* (Highland, California: Corvos Book, 20150.

Union's Lincoln greenbacks themselves may owe their origin to a hidden and secret purpose of supporting the research that the airships represented.

In some of my previous books I have argued for the existence of a breakaway civilization, borrowing and expanding upon that idea from Ufo researcher Richard Dolan. This breakaway civilization was created for and centered upon the development of an exotic technology far in advance of the public technologies known and available. The impetus for its development came following World War Two, with the arrival of nuclear weapons, UFOs, and the creation of the Communist bloc. I have argued that, faced with this triple strategic threat, a way had to be developed to confront and stalemate each threat, and this could only be done through a fantastic technological development, a development requiring a lot of money, in the billions and trillions of dollars, over a long time. A heavy tax for the purpose could hardly have been imposed, for that would have required disclosing the purpose of the tax, which would have exposed both the threat and technology. The only way, therefore, to develop the technology, which required a gigantic financial infrastructure to pay for it, would be through the creation of a large, and largely secret and hidden, system of finance.

With this in mind, let us look at various details of Bosley's NYMZA Hypothesis. "First," he says, "let me state my position.

> The breakaway civilizations of our time are not the product of Nazi Germany, nor are they the product of the postwar military industrial complex, and they are certainly not the result of reverse engineering of a crashed ET spacecraft.

271

He continues with a few points that outline a vast "revisionist" historiographic canvas, and the points which concern us here are italicized:

> 1. There was a technologically advanced human civilization in remote ancient history.
> 2. Secret societies and esoterically motivated hermetic organizations sought to recover and reconstruct the lost knowledge and technology of the forgotten ancient civilizations.
> 3. *The technology of the 19th Century airship builders was based on the lost technology of forgotten civilizations preserved and rediscovered.*
> 4. *Charles Dellschau was not simply an outsider artist—he was telling the truth.*
> 5. **American airship builders developed aero technology in the first 'black project' launched at the end of the Civil War.**
> 6. *20th Century Nazi Germany technology linked to the modern secret space program and breakaway civilization originated with the Prussian airship builders.*[6]

Dellschau, Bosley observes, was born in Brandenburg, Prussia, in 1830, and became the sole source of knowledge about an early group of pioneers experimenting with "airship" technology in late 1850s and early 1860s California.[7]

These "airships", however, were not the dirigibles of the late nineteenth and early twentieth centuries; Bosley writes—and anyone who has examined Dellschau's writings and his lifetime output of strange paintings of these "airships," or "aeros" as they were actually called, would have to concur; if the man was not nuts, and not painting

---

[6] Bosley, op. cit., pp. 9-10, all emphases added.
[7] Ibid., p. 103.

things he imagined or hallucinated, and if they were real, then what he was describing was truly shocking. The group in California doing all of this was, according to Dellschau, a "secretive group of German immigrants in Tuolumne County, California," a group "he said was called the Sonora Aero Club. This club," Bosley continues,

> ...was led by a man named Peter Mennis who, according to Dellschau, knew the secret recipe for the fuel used in the propulsion and lift mechanism of the flying machines the group referred to as 'aeros.' Dellschau's account makes it clear that these aeros were not balloons. They were apparently anti-gravity craft. The problem with that is that Dellschau said the club flew these anti-gravity craft in the mid to late 1850s.
>
> What's this? Practical anti-gravity isn't even supposed to exist now, how are we supposed to believe that men were flying anti-gravity machines before the US Civil War?[8]

Whatever the technology was or was not, what concerns us here is that *something* wild and exotic was going on in 1850s California German immigrant community.

That something was connected to an organization based in Prussia called "NYMZA" by Dellschau.[9] The name of this organization Bosley hypothesizes stands for

Nationlistische
Jagdflugzeug-
Maschinen
ZahlungsAmt,

---

[8] Bosley, op. cit, pp. 104-105.
[9] Ibid. p. 128.

or: "The National Pursuit-Flying-Machine Payment Office,"
or "National Aircraft-Flying Machine Payment Bureau."

However one wishes to translate the German, the
meaning and intention is clear: "NYMZA" is really an
English transliteration of the German letters for the
organization NJMZA, because the German "J" is pronounced
like an English "Y", as in the German word "ja" for "yea" or
"yes." As for the organization itself, it represents the key
financial component of the infrastructure supporting whatever
research the Sonora Aero club was doing in California.
Bosley writes:

> Like it or not, NYMZA was based in Germany, not in New
> York; Dellschau plainly says so, regardless whether my
> specific translation is exact or not. How am I so confident?
>
> For starters, once the Sonora Aero Club had success
> with their aero technology, Dellschau tells us that there
> soon followed a flirtation with the idea of developing aeros
> for commercial and military purposes. Then came the day,
> Dallschau relates, when a military officer approached the
> club and suggested they construct aeros designed for
> warfare.
>
> Whether this man was from the United States military or
> from Europe was supposedly unspecified, by Dellschau did
> specifically refer to him as "that Prussian officer". That
> statement alone makes it clear: the military officer was
> Prussian, thus ... he ... in my opinion represented the
> interests of the Prussian NYMZA.[10]

The Prussian connection here is important, for it means that
the Prussian *state* is actively involved in secretly funding a
research project within the territories of the United States,
thus making it *highly likely that the Prussian Chancellor,*

---

[10] Bosley, op. cit., p. 128.

Otto von Bismarck, would have been apprised of any special international financial arrangements involving the project, making his apocryphal comment more likely to have originated from him, at least in some form or fashion. Prussia, after all, had a direct stake in the outcome of the war, and with seeing its project brought to a successful conclusion.

In this respect, Bosley notes that there were Prussian and German officers attached to both sides of the war,[11] which may be explained either as the purely personal interests of German volunteers, *or as a deliberate policy of infiltrating agents of potential influence into the militaries of both sides in order to preserve the project regardless of who wins. The financial, and the research, infrastructures must be maintained.*

There is one final, crucial component to this emerging *post bellum* financial structure that, as I have argued, may have included re-hypothecated greenbacks as a component of a hidden system of finance to fund it all. Bosley observes that Prussia and the German Empire moved to a mono-metallic gold standard in the late nineteenth century.[12] If this is the case, and if it exercised any covert influence over American post war financial and currency policy—particularly in the covert re-hypothecation of greenbacks to support any ongoing efforts of NYMZA or the aero builders—then the policy would be a typically Bismarckian example of *Realpolitik*, for while it was contracting public money supply in America, it – and whomever else was involved in the project—was using those rehypothecated greenbacks to fund the project.

In his book Bosley refers often to the research of Michael Busby's singular and indispensable research on the

---

[11] Q.v., Bosley, op. cit., p. 176.
[12] Q.v. Bosley, op. cit. p. 200f.

airship mystery, *Solving the 1897 Airship Mystery*, tying it into the earlier Dellschau-NYMZA-Sonora Aero Club story. In effect, Bosley is arguing that the two stories are but the pre-bellum and post-bellum halves of *one* development, with the War Between the States intervening.

But as we seen, according to Dellschau the Sonora Aero Club was approached by a Prussian officer for the development of the technology for military purposes. Under such circumstances it would be foolish to assume that similar thoughts had not occurred to the Americans involved in the project.

*We have now arrived at the one final detail that ties **all** of this—the Lincoln Greenbacks, the Lincoln assassination, a nascent system of hidden finance, and the "exotic NYMZA technology" represented by the nineteenth century airships – together.* Busby states

> In a letter dated August 9, 1862, Dr. (Solomon) Andrews wrote President Lincoln, suggesting he could "produce an aerostat for reconnaissance, if nothing more, in aid of the armies of the Union."[13] Lincoln like the idea and asked the War Department to keep him informed of Dr. Andrews' progress. Lincoln further requested eyewitness accounts of the progress and test flights of Dr. Andrews' airship.[14]

---

[13] Michael Busby, *Solving the 1897 Airship Mystery* (Gretna, Louisiana: 2004, ISBN 1-58980-125-3), p. 293 citing Mary Kingsley, "The Flying New Jerseyman, Dr. Solomon Andrews of Perth Amboy," *Proceedings of the New Jersey Historical Society* (July 1954): 169.

[14] Busby, op. cit., pp. 293-294.

Andrews continued his work, and had a model ready for public exhibition and testing by September 4, 1863. The *New York Herald* reported:

> In October last Dr. Solomon Andrews, of Perth Amboy, N.J., commenced the construction of a war aerostat, for reconnoitering purposes, *on his own responsibility, not being able, after submitting his plans to the War Department, to make the honorable Secretary of War "see the utility" of a machine which would go over into [] and reconnoiter the force and position of the enemy. His plan showed on the face of them (sic) to any one not stupid that the machine could not do otherwise than go ahead in any direction in which the bow was pointed, and that, too, with any amount of power or force which might be desired, and which greenbacks would readily procure.*[15]

Note carefully what has just been stated by the newspaper report:

1) The "aerostat" was *not* mere balloon—which both the Union and Confederacy deployed for reconnoitering purposes throughout the war— because it was able to *move in any direction;* and,
2) It was able to move, apparently, under its own power;
3) *The project was ostensibly brought to fruition by Dr. Andrews himself, a point to which we shall momentarily return;* and

---

[15] Busby, op. cit., p. 294, emphasis added, citing *The New York Herald,* "Aerial Navigation/ An Extraordinary Invention— The Air Navigated Successfully—The Great Air Ships—Incidents of Their Trial Trips."

4) It was brought to the direct attention of the Secretary of the War Department, who was at that time, of course, Edwin Stanton(!); and finally,

5) The newspaper itself connected the project to greenback funding!

Five days later, in a letter to the newspaper, Dr. Andrews himself explained the "aerostat's" capabilities with a letter. The letter made it clear that the "aerostat" had performed remarkably well, becoming "lost to view in the upper strata of clouds" and with a speed in his estimation in excess of two hundred miles per hour.[16] But then Busby notes another significant clue:

> Dr. Andrews was frustrated in his efforts to promote his airship with the War Department, but he finally was able to schedule an appointment with President Lincoln, and report to him personally. Lincoln *ordered Secretary of War Edwin Stanton to form a congressional committee to investigate the invention and make recommendations for its acquisition.* Congressional hearings were held in March 1864, *The committee recommended the airship be purchased by the War Department immediately. Apparently, Edwin Stanton, a man of limited vision, squashed the recommendations,* and on March 22, 1865, Andrews received a letter from the House Military Affairs Committee stating they were really not that interested, and besides, the war was over, seemed to be their laconic attitude.[17]

---

[16] Busby, op. cit., p. 296.
[17] Ibid., p. 297, emphasis added. See also Busby's further comments on that page re. the airships and war veterans.

But was Stanton that much of a plodder and blockhead? In chapter two what emerged from our examination of Stanton's behavior during and after the murder of President Lincoln was a man who would stop at nothing to procure, and maintain, power, including outright defiance of direct orders from his boss! We also saw a man obsessed *with the secret exercise of power and its secret maintenance.*

It is not, in my opinion, very likely that Stanton would have passed by an opportunity to fund and acquire such a technology. It is far more likely that the secretive Stanton would have found some way to remove the project from view and, as per Bosley's "proto-typical" black projects world of the nineteenth century, found a covert war to *fund* it. This brings us back to Dr. Andrews himself. The newspaper article implies that Andrews brought his project to fruition using his own resources, which is unlikely. He had to have had some source, a covert one, for his research and activities. The newspaper article itself suggested the connection: greenbacks, the very greenbacks funding Stanton's War Department.

If these speculations be true, then we may arrive at two final speculations, and they are that

1) one of the reasons for the creation of the debt-free money in the first place was to fund such research into the then "exotic technologies;" and,

2) that Lincoln's perceived "soft" policy toward the post-war South might have been construed as also threatening to share or otherwise expose a technology to the former enemy, technology that the radical reconstructionists like Stanton wished to keep secret. Like Kennedy a century later, offering to share UFO information and thus potential technological secrets with the Soviet Union,

Lincoln had to be stopped. It was on this view *not* just "money" that was at stake, it was technology and the power it conferred.

But what, the reader might be asking, does all of this high and hidden finance, secret and covert technology projects, gold, silver, greenbacks, deflation, and assassination, have to do with the *Wonderful Wizard of Oz*?

B. The Wonderful Wizard of Oz as a Political and Monetary Allegory
1. Of Yellow Brick Roads, Silver (or Ruby) Slippers, Poppy Fields, Emerald Cities, Three Witches, and a Wizard

Little imagination is required to see what might have happened had the development of navigable aerial technologies been pursued as deployed weapons of war during the War Between the States, rather than being ushered—as Bosley outlined, and as I have embellished—into a covert project by the ever-dubious, power-hungry, and smarmy Union Secretary of War, Edwin Stanton. His possible role in the Lincoln assassination has now been given yet another potential motivation: the protection of "exotic technology".

The other half of those covert operations, as was seen, was Jefferson Davis' Continuity of Government flight, and his attempt to get to the Trans-Mississippi Department of the Confederacy, to continue the war and, hopefully, negotiate a peace.

That, too, appears to have some connection to the 19th century airship mystery. One of the recurring motifs of that mystery, at least in its *post bellum* manifestation, was that the airships were occasionally seen to *land*, disgorge human crewmembers, who would then interact and converse with the astonished citizenry, before returning to their vessels and lifting off.

One of these airship crewmembers who repeatedly was seen and conversed with was a man who gave his surname as "Wilson." There seems some connection to that Continuity of Government operation, for after the airships were initially spotted all over the upper Midwest and plains, the sightings gradually migrated south, where they ended in Texas, where not only "Wilson" was said to have lived in Fort Worth, but where, apparently, the airship operators maintained some sort of base of facility, and of course, Texas was the ultimate home of Dellschau.[18]

But again, what has all this to do with *The Wizard of Oz*? Oddly enough, it may have everything to do with it. In 1964, an article in *The American Quarterly* took what had been understood up to that point as a simply children's book by Frank L. Baum, a former newspaper editor from Aberdeen, South Dakota, and turned it into a carefully thought-out allegory of the nineteenth century American political debates over the philosophy of money, and the kind of money America should have. The article was by Henry M. Littlefield, and appeared in the Spring issue, perhaps significantly the first issue of *The American Quarterly* after the assassination of President Kennedy. Littlefield's article touched off an entirely new academic debate and trend, as ever since then it has become almost a pastime among some academics to decode Baum's clever allegory of nineteenth

---

[18] Busby, op. cit., pp. 21, 175, and esp. pp. 42-43, where Busby argues a case for some airship base in the environs of Sherman, Texas, north of Dallas and close to the Red River

century populism, while other academics stubbornly point out that Baum had intended to do no such thing, and only attempted, as the preface to his own book stated, to create an entertaining and moral children's tale.[19]

Briefly put, this interpretation of the book as a "populist political and monetary allegory" consists of seeing various key components of the story as symbols of the American financial and political debates. For example, the "yellow brick road" becomes the gold standard. Dorothy's ruby slippers, which are in the original book, *silver* slippers, become the remonetization of silver, and the "bi-metallic" standard of money being advocated by the Populists to expand the money supply, and end the deflationary and tight money cycle the country had been in since the end of the war. The Wicked Witch of the East becomes the symbol of the Eastern seaboard industrialists and financiers, who held the Munchkins of the land—the "little people"—in virtual thrall. In some cases, both Wicked Witches of East and West are understood to be the two "gold standard" presidents, Grover Cleveland and William McKinley. The Scarecrow becomes the supposedly (but not really) brainless farmers of the plains and South, the Tinman the heartless, almost robotized and "zombified" industrial workers of the East, and the Cowardly

---

[19] The best single volume compendium of all these allegorical interpretations and bibliography of the various other interpretations besides 19th century populism is that of Ranjit S. Dighe, Ed., *The Historian's Wizard of Oz: Reading L. Frank Baum's Classic as a Political and Monetary Allegory* (Westport, Connecticut: 2002 ISBN 0-275-97419-7). Another valuable source is Gretchen Ritter's *Goldbugs and Greenbacks: The Antimonopoly Tradition and the Politics of Finance in America, 1865-1896* (Cambridge: Cambridge University Press, 1999, ISBN 978-0-521-65392-3).

Lion by most readings symbolizes William Jennings Bryan, known for his mighty roar in his now famous "Cross of Gold" speech at the 1892 Democratic Party convention, a tour de force that earned him the presidential nomination both of the Populists and of the Democrats, but who was "cowardly" because of his opposition to American imperialism. The Emerald City, home and seat of the Powerful Wizard, becomes Washington DC.

The colors of the book, too, are all allegorical of money. Dorothy's silver slippers, which allow her to dance and skip her way along the yellow brick road, even when some bricks are missing, is yet another allegory of bi-metallism, as it means that silver would allow people to keep moving (producing) even when gold was in short supply. But the *heart* of the system was *green* of Emerald City, which comes to symbolize the greenback, and the greenback faction of nineteenth century populism. The Wizard in the book can shapeshift, and take on completely different forms to each of the four travelers, thus becomes a politician, a "very good man but a very poor wizard," to quote a description of himself that made it from the book into the lines of Frank Morgan, the actor who played the Wizard in the famous 1939 movie adaptation of the book.

The North and the South (and their respective witches) are thus "good" because not beholden to the wickedness of the Eastern industrialists and financiers nor to that of the western farm loaners, and so on.[20]

---

[20] Dighe, op. cit., pp. 42-130. Dighe's book reprints, in its entirety, the text of Baum's original book, with extensive footnotes summarizing the various interpretations of the book as a populist monetary-political allegory. I have attempted to summarize its salient features.

2. The Lack of Allegorical Treatment of the Movie and a Proposal in that Direction:
a. The Common Greenness of the Wicked Witch of the West and of the Emerald City

I am not here concerned with whether or not *The Wizard of Oz* was intended to be an allegory; I am concerned only with the fact that a great many intelligent people have *understood* it to be. It is to be noted, then, that the allegorical interpretations extend only to the *book*, and not to the classic 1939 Metro-Goldwyn-Mayer movie adaptation of the same, which I contend here has added its own allegorical motifs, and many of these appear to be uncharacteristically *morally inverted* from the populist-monetary reading.

In the movie, for example, there is a curious moral *identification* both of the Emerald City and of the Wicked Witch of the West, for both are colored *green*. The Wizard, however, when he first appears as himself, is not green at all, but almost a holographic projection between two cauldrons belching flame, and against a backdrop of what looks like pipes from a pipe organ. When the curtain is finally drawn back and his story is revealed, he turns out to be an ordinary man from the plains (Omaha) who is a very good man but a very poor wizard. He does not share the color, nor really belong, to Emerald city. The movie subtly suggests through this simple device that he is a usurper, and that the Wicked Witch of the West more properly belongs in Emerald City. The plain man from Omaha becomes a clear reference to Lincoln on this view.

b. "Oh We Love the Old One"
If anyone is like me, then people who have seen the movie version of *The Wizard of Oz* will recall that scene that

used to fascinate and mystify me as a boy. The scene was the changing of the guard outside the Wicked Witch of the West's castle, which was observed by the Scarecrow, Tin Man, and Cowardly Lion, who were trying to figure out how to rescue Dorothy, who had been captured by the Wicked Witch's flying monkeys. As the guards perform an elaborate choreographed ritual, they sing a song in unison, which to the ears of most people, sounds something like:

OH-EE-UHM-EE-OOOOH-UHM.

Nonsense and gibberish, just what one would expect from a narcissistic, sociopathic, and murderous ugly old witch.

But an actor who played the Munchkin Coroner who delivered the verdict in the movie to Glinda the Good Witch of the North and to Dorothy that the Wicked Witch of the East was truly dead, later revealed that in fact the Witch of the West's guards were in fact singing the words

OH WE LOVE THE OOOLD ONE.

Along our allegorical populist-monetarist interpretation what might *that* mean?

Within the monetary debates of the populist allegorical interpretation it might mean the *oldest* form of money, money that had *nothing* to do with metals, and which had everything to do with green, or debt-free money, the *oldest* form. Of course, in the movie, when Dorothy throws water on her, she "melts" and ultimately dies, vanishing away in a cloud of hissing steam, a metaphor perhaps of the evaporation of the greenbacks by Dorothy, who in the book is wearing silver, and not ruby, slippers, an "obvious" reference to the bi-metallic standard of money urged by some of the 19th century populists. She might, thus, even represent Lincoln himself, since his greenback policy would eventually "evaporate" in the 1875 Resumption Act.

But there's another potential clue as to the identity of the Wicked Witch of the West...

c. ...and Her Flying Monkeys

The scene in the movie is another classic one: actress Margaret Hamilton, in her green makeup and black witch's hat and clothes, her long spindly fingers and claw-like fingernails, summons the commander of her Flying Monkeys, and orders him to take Dorothy alive and bring her and her precious ruby slippers back to the Witch's castle. Having done so, we learn in a later scene that the ruby slippers are sought by the Witch because they will give her unequalled power in the land of Oz.

In the light of information presented in this chapter, I propose that the Wicked Witch of the West is Lincoln's Secretary of War, Edwin Stanton, himself, and not only because Stanton hailed from Ohio, which at that period of American history was still considered to be part of "the West," but because he is connected with the color green (greenbacks), *and, via Dr. Andrews and his "aerostat"* to the "flying monkeys," the *humans*, who were flying the airships. The Wicked Witch of the West, in other words, has *two* "technologies" that allow her to *navigate* and change direction in the air—her flying monkeys, and her broom— that the Wizard, with his simple balloon which must drift along with the pattern of the winds, does not. He is, again, a "very good man but a very poor Wizard." Small wonder, then, that he orders the four pilgrims to bring him the Wicked

Witch's *broom*, for that is a metaphor for stealing the technology from her.

But what of the change from silver to ruby slippers? Here I am tempted to read this as a bit of foresight, perhaps, of the Nazi Bell's "Xerum 525" and my speculative hypothesis that this cherry-red substance was some compound of mercury and thorium oxide.

However, I will resist the temptation, tidy as it may *appear* to be. This leaves us with yet another way to look at the ruby slippers as *some unknown, perhaps very hard, substance that confers great power to the Witch, perhaps even some power that can enhance her powers of flight.*

On the basis of this interpretive template of the allegory, the following "de-coding" of its specific elements emerges:

Element	"Decode"
The Wicked Witch of the East	In the standard view, the "Silver standard" powers of the Orient
The Wicked Witch of the West	In the standard view, the "Gold Standard" powers of the Occident; but in the Airship Allegory interpretation, her color, green, is that of the greenbacks enabling her technology. She represents Lincoln (a villain to the goldbugs), or better, Secretary of War Stanton, and her "melting" is the dissolution of the greenback policy after the assassination

287

Her "Flying Monkeys"	The "flying monkeys", or flying humans, of the 19th century airship mystery
Her Broom	A flying technology which allows her to control the direction and speed of flight, unlike the Wizard's Balloon
Her Crystal Ball	Television?
Glinda, the "good witch"	Orchestrating liquidation of the other witches
Dorothy Gale	Blind simplicity of populism
Scarecrow	Populist and "brainless" farmers
Tin Man	Heartless industrial barons, breakdown without oil
Cowardly Lion	Cowardly military
Munchins	Midgets of urban centers
The Wizard of Oz	Hidden manipulator of monetary and technological system; hidden finance *The Wizard as Wilson*
The Wizard's Balloon	The public technology of flight which is outclassed by the Witch's flying monkeys and broom
Emerald City	The debt free "Greenbacks" prosperous & advanced utopia, as the movie depicts the city in the distance as some modern and advanced vis a vis the simplicity and "old" feel of architecture in the rest of Oz

Ruby(Silver) Slippers	"Silver standard. monopoly"
Yellow Brick Road	"Gold standard, monopoly
The Poppy Field	Drug trade, effect of addiction on society, diversion from purpose

What all of this suggests is that if Bosley's hypothesis that we are looking at the nineteenth century proto-typing of the black projects world of the twentieth century is true, then perforce the elements of that world must be present as well, and that, I submit, the movie version of the *Wizard of Oz* and all of the preceding pages, provides. The crucial element of that hypothesis is the financial infrastructure to support it, and a robustness of government able to survive the cataclysm of war.

With the quiet involvement of European financiers and power brokers in the form of British and Prussian money, Lincoln's greenbacks, radical Republican reconstructionists, Confederate assassins who might potentially be double of even triple agents, Jefferson Davis' attempted continuity of government flight to the Trans-Mississippi, and the nineteenth century airship mystery which ends its tour of the country in the same department, we have arrived not at the *end* of the mystery, but at its beginning. The Rialto in Richmond did not cease to exist. It just went global, and wants to enslave everyone with monetized debt, and technology which only it has access to.

Or to put it country simple, "Houston, we have a problem…"

The Wizard of Oz's Balloon Accidentally Lifts Off (Pictured is Frank Morgan as the Wizard, and Jack Haley as the Tin Man)

1892 Presidential Campaign Poster for William Jennings Bryan. Many allegorical interpreters of "The Wonderful Wizard of Oz" believe Bryan to be the Wizard, since both were associated with plains states.

290

9
CONCLUSIONS AND EPILOGUE

*"Moreover, both the gold standard and the **bimetallic** (gold-and-silver) standard that preceded it were highly complex monetary and financial systems, the details of whose operations are still subject to debate and disagreement among economic historians."*
Ranjit S. Dighe[1]

W HAT WE HAVE ENDED UP WITH IN THIS BOOK is most definitely *not* a completed edifice. What we have managed to do is to survey the landscape, and perhaps to dig about on the ground, scratching the dirt here, moving a mound there, clearing some of the land. Perhaps we have even managed to pour a bit of the foundation, and maybe even raise some scaffolding. We have not, however, come anywhere close to erecting an edifice. The core hypothesis of this book,—that the *post bellum* financial history of America is intimately related to the radical Republican reconstructionist agenda, to the covert involvement of European financiers and politicians standing on the uppermost parapets of British power and German-French bankers embedded in the chateaus of Second Empire Paris, and perhaps even to the famous Prussian "Iron Chancellor" to the Continuity of Government fight of Jefferson Davis, and to the vortex of characters swirling around the assassination of Abraham Lincoln, to lots of missing Confederate money, to the 19th century's version of exotic technology in the airships mystery, and perhaps even

---

[1] Rankit S. Dighe, op. cit., p. 12.

to a South Dakota newspaper editor allegorizing all of it in a children's book that would become an international classic—all of this core hypothesis is a work under construction.

Why this is so requires a bit of an explanation, before I attempt to summarize the current state of the construction itself.

When I first began gathering the materials for this book (most of which were rare or hard-to-find books that were being thrown out [!] from this or that small college library) I *did* have in mind a book that tried to pull together all the threads outlined in this chapter's opening paragraph. What I did *not* realize was that all of the books—even those on the Lincoln assassination—were books authored in a complete disconnect from the other events of their time. The Union and Confederate financial policies were all in books in one box, full of eye-crossing statistics, but they led nowhere. The books about Lincoln's assassination were in another box, and while they all clearly hinted that there were connections between it and Stanton and a circle of radical Republicans around him, none wanted to deal with the association in other but vague terms, and the subject of Booth's diary was touched with all the light and gingerly tap of a child testing the heat of a red hot burner on a stove, and quickly withdrawn. And out of all of these books, none wanted to deal with the flight and capture of the Confederate President, nor his exceedingly strange *post bellum* career, nor with all the questions and implications of that career, much less try to tie all of *that* to all of the *rest* of it. Writing of this book therefore stalled for many months because I simply could not figure out how to take the mountain of Civil War statistics and interconnections and integrate them into a smooth and readable narrative about the true extent of what I thought was going on; to do so ran the risk of burying people in a blizzard of footnotes and numbers to the extent that the narrative scaffolding would collapse.

All of that literally changed in a matter of a couple of days when I reached for two books that had finally worked their way to the top of my research reading pile, and in their statements about the Confederacy's Erlanger loan. These two books were Dr. John Christopher Schwab's *The Confederate States of America, 1861-1865: A Financial and Industrial History of the South During the Civil War*, and Richard I. Lester's *Confederate Finance and Purchasing in Great Britain*. The latter, as the previous pages of this book have stated, clearly revealed the participation of the upper reaches of British power and finance, with two very powerful and clear connections to the Bank of England. The months of reading about Lincoln's assassination and Davis' flight, of pondering the declarations printed on Union and Confederate currency, suddenly just clicked into place, enabling me to write this book in a furious cyclone of typing lest my thoughts be lost.

What has resulted, to draw upon yet another metaphor, is not a blueprint, but an architect's initial sketch of an idea.

Whether time will add details to vindicate, elaborate, obfuscate, or confute this complex hypothesis remains to be seen.

So when all is said and done, where have we ended? What are the precise and precisely formulated elements of this complex hypothesis? There are three major components, each with subtle and nuanced sub-components which in turn all interlock with those of the other major elements:

1) The flight of Confederate President at the end of the War Between the States must be viewed as a Continuity of Government operation and nothing

else, because his flight party contained, controlled, or otherwise had jurisdiction over the following elements:

a) The state seals of the departments of the Confederacy, presumably largely those of the Confederate executive, but by implication, those of its Congress and Judiciary. Such seals would be necessary for the continuing function of the government and particularly for formalities involving official documents and communications;

b) A sum of specie, which most scholarship believes was somewhere between $200,000 and $500,000, but as this book has argued, had to be much more because

   i) Davis's flight was a Continuity of Government flight, and attempting to link up with the armies of Generals Lee and Johnston; a much larger sum of specie would be needed to pay and supply the vast numbers of soldiers involved; and,

   ii) as a Continuity of Government operation, Davis' administration would have to continue to service its foreign debt, which was serviceable only in specie; and,

   iii) it is clearly recorded that his flight party removed the specie of Richmond banks, an amount which the Richmond bankers informed the occupying Union troops was somewhere between six and thirteen million dollars; and,

   iv) because this specie also included an unknown amount of Mexican silver specie;

c) a sum of paper money, consisting of
   i) a sum of Confederate notes which were burnt
      along the flight, *not* because "all was lost"
      but because, as I argued, it was not wished
      nor desired to inflate the money supply
      within the Confederacy's Trans-Mississippi
      department which was the goal of Davis'
      Continuity of Government operation and
      thereby depreciate the value of its
      circulating currency;
d) The objective of the flight, the Trans-Mississippi
   department, was the logical objective because it
   was capable of sustaining government
   operations; it was able to do so because:
   i) President Davis had authorized the
      department to assume a kind of semi-
      autonomous status after the Fall of
      Vicksburg in 1863;
   ii) The region was more than agriculturally self-
      sufficient;
   iii) The region produced a small amount of its
      own textiles, small arms, wagons, and heavy
      ordnance, and could thus equip, supply, and
      sustain field armies;
   iv) as the war continued and became worse for
      the Confederacy, the Trans-Mississippi de-
      partment became crucial to its blockade-
      running because of its long Gulf of Mexico
      coastline, and because of its common
      international border with Mexico;
   v) the vastness of the territory and its "military
      topography" favored guerilla style warfare
      and would have been difficult for Union

armies to invade and occupy the region, enabling the Continuity of Government.

2) The Assassination of Union President Lincoln was at the minimum the result of a penetrated operation, if one is to believe the assertions of the missing pages of the Booth diary; that is to say, behind the Southern partisans and assassins—Booth, Atzerodt, Payne, and Surratt—there was another, deeper layer, consisting of

    a) the Radical Republicans mentioned in Booth's diary's missing pages, including:

        i) Secretary of War Edwin Stanton;

        ii) His assistant secretary of war Major Eckert, whom, it will be recalled, Lincoln wanted on the night of his murder for personal security, and whose service Stanton refused;

        iii) California U.S. Senator John Conness;

        iv) Michigan U.S. Senator and one-time Republican National Committee and Lincoln Campaign Chairman Zechariah Chandler;

        v) Indiana Congressman George W. Julian;

        vi) Ohio U.S. Senator Benamin Wade;

    b) Booth's diary's missing pages also mention money payments from the Confederate secret service cell in Canada to the Radical Republicans via moneys conveyed to Booth, thence to Conness, and also mentions Booth's contacts with northeastern Yankee industrialists and financiers. All of this strongly suggests an even *deeper* layer of involvement with the assassination with international connections. Thus, the Lincoln assassination appears to have the outlines and profile of an operation-within-an-operation-within-an operation; thus,

c) the motivation at least in part appears financial, and *given the heavy foreign investments in the Confederacy and heavy speculations in its cotton, one means available to the European bankers to recoup their losses was to back the radical republican platform for the "reconstruction" of the South, i.e., for the acquisition of hard southern assets for pennies on the dollar, or pence on the pound, or centimes on the franc, or pfennigen on the goldmarks;* this deeper connection led, via the Erlanger loan, all the way to

    i) the personal secretary to the then British Prime Minister, Lord Palmerston;

    ii) the Chancellor of the Exchequer in Palmerston's cabinet, and himself a future prime minister, William E. Gladstone;

    iii) the Lord High Chancellor (and previous Lord Chief Justice(!), and thus a member of the privy council and the keeper of the British Great Seal;

    iv) a director of the Bank of England (and thus, a second connection to the British Central bank besides Gladstone)

    v) Emile d'Erlanger himself, with his banking connections both in Paris and Frankfurt, and via the latter all the way to Vienna and Berlin;

d) the other financial motivation for the assassination was to put an end to its policy of the issuance of debt-free paper notes defined or declared to be legal tender; this was effectively accomplish by the deliberate contraction of the money supply via the Resumption act and the redemption of greenbacks by gold or some equivalent; I have argued that there does not seem to be enough gold in reserve to redeem all greenbacks; this leads to the next motivation:

e) the deeper motivation behind the assassination may have been technological, i.e., to maintain control over the secret development of airship technology; it was seen that Stanton and Lincoln both were aware of it, and that Lincoln wanted it developed; Stanton ostensibly did not do so, but I have argued that it was more likely that someone of his character ordered its *secret* development, and funded that *by means of the resumed and redeemed greenbacks which were re-hypothecated, rather than being destroyed*, thus creating a hidden reserve and proto-typical hidden system of funding. The previous points confirm Walter Bosley's NYMZA hypothesis, and go further, and suggest connections that can provide covert sources of funding for a covert research project;

i) this project ends up itself in the Trans-Mississippi Department, for the 19th century airship sightings appear to trail off there, centering their last sightings in the environs around Sherman, Texas; and,

ii) one of the oft-sighted members of the airship crew, the man calling himself "Wilson", appears to end up in Fort Worth, and Dellschau, whose paintings of the airships

298

and allegations concerning the Sonora Aero Club, also ends in Texas. While this may be purely coincidental, I believe that this is an indicator of deeper connections between the airship mystery and sightings, and the Confederacy's Trans-Mississippi depart-ment, and that it may represent some unknown connection to Davis' Continuity of Government operation. This assumes that the operation continued long after Davis himself was captured and forced to abandon it, and that its role at that point may have been as a hidden source of funding, perhaps accessible only by use of Confederate state seals. This, it is to be acknowledge, is highly speculative.

3) Besides the underlying technological theme and thread running through all of this, there are also the twin threads of monetary and fiscal philosophy, and the threads of the relationships of culture and politics. If before the war it may be reasonably stated that the United States were two countries and/or two cultures[2] held uneasily together by a common government; then it may also be

---

[2] Consider one the one hand only the northeastern "Yankee secularized Calvinism" in the form of its Unitarianism or its earlier pre-war revivalism, the Puritan background of Cotton Mather and so on, forms of religion close resembling modern American evangelicalism, and on the other hand Southern Episcopalianism, and its "more tolerant" attitudes to Roman Catholicism or Judaism, as evident in Confederate general Leonidas Polk (a former Episcopalian bishop), or General Beauregard (A Roman Catholic), or Confederate Secretary of State Judah Benjamin, a Jew.

reasonably said that they split along sectional and cultural lines during the war into two countries and two governments which shared a more-or-less identical *system* of government;[3] and again it may reasonably be said that after the war it appears that the cultural and monetary problems were only exacerbated even more, with new sectionalist tensions added to the old ones, and everything forcibly jammed together once again into the Lincolnian version of the suicide pact of the "indissoluble" union, with no genuinely deep resolution of the monetary and cultural issues whatsoever; there was merely plunder to be had on the backs of newly manumitted and impoverished southern blacks, and newly impoverished southern planters. This means that

a) The experiments in fiat currencies by the Union and by the Confederacy have as many similarities as they do differences, for both the Union and the Confederacy suffered inflation of prices and depreciation of their currency as a result of their paper currency policies; but here the similarities end, for not only was the Union inflation relatively mild compared to the Confederate, the two fiat currency systems were very dissimilar in that:

---

[3] With obvious and well-known and well-rehearsed differing interpretations of what that system meant, the North arguing that the Union was a kind of secularized version of the Roman Catholic view of marriage, once-married-never-divorced, and the South arguing (more correctly in my opinion) that it was never intended to be an irrevocable suicide pact.

i) the Confederate issues were always tied to debt in some form or fashion, and its early experiment with actual interest-bearing money in the 1862 issue ended in failure, because rather than circulating as they were intended to do, the notes were used as reserves; and,

ii) the Union's Lincoln greenbacks were debt free entirely, the Union only adopting a more "Confederate" policy in the currency act of 1864-1865; and

iii) Both countries suffered a drain on their specie, but this drain affected the Confederacy much more than the Union. Nonetheless, the Confederacy was scrupulous in its servicing interest payments via gold specie during the war, raising a significant and unanswered question: where did they get it? The conventional explanation that these were all donations of silver and gold appointments cannot, it would seem, account for all of it, implying that the source for some of it may be either a hidden *source*, or a hidden *supply line* to that source.

b) Both the Union and the Confederacy owed much of their war-making finance and currency philosophy to the twin experiences of the American and French revolutions, the first attempts in modern history to revisit and revive a very ancient idea of debt-free money. In doing so the French, and the American colonies, both ran afoul of banking interests that were able to mobilize considerable military power in an effort to put the financial rebellions down, but at considerable cost in France's—and Europe's—case, and to their defeat in America's case, a defeat rectified, it would seem, by the post-Civil War effort to refasten their debt system on the country.

These, then, are our surveys, sketches, blueprints, and scaffolds. That they do not constitute a finished edifice with doorways, windows, cornices, porches, and various utile rooms should be abundantly clear. Perhaps there are not even enough materials here from which to build anything at all. That is for the reader to decide.

We began this book with the two American Presidents. Neither man was by any stretch of the imagination, nor by their own self-assessments and admissions, perfect. But they were both *men*, and they were both *good* men, unafraid to stand and fight for their principles. If there was a fault with either man and the nations they led, it was perhaps—and to a degree which we would not acknowledge today—that they allowed themselves to be caught up in a conflict where the perfect was allowed to fight and conquer the good. As is always the case, when one ceases to fight for the good in order to fight for perfection, the perfection never comes, and the good is always ruined. Both men knew their Bibles well, and knew that God did not create a perfect world; He created a *good* one. All else, and anything more, was idolatry.

"We shall nobly save or meanly lose the last best hope of earth," said one of those Presidents. And the other President, with no less eloquence, and in his own way, agreed: "To save ourselves from a revolution which, in its silent but rapid progress, was about to place us under the despotism of numbers... we determined to make a new association...". Both men, and their country, paid a high cost for those words, because the cost of those words was, in the final analysis, worth it, for it was never about mere money.

The Two Presidents:
Left: Confederate States President Jefferson Davis;
Right: United States President Abraham Lincoln.

BIBLIOGRAPHY

BOOKS CITED OR CONSULTED FOR THE PRESENT WORK
(AN ASTERISK, *, DESIGNATES A WORK ACTUALLY CITED
IN THE PRESENT WORK)

Ball, Douglas B. *Financial Failure and Confederate Defeat*. Urbana, Illinois. University of Illinois Press. ISBN 0-252-01755-2. 1991.

*Balsiger, David, and Sellier, Charles, E., Jr. *The Lincoln Conspiracy*. Los Angeles. Schick Sunn Classic Books. Obsolete ISBN 0-917214-03-X. 1977.

Baum, L. Frank. *The Wonderful Wizard of Oz*. Reprint of original edition with the original artwork of W.W. Denslow.) Orinda, California. Sea Wolf Press. ISBN 978-1950435432. 2019-2023.

*Booth, John Wilkes. *The Assassination of Abraham Lincoln: John Wilkes Booth's Diary, Excerpts from Newspapers, and Other Sources*. London. Forgotten Books. (Lincoln Financial Foundation Collection.) ISBN 978-0-282-85287-0. 2018.

*Bosley, Walter. *Origin: The Nineteenth Century Emergence of the 20th Century Breakaway Civilizations*. Highland, California. No ISBN. 2015.

*Brown, Ellen Hodgson, J.D. *The Web of Debt: The Shocking Truth About Our Money System and How We Can Break Free*. Revised and Expanded with 2008 update. Baton Rouge, Louisiana. Third Millennium Press. ISBN 978-0-9795608-2-8. 2008.

Bulloch, James D. *The Secret Service of the Confederate States in Europe.* New York. Thomas Yoseloff. No ISBN. 1959.

*Busby, Michael. *Solving the 1897 Airship Mystery.* Gretna, Louisiana. Pelican Publishing Co., Inc. 2004. ISBN 1-58980-125-3.

Capers, Henry D., A.M. *The Life and Times of C.G. Memminger.* Richmond, Virginia. Everett Waddey Co., Publishers. 1893. (Modern reprint, Legare Street Press. ISBN 978-1016-319225.

*Cutrer, Thomas W. *Theater of a Separate War: The Civil War West of the Mississippi River, 1861-1865.* Chapel Hill. The University of North Carolina Press. ISBN 978-1-4696-3156-1. 2017.

Davis, Charles S. *Colin J. McRae: Confederate Financial Agent.* Confederate Centennial Studies, Number Seventeen. Tuscaloosa, Alabama. Confederate Publishing Company, Inc. No ISBN. 1961. (This work also contains important information on the Erlanger Bonds.)

*Davis, Jefferson. *The Rise and Fall of the Confederate Government.* New York. Thomas Yoseloff. No ISBN. 1958.

*Dighe, Ranjit S., Ed. *The Historian's Wizard of Oz: Reading L. Frank Baum's Classic as a Political and Monetary Allegory.* Westport, Connecticut. ISBN 0-275-97419-7. 2002.

*Eisenschiml, Otto. *Why Was Lincoln Murdered?* New York. Little Brown and Company (Grosset's Universal Library, Grosset & Dunlap). No ISBN. 1937. (Indispensable.)

*Geise, William Royston (Michael J. Forsyth, Editor). *The Confederate Military Forces in the Trans-Mississippi West, 1861-1865: A Study in Command.* El Dorado Hills, California. Savas Beatire. ISBN 978-1-61121-621-9. 2022.

Huse, Caleb, Major (C.S.A.). *The Supplies for the Confederate Army.* No publication location given. Okitoks Press. ISBN 978-1984911964. 2018.

*Lester, Richard I. *Confederate Finance and Purchasing in Great Britain.* Charlottsville, Virginia. University Press of Virginia. Old ISBN Number 0-8139-0513-3. 1975. (Contains the vital information on Erlanger bond subscribers.)

*McNeely, Patricia G. *President Abraham Lincoln, General William t. Sherman, President Jefferson Davis, and the Lost Confederate Gold.* No Publication location. ISBN 978-1517-212384. 2015. (Despite some online panning reviews, this is a well-argued, well-referenced, and indispensable source.)

Memminger, Christopher Gustavus. *Instructions for Collectors of Taxes: Confederate States of America Treasury Department, Richmond, May 15, 1863.* London. Forgotten Books. ISBN 978-0-243-15137-0. 2018.

*Memminger, Hon. C.G. *Address of the Hon. C.G. Memminger.* No Publication location. Gale Archival Editions on Demand. ISBN 978-1432-801397. No Publication date. Remarks to Virginia Legislature, January 19, 1860. (The date in the original appears to be a misprint, as the remarks would have been made in 1861.)

*Nepveux, Ethel Trenholm Seabrook. *George A. Trenholm, Financial Genius of the Confederacy: His Associates and His Ships that Ran the Blockade.* Anderson, South Carolina. The Electric City Printing Company. ISBN 0-9668843-1-0. 1999.

Owsley, Frank Lawrence. *King Cotton Diplomacy: Foreign Relations of the Confederate States of America.* (Second Edition, Revised by Harriet Chappell Owsley.) Chicago. The University of Chicago Press. No ISBN. 1959.

Richardson, James D., Ed.. *A Compilation of the Messages and Papers of the Confederacy, Including the Diplomatic Correspondence, 1861-1865.* Coppell, Texas. University of Michigan Library reprint of the 1905 edition. M0D1002570334.

*Ritter, Gretchen. *Goldbugs and Greenbacks: The Antimonopoly Tradition and the Politics of Finance in America, 1865-1896.* Cambridge. Cambridge University Press. ISBN 978-0-521-65392-3. 1997.

*Roscoe, Theodore. *The Web of Conspiracy: The Complete Story of the Men Who Murdered Abraham Lincoln.* Englewood Cliffs, New Jersey. Prentice Hall, Inc. No ISBN. 1959. (Roscoe's work, along with Eisenschiml's, is indispensable for any Lincoln assassination research.)

*Schwab, John Christopher, A.M., Ph.D., *The Confederate States of America, 1861-1865: A Financial and Industrial History of the South During the Civil War.* New York. Burt Franklin. No ISBN. 1968 reprint of the 1901 original. (Also contains critical information on the Erlanger bonds.)

*Smith, Ernest Ashton. *The History of the Confederate Treasury.* University of Michigan Library reprint. ISBN M0D1002256297. Original publication: Southern History Association, Namuary, March, May 1902 of Smith's Ph.D. Dissertation to Johns Hopkins University.

Todd, Richard Cecil. *Confederate Finance.* Athens, Georgia. The University of Georgia Press. No ISBN. 1954.

*Warren, Robert Penn. *Jefferson Davis Gets His Citizenship Back.* Lexington, Kentucky. The University Press of Kentucky. ISBN 0-8131-1445-4. 1981.

*Warren, Robert Penn. *The Legacy of the Civil War.* Lincoln, Nebraska. The University of Nebraska Press. ISBN 0-8032-9801-3. 1998.

Get these fascinating books from your nearest bookstore or directly from: Adventures Unlimited Press
www.adventuresunlimitedpress.com

COVERT WARS AND BREAKAWAY CIVILIZATIONS
By Joseph P. Farrell

Farrell delves into the creation of breakaway civilizations by the Nazis in South America and other parts of the world. He discusses the advanced technology that they took with them at the end of the war and the psychological war that they waged for decades on America and NATO. He investigates the secret space programs currently sponsored by the breakaway civilizations and the current militaries in control of planet Earth. Plenty of astounding accounts, documents and speculation on the incredible alternative history of hidden conflicts and secret space programs that began when World War II officially "ended."

292 Pages. 6x9 Paperback. Illustrated. $19.95. Code: BCCW

THE ENIGMA OF CRANIAL DEFORMATION
Elongated Skulls of the Ancients
By David Hatcher Childress and Brien Foerster

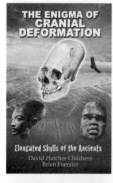

In a book filled with over a hundred astonishing photos and a color photo section, Childress and Foerster take us to Peru, Bolivia, Egypt, Malta, China, Mexico and other places in search of strange elongated skulls and other cranial deformation. The puzzle of why diverse ancient people—even on remote Pacific Islands—would use head-binding to create elongated heads is mystifying. Where did they even get this idea? Did some people naturally look this way—with long narrow heads? Were they some alien race? Were they an elite race that roamed the entire planet? Why do anthropologists rarely talk about cranial deformation and know so little about it? Color Section.

250 Pages. 6x9 Paperback. Illustrated. $19.95. Code: ECD

ARK OF GOD
The Incredible Power of the Ark of the Covenant
By David Hatcher Childress

Childress takes us on an incredible journey in search of the truth about (and science behind) the fantastic biblical artifact known as the Ark of the Covenant. This object made by Moses at Mount Sinai—part wooden-metal box and part golden statue—had the power to create "lightning" to kill people, and also to fly and lead people through the wilderness. The Ark of the Covenant suddenly disappears from the Bible record and what happened to it is not mentioned. Was it hidden in the underground passages of King Solomon's temple and later discovered by the Knights Templar? Was it taken through Egypt to Ethiopia as many Coptic Christians believe? Childress looks into hidden history, astonishing ancient technology, and a 3,000-year-old mystery that continues to fascinate millions of people today. Color section.

420 Pages. 6x9 Paperback. Illustrated. $22.00 Code: AOG

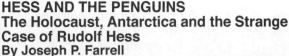

HESS AND THE PENGUINS
The Holocaust, Antarctica and the Strange Case of Rudolf Hess
By Joseph P. Farrell
Farrell looks at Hess' mission to make peace with Britain and get rid of Hitler—even a plot to fly Hitler to Britain for capture! How much did Göring and Hitler know of Rudolf Hess' subversive plot, and what happened to Hess? Why was a doppleganger put in Spandau Prison and then "suicided"? Did the British use an early form of mind control on Hess' double? John Foster Dulles of the OSS and CIA suspected as much. Farrell also uncovers the strange death of Admiral Richard Byrd's son in 1988, about the same time of the death of Hess.
288 Pages. 6x9 Paperback. Illustrated. $19.95. Code: HAPG

HIDDEN FINANCE, ROGUE NETWORKS & SECRET SORCERY
The Fascist International, 9/11, & Penetrated Operations
By Joseph P. Farrell
Farrell investigates the theory that there were not *two* levels to the 9/11 event, but *three*. He says that the twin towers were downed by the force of an exotic energy weapon, one similar to the Tesla energy weapon suggested by Dr. Judy Wood, and ties together the tangled web of missing money, secret technology and involvement of portions of the Saudi royal family. Farrell unravels the many layers behind the 9-11 attack, layers that include the Deutschebank, the Bush family, the German industrialist Carl Duisberg, Saudi Arabian princes and the energy weapons developed by Tesla before WWII.
296 Pages. 6x9 Paperback. Illustrated. $19.95. Code: HFRN

THRICE GREAT HERMETICA & THE JANUS AGE
By Joseph P. Farrell
What do the Fourth Crusade, the exploration of the New World, secret excavations of the Holy Land, and the pontificate of Innocent the Third all have in common? Answer: Venice and the Templars. What do they have in common with Jesus, Gottfried Leibniz, Sir Isaac Newton, Rene Descartes, and the Earl of Oxford? Answer: Egypt and a body of doctrine known as Hermeticism. The hidden role of Venice and Hermeticism reached far and wide, into the plays of Shakespeare (a.k.a. Edward DeVere, Earl of Oxford), into the quest of the three great mathematicians of the Early Enlightenment for a lost form of analysis, and back into the end of the classical era, to little known Egyptian influences at work during the time of Jesus.
354 Pages. 6x9 Paperback. Illustrated. $19.95. Code: TGHJ

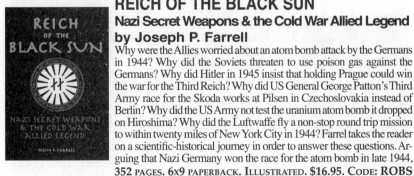

REICH OF THE BLACK SUN
Nazi Secret Weapons & the Cold War Allied Legend
by Joseph P. Farrell
Why were the Allies worried about an atom bomb attack by the Germans in 1944? Why did the Soviets threaten to use poison gas against the Germans? Why did Hitler in 1945 insist that holding Prague could win the war for the Third Reich? Why did US General George Patton's Third Army race for the Skoda works at Pilsen in Czechoslovakia instead of Berlin? Why did the US Army not test the uranium atom bomb it dropped on Hiroshima? Why did the Luftwaffe fly a non-stop round trip mission to within twenty miles of New York City in 1944? Farrel takes the reader on a scientific-historical journey in order to answer these questions. Arguing that Nazi Germany won the race for the atom bomb in late 1944,
352 PAGES. 6x9 PAPERBACK. ILLUSTRATED. $16.95. CODE: ROBS

ROSWELL AND THE REICH
The Nazi Connection
By Joseph P. Farrell

Farrell has meticulously reviewed the best-known Roswell research from UFO-ET advocates and skeptics alike, as well as some little-known source material, and comes to a radically different scenario of what happened in Roswell, New Mexico in July 1947, and why the US military has continued to cover it up to this day. Farrell presents a fascinating case sure to disturb both ET believers and disbelievers, namely, that what crashed may have been representative of an independent postwar Nazi power—an extraterritorial Reich monitoring its old enemy, America, and the continuing development of the very technologies confiscated from Germany at the end of the War.

540 pages. 6x9 Paperback. Illustrated. $19.95. Code: RWR

SECRETS OF THE UNIFIED FIELD
The Philadelphia Experiment, the Nazi Bell, and the Discarded Theory
by Joseph P. Farrell

Farrell examines the now discarded Unified Field Theory. American and German wartime scientists and engineers determined that, while the theory was incomplete, it could nevertheless be engineered. Chapters include: The Meanings of "Torsion"; Wringing an Aluminum Can; The Mistake in Unified Field Theories and Their Discarding by Contemporary Physics; Three Routes to the Doomsday Weapon: Quantum Potential, Torsion, and Vortices; Tesla's Meeting with FDR; Arnold Sommerfeld and Electromagnetic Radar Stealth; Electromagnetic Phase Conjugations, Phase Conjugate Mirrors, and Templates; The Unified Field Theory, the Torsion Tensor, and Igor Witkowski's Idea of the Plasma Focus; tons more.

340 pages. 6x9 Paperback. Illustrated. $18.95. Code: SOUF

NAZI INTERNATIONAL
The Nazi's Postwar Plan to Control Finance, Conflict, Physics and Space
by Joseph P. Farrell

Beginning with prewar corporate partnerships in the USA, including some with the Bush family, he moves on to the surrender of Nazi Germany, and evacuation plans of the Germans. He then covers the vast, and still-little-known recreation of Nazi Germany in South America with help of Juan Peron, I.G. Farben and Martin Bormann. Farrell then covers Nazi Germany's penetration of the Muslim world including Wilhelm Voss and Otto Skorzeny in Gamel Abdul Nasser's Egypt before moving on to the development and control of new energy technologies including the Bariloche Fusion Project, Dr. Philo Farnsworth's Plasmator, and the work of Dr. Nikolai Kozyrev. Finally, Farrell discusses the Nazi desire to control space, and examines their connection with NASA, the esoteric meaning of NASA Mission Patches.

412 pages. 6x9 Paperback. Illustrated. $19.95. Code: NZIN

ARKTOS
The Polar Myth in Science, Symbolism & Nazi Survival
by Joscelyn Godwin

Explored are the many tales of an ancient race said to have lived in the Arctic regions, such as Thule and Hyperborea. Progressing onward, he looks at modern polar legends: including the survival of Hitler, German bases in Antarctica, UFOs, the hollow earth, and the hidden kingdoms of Agartha and Shambala. Chapters include: Prologue in Hyperborea; The Golden Age; The Northern Lights; The Arctic Homeland; The Aryan Myth; The Thule Society; The Black Order; The Hidden Lands; Agartha and the Polaires; Shambhala; The Hole at the Pole; Antarctica; more.

220 Pages. 6x9 Paperback. Illustrated. Bib. Index. $16.95. Code: ARK

SAUCERS, SWASTIKAS AND PSYOPS
A History of a Breakaway Civilization
By Joseph P. Farrell
Farrell discusses SS Commando Otto Skorzeny; George Adamski; the alleged Hannebu and Vril craft of the Third Reich; The Strange Case of Dr. Hermann Oberth; Nazis in the US and their connections to "UFO contactees"; The Memes—an idea or behavior spread from person to person within a culture— are Implants. Chapters include: The Nov. 20, 1952 Contact: The Memes are Implants; The Interplanetary Federation of Brotherhood; Adamski's Technological Descriptions and Another ET Message: The Danger of Weaponized Gravity; Adamski's Retro-Looking Saucers, and the Nazi Saucer Myth; Dr. Oberth's 1968 Statements on UFOs and Extraterrestrials; more.
272 Pages. 6x9 Paperback. Illustrated. $19.95. Code: SSPY

LBJ AND THE CONSPIRACY TO KILL KENNEDY
By Joseph P. Farrell
Farrell says that a coalescence of interests in the military industrial complex, the CIA, and Lyndon Baines Johnson's powerful and corrupt political machine in Texas led to the events culminating in the assassination of JFK. Chapters include: Oswald, the FBI, and the CIA: Hoover's Concern of a Second Oswald; Oswald and the Anti-Castro Cubans; The Mafia; Hoover, Johnson, and the Mob; The FBI, the Secret Service, Hoover, and Johnson; The CIA and "Murder Incorporated"; Ruby's Bizarre Behavior; The French Connection and Permindex; Big Oil; The Dead Witnesses: Guy Bannister, Jr., Mary Pinchot Meyer, Rose Cheramie, Dorothy Killgallen, Congressman Hale Boggs; LBJ and the Planning of the Texas Trip; LBJ: A Study in Character, Connections, and Cabals; LBJ and the Aftermath: Accessory After the Fact; The Requirements of Coups D'État; more.
342 Pages. 6x9 Paperback. $19.95 Code: LCKK

THE TESLA PAPERS
Nikola Tesla on Free Energy & Wireless Transmission of Power
by Nikola Tesla, edited by David Hatcher Childress
David Hatcher Childress takes us into the incredible world of Nikola Tesla and his amazing inventions. Tesla's fantastic vision of the future, including wireless power, anti-gravity, free energy and highly advanced solar power. Also included are some of the papers, patents and material collected on Tesla at the Colorado Springs Tesla Symposiums, including papers on: •The Secret History of Wireless Transmission •Tesla and the Magnifying Transmitter •Design and Construction of a Half-Wave Tesla Coil •Electrostatics: A Key to Free Energy •Progress in Zero-Point Energy Research •Electromagnetic Energy from Antennas to Atoms
325 PAGES. 8x10 PAPERBACK. ILLUSTRATED. $16.95. CODE: TTP

COVERT WARS & THE CLASH OF CIVILIZATIONS
UFOs, Oligarchs and Space Secrecy
By Joseph P. Farrell
Farrell's customary meticulous research and sharp analysis blow the lid off of a worldwide web of nefarious financial and technological control that very few people even suspect exists. He elaborates on the advanced technology that they took with them at the "end" of World War II and shows how the breakaway civilizations have created a huge system of hidden finance with the involvement of various banks and financial institutions around the world. He investigates the current space secrecy that involves UFOs, suppressed technologies and the hidden oligarchs who control planet earth for their own gain and profit.
358 Pages. 6x9 Paperback. Illustrated. $19.95. Code: CWCC

THE GIZA DEATH STAR REVISITED
An Updated Revision of the Weapon Hypothesis of the Great Pyramid
By Joseph P. Farrell

Join revisionist author Joseph P. Farrell for a summary, revision, and update of his original *Giza Death Star* trilogy in this one-volume compendium of the argument, the physics, and the all-important ancient texts, from the Edfu Temple texts to the Lugal-e and the Enuma Elish that he believes may have made the Great Pyramid a tremendously powerful weapon of mass destruction. Those texts, Farrell argues, provide the clues to the powerful physics of longitudinal waves in the medium that only began to be unlocked centuries later by Sir Isaac Newton and Nikola Tesla's "electro-acoustic" experiments.
360 Pages. 6x9 Paperback. Illustrated. $19.95. Code: GDSR

THE DEMON IN THE EKUR
Angels, Demons, Plasmas, Patristics, and Pyramids
By Joseph P. Farrell

Farrell looks at the Demon in the *Ekur* (the gathering place of the gods in Sumerian tradition) and the Great Pyramid Weapon Hypothesis. He delves deep into the realm of angels, presenting John of Damascus' Angelology and examines the "Immaterial Materiality" of angels; their ability to penetrate ordinary matter and "unlimited" nature; their ability to shapeshift; and the everlasting temporality, or "Sempiternity," of angels. Farrell also explores "Plasma Cosmotheology" and the Plasma Life Hypothesis. He presents intriguing pictures of nuclear detonations and discusses the Hyper-Dimensional Transduction Hypothesis. He includes a discussion of crystals as tuners and transducers, and explores the planetary associations of crystals with angels.
160 Pages. 6x9 Paperback. Illustrated. $16.95. Code: DITE

VRIL: SECRETS OF THE BLACK SUN
By David Childress

A remnant of the Nazi military—particularly the SS—continued to operate aircraft and submarines around the world in the decades after the end of the war. This volume closes with how the SS operates today in the Ukraine and how the Wagner second in command, Dimitry Utkin, killed in the fiery crash of Yevgeny Prigozhin's private jet between Moscow and St. Petersburg in August of 2023, had SS tattoos on his shoulders and often signed his name with the SS runes. Chapters include: Secrets of the Black Sun; The Extra-Territorial Reich; The Rise of the SS; The SS Never Surrendered; Secret Submarines, Antarctica & Argentina; The Marconi Connection; Yellow Submarine; Ukraine and the Battalion of the Black Sun; more. Includes an 8-page color section.
382 Pages. 6x9 Paperback. Illustrated. $22.00 Code: VSBS

ANTARCTICA AND THE SECRET SPACE PROGRAM
Hatcher Childress

David Childress, popular author and star of the History Channel's show *Ancient Aliens*, brings us the incredible tale of Nazi submarines and secret weapons in Antarctica and elsewhere. He then examines Operation High-Jump with Admiral Richard Byrd in 1947 and the battle that he apparently had in Antarctica with flying saucers. Through "Operation Paperclip," the Nazis infiltrated aerospace companies, banking, media, and the US government, including NASA and the CIA after WWII. Does the US Navy have a secret space program that includes huge ships and hundreds of astronauts?
392 Pages. 6x9 Paperback. Illustrated. $22.00 Code: ASSP

ORDER FORM

10% Discount When You Order 3 or More Items!

One Adventure Place
P.O. Box 74
Kempton, Illinois 60946
United States of America
Tel.: 815-253-6390 • Fax: 815-253-6300
Email: auphq@frontiernet.net
http://www.adventuresunlimitedpress.com

ORDERING INSTRUCTIONS

✓ Remit by USD$ Check, Money Order or Credit Card

✓ Visa, Master Card, Discover & AmEx Accepted

✓ Paypal Payments Can Be Made To:

    info@wexclub.com

✓ Prices May Change Without Notice

✓ 10% Discount for 3 or More Items

SHIPPING CHARGES

United States

✓ POSTAL BOOK RATE

✓ Postal Book Rate { $5.00 First Item / 50¢ Each Additional Item

✓ Priority Mail { $8.50 First Item / $2.00 Each Additional Item

✓ UPS { $9.00 First Item (Minimum 5 Books) / $1.50 Each Additional Item

NOTE: UPS Delivery Available to Mainland USA Only

Canada

✓ Postal Air Mail { $19.00 First Item / $3.00 Each Additional Item

✓ Personal Checks or Bank Drafts MUST BE US$ and Drawn on a US Bank

✓ Canadian Postal Money Orders OK

✓ Payment MUST BE US$

All Other Countries

✓ Sorry, No Surface Delivery!

✓ Postal Air Mail { $29.00 First Item / $7.00 Each Additional Item

✓ Checks and Money Orders MUST BE US$ and Drawn on a US Bank or branch.

✓ Paypal Payments Can Be Made in US$ To:
    info@wexclub.com

SPECIAL NOTES

✓ RETAILERS: Standard Discounts Available

✓ BACKORDERS: We Backorder all Out-of-Stock Items Unless Otherwise Requested

✓ PRO FORMA INVOICES: Available on Request

✓ DVD Return Policy: Replace defective DVDs only

ORDER ONLINE AT: www.adventuresunlimitedpress.com

10% Discount When You Order 3 or More Items!

Please check: ✓

☐ This is my first order   ☐ I have ordered before

Name			
Address			
City			
State/Province		Postal Code	
Country			
Phone: Day		Evening	
Fax		Email	

Item Code	Item Description	Qty	Total

Please check: ✓

	Subtotal ▶	
	Less Discount-10% for 3 or more items ▶	
☐ Postal-Surface	Balance ▶	
☐ Postal-Air Mail (Priority in USA)	Illinois Residents 6.25% Sales Tax ▶	
	Previous Credit ▶	
☐ UPS	Shipping ▶	
(Mainland USA only)	Total (check/MO in USD$ only) ▶	

☐ Visa/MasterCard/Discover/American Express

Card Number:

Expiration Date: Security Code:

✓ SEND A CATALOG TO A FRIEND: